OXFORD WORLD'S CLASSICS

WILLIAM BLAKE
SELECTED POETRY

WILLIAM BLAKE was born in 1757, the son of a West End shop-keeper. His own trade was that of craftsman engraver, and until he was in his thirties there was little to distinguish him outwardly from the ordinary man of his profession. In 1789 he produced *Songs of Innocence*, the first in a beautiful series of small hand-made volumes of illustrated poetry in lyric and blank-verse—sometimes obscure, but always arresting—issued by Blake over the next six years: among them *The Book of Thel*, *The Marriage of Heaven and Hell* (chiefly prose), *Visions of the Daughters of Albion*, *America*, *Songs of Experience*, *Europe*, and *The Book of Urizen*. In 1800 Blake tried to break free from London and commercial engraving by accepting an invitation to work under the patronage of the poet and critic William Hayley near his home in Sussex. Blake's mind was already turning to mythological narrative on a much larger scale than hitherto, and his new situation was not congenial. He returned to London in 1803, and worked heroically on the etching of his grand narratives *Milton* and *Jerusalem*, and on ambitious and highly personal painting and illustrating projects. For years he was a derided or ignored figure but towards the end of his life he attracted around him a deeply admiring group of young artists of the next generation. To them is largely due the survival, alongside Blake's etched and printed works, of a body of manuscript that remains full of pungent aphorisms and haunting lyrics. Blake died in 1827.

MICHAEL MASON is Professor in English at University College London. He has published many studies of nineteenth-century poetry and fiction, including an edition of Wordsworth's *Lyrical Ballads* (Longman, 1992).

OXFORD WORLD'S CLASSICS

For almost 100 years Oxford World's Classics have brought readers closer to the world's great literature. Now with over 700 titles—from the 4,000-year-old myths of Mesopotamia to the twentieth century's greatest novels—the series makes available lesser-known as well as celebrated writing.

The pocket-sized hardbacks of the early years contained introductions by Virginia Woolf, T. S. Eliot, Graham Greene, and other literary figures which enriched the experience of reading. Today the series is recognized for its fine scholarship and reliability in texts that span world literature, drama and poetry, religion, philosophy and politics. Each edition includes perceptive commentary and essential background information to meet the changing needs of readers.

OXFORD WORLD'S CLASSICS

==

WILLIAM BLAKE

Selected Poetry

==

Edited with an Introduction and Notes by
MICHAEL MASON

Oxford New York

OXFORD UNIVERSITY PRESS

Oxford University Press, Great Clarendon Street, Oxford OX2 6DP

Oxford New York

Athens Auckland Bangkok Bogotá Buenos Aires Calcutta
Cape Town Chennai Dar es Salaam Delhi Florence Hong Kong Istanbul
Karachi Kuala Lumpur Madrid Melbourne Mexico City Mumbai
Nairobi Paris São Paulo Singapore Taipei Tokyo Toronto Warsaw
and associated companies in Berlin Ibadan

Oxford is a registered trade mark of Oxford University Press

First published as a World's Classics paperback 1996
Reissued as an Oxford World's Classics paperback 1998

British Library Cataloguing in Publication Data

Data available

Library of Congress Cataloging in Publication Data
Blake, William, 1757–1827.
[Poems. Selections]
William Blake : selected poetry / edited by Michael Mason.
p. cm.—(World's classics)
I. Mason, Michael, 1941– . II. Title. III. Series.
PR4142.M37 1996 821'.7—dc20 96–14953
ISBN 0-19-283489-4

3 5 7 9 10 8 6 4 2

Printed in Great Britain by
Cox & Wyman Ltd.
Reading, Berkshire

Contents

Introduction

How should the modern reader approach William Blake? He was a 'Romantic', which at least pigeonholes him—but into a cultural-historical category which is not simple. Worse is to come. He was not just a writer, but also a visual artist. Indeed, work for work, Blake can claim to have been more of the latter than the former. When the fact is added that almost all his serious poetry was issued by him with accompanying illustrations, it is clear that Blake-the-writer was a very unusual entity, much less coextensive with Blake-the-creator than we expect poets to be. In fact there is no parallel for Blake's artistic duality in the rest of English literature.

The idiosyncratic manner in which the texts of such works as *The Marriage of Heaven and Hell*, *America*, *Songs of Innocence and Experience*, and *Jerusalem* were issued artistically is only the beginning of the strange story of Blake's production. Blake is by no means the only writer ignored or derided in the past whom we now believe to have been great, but the gap between Blake's standing in his own day and his modern reputation exceeds all other cases. Apart from two Innocence lyrics pirated towards the end of his life not a single item of text by Blake achieved commercial publication. This was a different kind of invisibility from that affecting the great poets of the seventeenth century, for example, such as Donne, whose work circulated in manuscript. In the 1780s and 1790s, when Blake wrote most of his short- and medium-length poems, it was not hard to get into print, and printed publication was certainly the usual way to bring yourself to the attention of readers and critics. Blake did start to go down the road of orthodox publication, but the conventionally printed sheets of his *Poetical Sketches* (1783) were never bound into book form for commercial issue. Eight years later the first two books of a projected epic, *The French Revolution*, were typeset by the publisher Joseph Johnson—but never got beyond proof stage. It may be argued that Blake deliberately adopted the technique of printing his poetry from engraved plates as an alternative to conventional printing from movable type. If so, the strategy failed as a means of reaching a numerous readership. Blake's most successful engraved work was *The Songs of Innocence*, but he probably produced less than a hundred copies of this in his lifetime. *Jerusalem*, the product of perhaps fifteen years of arduous work, seems only to have been printed six times.

The orthodox way of issuing poetry has the effect of tidying up a poet's output as far as the reader is concerned, of creating a canon of public work, behind which lies a body of private manuscript which we may or may not care to read. This kind of tidy distinction between private and public does not exist in Blake's case, because of his unusual publishing methods. There are awkward borderline cases between the canonical and the non-canonical, such as the poem *Tiriel*, which exists only in manuscript but for which a sequence of illustrations was executed, perhaps indicating that it was one step from being engraved by the poet. There has been a long tradition of searching out, preserving, and transcribing Blake's manuscript remains, and one difficulty for the modern reader approaching a standard collection of Blake's poetry is that about a quarter of it is likely to consist of manuscript verse, sometimes with all his deletions and corrections carefully reproduced. This unusual situation has been assisted by bibliophiliac obsession, but it is apt for Blake. He himself seems to have regarded some of his manuscript work as having a quasi-canonical status: most of the manuscript lyrics, for example, are preserved in one small notebook which he acquired from his dead brother Robert in 1787, and then over the next forty years crammed with writings and drawings. The first marginal annotations by Blake which have survived—those he made in a copy of Lavater's *Aphorisms on Man*—were definitely intended for showing to one or more close friends, and it may be that the later annotations he wrote in books such as Reynolds's *Discourses* and Watson's *Apology for the Bible* were also semi-public utterances. It is interesting that purely personal written documents by Blake, such as letters, have hardly survived.

I have envisaged the modern reader as approaching a collection of Blake's poetry with a certain wish to simplify. This is a very natural wish, and one that arises whenever we confront a writer's output *en masse*. To group texts together for their affinities of form and content; to rank, perhaps, some groupings above others; to de-emphasize the individuality of texts at the expense of what they have in common; to bring out the similarities as somehow the essence of the writer: these are inevitable responses to the spectacle of assembled work. In Blake's case the flight to simplification appears to be further endorsed by the texts in two specific respects. Because he is a daunting poet readers have been inclined to receive this endorsement with gratitude and relief, and thus carry the tidying-up process, in this writer's case, to an extreme.

One of the encouragements to simplification has been *Songs of Innocence and Experience*, and the other is the myth of Blake's 'mythology'. Amid the welter of strange materials that make up Blake's output there is a manageably short work, the *Songs*, which is certainly canonical in the sense that Blake printed and published it. It also uses the poetic form, namely lyric, which modern taste feels most comfortable with, and takes to be distinctive of Romanticism. There is admittedly the oddity that these poems, as issued by the author, are all decorated with ornament and illustration, but this does not take the collection beyond manageability. Hence it comes about that the necessary moving to close-up—equivalent to the picking out of the 'Songs and Sonnets' from Donne's work, say, or the odes from Keats's—commonly with Blake becomes an exclusive attention to only about a twentieth of his poetic production. The remainder is not all obscure blank verse, it should be said. Eng. Lit. students who boil Blake down to the *Songs* are depriving themselves of an encounter with some of the most fascinating lyrics in the language, such as 'The Mental Traveller'.

Songs of Innocence and Experience also has, in itself, an unusual and welcome appearance of clear structure. Indeed no lyric collection in English before or since has seemed to offer such definite indications of how, and under what headings, its materials are to be grouped. But Blake did say that 'to generalize is to be an idiot', and it is evident on a quite cursory inspection that 'innocence' and 'experience' were for him provisional and unstable concepts, fuzzy almost to the point of being reversible into their opposites. Some of the songs turn up first of all in different environments and alignments in the satire called 'An Island in the Moon'; some were moved from one half of the collection to the other. It is a mistaken enterprise to struggle to make a hard-and-fast contrast between, say, the two 'Chimney-Sweeper' poems, or the two 'Holy Thursday' poems. The difficulty one will inevitably encounter in the attempt is some part of their meaning.

It is true that Blake's title, 'Songs of Innocence and Experience', sounds downright and confident about moral distinctions, while many of the individual poems have a strong, simple emotional colouring. Throughout Blake's writing, in fact, one finds the disconcerting conjunction of a bold and vehement tone with a moral vision which is thoroughly fluid and ambiguous. The simplifications of the tone (as with 'Innocence' and 'Experience') are often adversarial, and tempt readers into assertions about Blake's values. But it is interestingly hard actually to state a belief of Blake's about ethics, politics, or even religion and art, although one may embark confidently enough on the exercise, spurred by the general sense that Blake had firm views on such things. If Blake held consistently to a moral view it was one which tends to exclude moral judgement: 'every thing that lives is holy'.

But why the appearance of black-and-white judgement? Blake may not have been pro-Orc and anti-Urizen, for example, but he was certainly prone to writing about these figures in a way that lures the unwary reader into mistaking his meaning. On page 138 of this edition there is reproduced a fascinating observation by Blake about poetry which goes some way towards illuminating the strange coexistence in his writing of moral structures with a groundwork of value-free belief. It concludes, 'poetry is to excuse vice, and show its reason and necessary purgation'. Among the characters Blake lists as requiring 'excusing' by the poet are not only Jesus (who could fall foul, he jokingly suggests, of the accusation of being a 'wine-bibber'), but *also* Jehovah. On a simplistic reading of Blake's beliefs, Jehovah, god of the Old Testament, is a villain. Here Blake clearly implies that his formidable depictions of this entity are meant to take us beyond moralism, even transgressive moralism. It is the extreme challenge of the conviction that every thing that lives is holy to accept all other subjectivities in the world: to realize that 'every bird that cuts the airy way is an immense world of delight, closed by your senses five'.

I have referred to Orc and Urizen, two figures from the blank-verse narrative writing that so greatly outweighs the *Songs* in its extent. This side of Blake's output has also suffered from excessive simplification. There is no single mythological system which the blank-verse narratives expound. There are two epics, *Milton* and *Jerusalem*, which have a systematic machinery involving Blake's personal life, the history of Britain, and parts of the Bible, especially Genesis, Exodus, Joshua, and Revelation. These were preceded by a series of mainly short poems, climaxing with the abandoned epic *Vala*, which deploy a cast of figures invented by the author. Blake wrote that 'unity is the cloak of folly'. He does show a certain taste for pattern-making in the two late epics (he identifies each tribe of Israel with a group of English counties, for example), but his invented mythology in the earlier narratives is not consistent and not meant to be. It is created out of a minimum of antecedent materials, and then added to, and sometimes reshaped, with almost every appearance. Its complexity is related to Blake's vision of a plural, holy universe, composed of an infinity of diverse, equally valuable subjectivities. As Los proclaims early in *Jerusalem*, 'I must create a system, or be enslaved by another man's | I will not reason and compare; my business is to create'. Blake's mythology was a device for virtually unlimited multiplication and diversification, and if it could be summarized in a table it would have failed in its purpose.

Blake, who is so readily simplified by his readers, was the great anti-simplifier, always probing for contradiction and tension. He seems to have become especially absorbed by the theme of self-contradiction, so that even in the two epics the relatively stable nature of the main machinery is balanced by an extreme volatility and multiplicity in such figures as Milton, Albion, and Los—as if Blake has become more strongly aware, or wants to make us more aware, that 'the contrary states of the human soul' (to borrow from the subtitle of *Songs of Innocence and Experience*) are a personal, individual phenomenon. The sense of the moral imperative of diversity survives: 'Man ... requires a new selfhood continually, and must continually be changed into his direct contrary'.

I would advise the reader of Blake to read beyond *Songs of Innocence and Experience*, to abandon the search for easy symmetries and moral judgements in the former, and to attend to local effects in the mythological narratives rather than trying to construct overarching histories. This may sound dismayingly like a recipe for chaos, from which we are at least rescued by the strategic simplifications I have been criticizing. But declining to impose structures on Blake is compatible with discovering structure and shape elsewhere, namely, in our responses to his verse. One of Blake's ways of expressing his own mental and emotional ambivalence was, interestingly, to depict himself as at a certain remove from his text, and thus in effect as a reader. He refers to the physical processes of writing, engraving, and printing his text. He creates an image of himself within his narratives, the blacksmith-bard Los, who is often alienated in various ways, as if from the very stuff the poet has written.

So Blake is alive to what it might be like for us to encounter his poetry, and he does not wish to constrain our responses, which in each of us belong to a subjective 'world of delight' which he must respect. There is something very generous and self-effacing in Blake's attitude towards his readers: as he wrote of one of his paintings, 'if the spectator could enter into these images in his imagination, approaching them on the fiery chariot of his contemplative thought, if he could . . . make a friend and companion of one of these images of wonder . . . then he would be happy'. Earlier I mentioned that the serial processes which Blake used in issuing his poetry did not bring him a wide audience. One may look at the matter the other way round, and see these texts as essentially private manuscript-like objects which have been transformed so that each reader may possess them for himself or herself. Blake leads into *Songs of Innocence* as follows: 'And I wrote my happy songs | Every child may joy to hear'. We are invited to hear something more doleful from 'the bard' at the beginning of *Experience*, but even these are still 'songs'—in other words, just about the most widely possessed form of poetry in modern Western culture. Of the three nouns in Blake's title, songs . . . innocence . . . experience, the last two have attracted too much of our attention. The first, simple one deserves at least as much of our notice, and trust.

Chronology

1757   Blake born (28 November) in Broad Street, Soho, where his father ran a hosiery business.

1759   Death of the poet William Collins.

1760   The first 'Ossian' poems of James Macpherson.

1762   Catherine Boucher, Blake's future wife, born (25 April). Her father was a financially hard-pressed market gardener in Battersea.

1763   Christopher Smart's *Song to David*.

1765   Thomas Percy's *Reliques of Ancient English Poetry*.

1767   Robert Blake, Blake's favourite brother, born (4 August).

1770   Death of George Whitefield.

1772   Death of Emanuel Swedenborg. Blake is apprenticed (4 August) for seven years to James Basire, the most distinguished topographical and antiquarian engraver in London.

1774   Jacob Bryant's *New System* starts to be published.

1776   Declaration of Independence in America. Death of the philosopher David Hume.

1777   Thomas Chatterton's *Poems ... by Thomas Rowley*. Thomas Warton's *Poems*.

1778   Death of Voltaire.

1779   Death of the poet William Cowper. Blake admitted (8 October) as a student of the Royal Academy (founded in 1768), after submitting work to prove a basic proficiency in academic drawing. He is entitled to attend classes and use the Academy's resources for six years. For many further years Blake showed drawings in the Academy's annual exhibitions.

c.1780   Blake makes the acquaintance of Flaxman, Stothard, and Cumberland.

1782   Blake marries Catherine Boucher (18 August), and the couple take rooms near the modern Leicester Square.

1783   *Poetical Sketches* printed.

1784   Blake's father dies (4 July). Soon afterwards Blake tries unsuccessfully to start a print-selling business next door to his father's old establishment.

1785   The Blakes move to Poland Street, Soho.

1787   Thomas Taylor's *The . . . Hymns of Orpheus*. In February Blake's
       beloved brother Robert dies. At about this time Blake becomes
       intimate with Fuseli, and through him probably meets political
       radicals of the day.

1789   *The Book of Thel, Songs of Innocence*, and, probably, *Tiriel*. Blake and
       Catherine attend the first session of the general conference of the
       Swedenborgian New Jerusalem Church (13 April), and are among
       the sixty-odd signatories of a resolution to establish the church.
       Fall of the Bastille (14 July).

1790   *The Marriage of Heaven and Hell*. In the autumn the Blakes move
       to Hercules Buildings, Lambeth, and Blake enters a period of
       relative prosperity as a commercial engraver.

1791   *The French Revolution*. Death of John Wesley.

1792   Death of Sir Joshua Reynolds. Blake's mother dies (7 September).

1793   *Songs of Experience, Visions of the Daughters of Albion, America*.
       Execution of Louis XVI (21 January). In February war is declared
       between Britain and France.

1794   *Europe, The Book of Urizen*. Trial and acquittal of the radicals Horne
       Tooke, Holcroft, and Thelwall. Execution of Robespierre (28
       July).

1795   *Africa, Asia, The Book of Los*. Blake is commissioned to do an
       elaborate series of illustrations for a new edition of Young's *Night
       Thoughts*, which were partly published, without success, about two
       years later. Passage of the Seditious Meetings and Treasonable
       Practices Acts.

1799   Outlawing of Corresponding Societies and other radical groups.
       In January Flaxman arranges for Blake to engrave two illustrations
       for his friend William Hayley's *Essay on Sculpture*: the beginning of
       Blake's association with the connoisseur and poet.

1800   Probable date of composition of *The Four Zoas*. Around June Blake
       visits Hayley at his house in Felpham, Sussex and becomes
       involved in painting a series of portraits of great authors to adorn
       the library, and in other projects of Hayley's. Blake moves into a
       cottage in Felpham (18 September) with his wife and sister-in-law
       to work under Hayley's patronage. By January 1802 he is express-
       ing himself extremely discontented with his physical and artistic
       situation. By July 1803 he has resolved to leave.

1802   Britain signs the Peace of Amiens with France (March).

1803   War with France is renewed (May). On 12 August Blake is
       involved in an altercation outside his cottage with a private soldier,
       John Scolfield, who is quartered in the Felpham inn. On 15 August
       Scolfield deposes before a magistrate that Blake had assaulted him

and uttered seditious opinions in the course of their altercation, 'damning' the King, and calling the army and the people 'slaves' whom Napoleon could easily conquer. Blake denies the charges, and is bailed by Hayley and a local printer. In September the Blakes return to London, and by October are living in South Molton Street.

1804   Probable date of composition of *Milton*, and of first work on *Jerusalem*. Blake stands trial at Chichester Quarter Sessions (11 January) and is acquitted. Hayley pays for his defence. Napoleon becomes Emperor (May).

1805/6 At the turn of the year, after two fairly prosperous years in London during which he charged more for his work than hitherto, Blake is let down or shabbily treated over several illustration projects. He now breaks with most old patrons and associates, including Flaxman and Hayley, and abandons commercial engraving for about ten years. Thomas Butts, who paid unhesitatingly for a large quantity of paintings, prints, and illuminated writing, was for a considerable period Blake's only known source of livelihood. Even this provision seems to have ceased around 1810, and thereafter the Blakes lived in poverty and obscurity for four or five years.

1806   Death of James Barry.

1808   Blake's illustrations to Blair's *The Grave*, one of the projects he had been partly ousted from, reviewed in a hostile and even abusive fashion in *The Examiner* and *The Antijacobin Review*.

1809   In May Blake mounts an exhibition of his work (for which he composes the *Descriptive Catalogue*) at his brother James's house, the old family home and hosiery establishment in Broad Street that James had inherited from his father. *The Examiner* runs the only review, which calls Blake 'an unfortunate lunatic'.

1814   Abdication of Napoleon.

1815   Final defeat of Napoleon. Blake starts to undertake a limited amount of commercial engraving again. From roughly this period also knowledge of at least his lyric poetry spreads in literary circles.

1818   Probable date of composition of *The Everlasting Gospel*. The painter John Linnell is introduced to Blake (June). He quickly obtains engraving work for Blake, and becomes a close friend, though some 35 years his junior. From now on there gathers round Blake a group of younger artists who genuinely admire his work and thought and do much on his behalf, though the Blakes remain relatively poor. The core of this group calls itself 'The Ancients', and includes Linnell, Samuel Palmer, and Edward Calvert. Several substantial (and superbly executed) illustration projects flow from the encouragement and assistance of Linnell: for Thornton's *The*

Pastorals of Virgil (1819), for *The Book of Job* (1821), and for *The Divine Comedy* (1824).

1820   Death of Hayley.

1821   The Blakes move to a pair of rooms in Fountain Court, between the Strand and the Thames. Here Blake lived and worked until his death.

1825   Death of Fuseli.

1826   Death of Flaxman.

1827   Blake dies serenely on 12 August. Just before his death, according to one account, he 'burst out in singing of the things he saw in Heaven'.

LYRICS FROM *POETICAL SKETCHES* (1783)

To Spring

O thou, with dewy locks, who lookest down
Through the clear windows of the morning: turn
Thine angel eyes upon our western isle,
Which in full choir hails thy approach, O Spring!

The hills tell each other, and the list'ning
Valleys hear; all our longing eyes are turned
Up to thy bright pavilions. Issue forth,
And let thy holy feet visit our clime.

Come o'er the eastern hills, and let our winds
Kiss thy perfumed garments; let us taste   10
Thy morn and evening breath; scatter thy pearls
Upon our love-sick land that mourns for thee.

Oh deck her forth with thy fair fingers; pour
Thy soft kisses on her bosom; and put
Thy golden crown upon her languished head,
Whose modest tresses were bound up for thee!

To Summer

O thou, the passest through our valleys in
Thy strength, curb thy fierce steeds, allay the heat
That flames from their large nostrils! Thou, O Summer,
Oft pitched'st here thy golden tent, and oft
Beneath our oaks hast slept, while we beheld
With joy thy ruddy limbs and flourishing hair.

Beneath our thickest shades we oft have heard
Thy voice, when noon upon his fervid car
Rode o'er the deep of heaven; beside our springs
Sit down, and in our mossy valleys; on   10
Some bank beside a river clear throw thy

Silk draperies off, and rush into the stream.
Our vallies love the Summer in his pride.

Our bards are famed who strike the silver wire;
Our youth are bolder than the southern swains;
Our maidens fairer in the sprightly dance;
We lack not songs, nor instruments of joy,
Nor echoes sweet, nor waters clear as heaven,
Nor laurel wreaths against the sultry heat.

To Autumn

O Autumn, laden with fruit, and stained
With the blood of the grape, pass not, but sit
Beneath my shady roof; there thou may'st rest,
And tune thy jolly voice to my fresh pipe;
And all the daughters of the year shall dance!
Sing now the lusty song of fruits and flowers.

'The narrow bud opens her beauties to
The sun, and love runs in her thrilling veins;
Blossoms hang round the brows of morning, and
Flourish down the bright cheek of modest eve,   10
Till clust'ring Summer breaks forth into singing,
And feathered clouds strew flowers round her head.

'The spirits of the air live on the smells
Of fruit; and joy, with pinions light, roves round
The gardens, or sits singing in the trees.'
Thus sang the jolly Autumn as he sat;
Then rose, girded himself, and o'er the bleak
Hills fled from our sight; but left his golden load.

To Winter

O Winter! bar thine adamantine doors;
The north is thine; there hast thou built thy dark
Deep-founded habitation. Shake not thy roofs,
Nor bend thy pillars with thine iron car.

He hears me not, but o'er the yawning deep
Rides heavy; his storms are unchained; sheathed
In ribbed steel, I dare not lift mine eyes;
For he hath reared his sceptre o'er the world.

Lo! now the direful monster, whose skin clings
To his strong bones, strides o'er the groaning rocks.　10
He withers all in silence, and his hand
Unclothes the earth, and freezes up frail life.

He takes his seat upon the cliff; the mariner
Cries in vain. Poor little wretch! that deal'st
With storms; till heaven smiles, and the monster
Is driv'n yelling to his caves beneath Mount Hecla.

To the Evening Star

Thou fair-haired angel of the evening,
Now, whilst the sun rests on the mountains, light
Thy bright torch of love; thy radiant crown
Put on, and smile upon our evening bed!
Smile on our loves; and, while thou drawest the
Blue curtains of the sky, scatter thy silver dew
On every flower that shuts its sweet eyes
In timely sleep. Let thy west wind sleep on
The lake; speak silence with thy glimmering eyes,
And wash the dusk with silver. Soon, full soon,　10
Dost thou withdraw; then the wolf rages wide,
And the lion glares through the dun forest.
The fleeces of our flocks are covered with
Thy sacred dew; protect them with thine influence.

To Morning

O holy virgin! clad in purest white,
Unlock heav'n's golden gates, and issue forth;
Awake the dawn that sleeps in heaven; let light
Rise from the chambers of the east, and bring
The honied dew that cometh on waking day.
O radiant morning, salute the sun,
Roused like a huntsman to the chase; and, with
Thy buskined feet, appear upon our hills.

Song

How sweet I roamed from field to field,
   And tasted all the summer's pride,
Till I the prince of love beheld,
   Who in the sunny beams did glide!

He showed me lilies for my hair,
   And blushing roses for my brow;
He led me through his gardens fair,
   Where all his golden pleasures grow.

With sweet May dews my wings were wet,
   And Phoebus fired my vocal rage;   10
He caught me in his silken net,
   And shut me in his golden cage.

He loves to sit and hear me sing;
   Then, laughing, sports and plays with me;
Then stretches out my golden wing,
And mocks my loss of liberty.

Song

My silks and fine array,
　My smiles and languished air,
By love are driv'n away,
　And mournful lean Despair
Brings me yew to deck my grave;
Such end true lovers have.

His face is fair as heav'n
　When springing buds unfold;
Oh why to him was't giv'n,
　Whose heart is wintry cold?   10
His breast is love's all worshipped tomb,
Where all love's pilgrims come.

Bring me an axe and spade;
　Bring me a winding sheet.
When I my grave have made,
　Let winds and tempests beat;
Then down I'll lie, as cold as clay.
True love doth pass away!

Song

Love and harmony combine,
And around our souls intwine,
While thy branches mix with mine,
And our roots together join.

Joys upon our branches sit,
Chirping loud, and singing sweet;
Like gentle streams beneath our feet
Innocence and virtue meet.

Thou the golden fruit dost bear;
I am clad in flowers fair;   10
Thy sweet boughs perfume the air,
And the turtle buildeth there.

There she sits and feeds her young;
Sweet I hear her mournful song;
And thy lovely leaves among,
There is love: I hear her tongue.

There his charming nest doth lay;
There he sleeps the night away;
There he sports along the day,
And doth among our branches play.   20

Song

I love the jocund dance,
    The softly-breathing song,
Where innocent eyes do glance,
    And where lisps the maiden's tongue.

I love the laughing vale,
    I love the echoing hill,
Where mirth does never fail,
    And the jolly swain laughs his fill.

I love the pleasant cot,
    I love the innocent bow'r,   10
Where white and brown is our lot,
    Or fruit in the midday hour.

I love the oaken seat,
    Beneath the oaken tree,
Where all the old villagers meet,
    And laugh our sports to see.

I love our neighbours all,
    But, Kitty, I better love thee;
And love them I ever shall,
    But thou art all to me.   20

Song

Memory, hither come,
  And tune your merry notes;
And, while upon the wind
  Your music floats,
  I'll pore upon the stream,
  Where sighing lovers dream,
  And fish for fancies as they pass
  Within the watery glass.

I'll drink of the clear stream,
  And hear the linnet's song;   10
And there I'll lie and dream
  The day along.
And, when night comes, I'll go
  To places fit for woe,
Walking along the darkened valley,
  With silent Melancholy.

Mad Song

The wild winds weep,
  And the night is a-cold;
Come hither, Sleep,
  And my griefs infold.
But lo! the morning peeps,
  Over the eastern steeps,
And the rustling birds of dawn
The earth do scorn.

Lo! to the vault
  Of paved heaven,   10
With sorrow fraught,
  My notes are driven.
They strike the ear of night,
  Make weep the eyes of day;
They make mad the roaring winds,
  And with tempests play.

Like a fiend in a cloud,
  With howling woe
After night I do crowd,
  And with night will go.   20
I turn my back to the east,
From whence comforts have increased;
For light doth seize my brain
With frantic pain.

Song

Fresh from the dewy hill, the merry year
Smiles on my head, and mounts his flaming car;
Round my young brows the laurel wreathes a shade,
And rising glories beam around my head.

My feet are winged, while o'er the dewy lawn
I meet my maiden, risen like the morn.
Oh, bless those holy feet, like angels' feet!
Oh, bless those limbs, beaming with heav'nly light!

Like as an angel glitt'ring in the sky,
In times of innocence and holy joy.   10
The joyful shepherd stops his grateful song,
To hear the music of an angel's tongue.

So when she speaks, the voice of Heaven I hear;
So when we walk, nothing impure comes near.
Each field seems Eden, and each calm retreat;
Each village seems the haunt of holy feet.

But that sweet village where my black-eyed maid
Closes her eyes in sleep beneath night's shade,
Whene'er I enter, more than mortal fire
Burns in my soul, and does my song inspire.   20

Song

When early morn walks forth in sober grey,
Then to my black-eyed maid I haste away.
When evening sits beneath her dusky bow'r,
And gently sighs away the silent hour,
The village bell alarms, away I go—
And the vale darkens at my pensive woe.

To that sweet village, where my black-eyed maid
Doth drop a tear beneath the silent shade,
I turn my eyes; and, pensive as I go,
Curse my black stars, and bless my pleasing woe.   10

Oft when the summer sleeps among the trees,
Whisp'ring faint murmurs to the scanty breeze,
I walk the village round; if at her side
A youth doth walk in stolen joy and pride,
I curse my stars in bitter grief and woe,
That made my love so high, and me so low.

O should she e'er prove false, his limbs I'd tear,
And throw all pity on the burning air;
I'd curse bright fortune for my mixed lot,
And then I'd die in peace, and be forgot.   20

King Edward the Third (1783)

SCENE I

The coast of France. King Edward and nobles. The army

KING. O thou, to whose fury the nations are
    But as dust! maintain thy servant's right.
    Without thine aid the twisted mail, and spear,
    And forged helm, and shield of seven times beaten brass,
    Are idle trophies of the vanquisher.
    When confusion rages, when the field is in a flame,
    When the cries of blood tear horror from heav'n,
    And yelling death runs up and down the ranks,
    Let Liberty, the chartered right of Englishmen,
    Won by our fathers in many a glorious field,   10
    Enerve my soldiers; let Liberty
    Blaze in each countenance, and fire the battle.
    The enemy fight in chains, invisible chains, but heavy;
    Their minds are fettered; then how can they be free,
    While, like the mounting flame,
    We spring to battle o'er the floods of death?
    And these fair youths, the flow'r of England,
    Vent'ring their lives in my most righteous cause,
    Oh sheathe their hearts with triple steel, that they
    May emulate their fathers' virtues.   20
    And thou, my son, be strong; thou fightest for a crown
    That death can never ravish from thy brow,
    A crown of glory; but from thy very dust
    Shall beam a radiance, to fire the breasts
    Of youth unborn! Our names are written equal
    In fame's wide trophied hall; 'tis ours to gild

The letters, and to make them shine with gold
That never tarnishes: whether Third Edward,
Or the Prince of Wales, or Montacute, or Mortimer,
Or ev'n the least by birth, shall gain the brightest fame,   30
Is in his hand to whom all men are equal.
The world of men are like the num'rous stars,
That beam and twinkle in the depth of night,
Each clad in glory according to his sphere;
But we, that wander from our native seats,
And beam forth lustre on a darkling world,
Grow larger as we advance! And some perhaps
The most obscure at home, that scarce were seen
To twinkle in their sphere, may so advance
That the astonished world, with up-turned eyes,   40
Regardless of the moon, and those that once were bright,
Stand only for to gaze upon their splendour!
                    [*He here knights the Prince, and other young nobles*
Now let us take a just revenge for those
Brave lords, who fell beneath the bloody axe
At Paris. Thanks, noble Harcourt, for 'twas
By your advice we landed here in Brittany—
A country not yet sown with destruction,
And where the fiery whirlwind of swift war
Has not yet swept its desolating wing.
Into three parties we divide by day,   50
And separate march, but join again at night;
Each knows his rank, and Heav'n marshall all.

                                              [*Exeunt*

SCENE II

*English Court. Lionel Duke of Clarence, Queen Philippa,
lords, bishop, etc*

CLARENCE. My Lords, I have, by the advice of her
Whom I am doubly bound to obey, my parent
And my sovereign, called you together.
My task is great, my burden heavier than
My unfledged years;
Yet, with your kind assistance, Lords, I hope
England shall dwell in peace; that while my father
Toils in his wars, and turns his eyes on this

His native shore—and sees Commerce fly round
With his white wings, and sees his golden London   10
And her silver Thames thronged with shining spires
And corded ships, her merchants buzzing round
Like summer bees, and all the golden cities
In his land overflowing with honey—
Glory may not be dimmed with clouds of care.
Say, Lords, should not our thoughts be first to commerce?
My Lord Bishop, you would recommend us agriculture?
BISHOP. Sweet Prince! the arts of peace are great,
And no less glorious than those of war,
Perhaps more glorious in the philosophic mind,   20
When I sit at my home, a private man,
My thoughts are on my gardens, and my fields,
How to employ the hand that lacketh bread.
If Industry is in my diocese,
Religion will flourish; each man's heart
Is cultivated, and will bring forth fruit:
This is my private duty and my pleasure.
But as I sit in council with my prince,
My thoughts take in the gen'ral good of the whole,
And England is the land favoured by Commerce;   30
For Commerce, though the child of Agriculture,
Fosters his parent, who else must sweat and toil,
And gain but scanty fare. Then, my dear Lord,
Be England's trade our care; and we, as tradesmen,
Looking to the gain of this our native land.
CLAR. O my good Lord, true wisdom drops like honey
From your tongue, as from a worshipped oak!
Forgive, my Lords, my talkative youth, that speaks
Not merely what my narrow observation has
Picked up, but what I have concluded from your lessons.
Now, by the Queen's advice, I ask your leave   40
To dine to-morrow with the Mayor of London.
If I obtain your leave, I have another boon
To ask, which is, the favour of your company.
I fear Lord Percy will not give me leave.
PERCY. Dear Sir, a prince should always keep his state,
And grant his favours with a sparing hand,
Or they are never rightly valued.
These are my thoughts, yet it were best to go;

But keep a proper dignity, for now   50
You represent the sacred person of
Your father; 'tis with princes as 'tis with the sun,
If not sometimes o'er-clouded, we grow weary
Of his officious glory.

CLAR. Then you will give me leave to shine sometimes,
My Lord?

LORD. Thou hast a gallant spirit, which I fear
Will be imposed on by the closer sort!   [*Aside*.

CLAR. Well, I'll endeavour to take
Lord Percy's advice; I have been used so much   60
To dignity, that I'm sick on't.

QUEEN PHILIPPA. Fie, fie, Lord Clarence; you proceed not to
business,
But speak of your own pleasures.
I hope their Lordships will excuse your giddiness.

CLAR. My Lords, the French have fitted out many
Small ships of war, that, like to ravening wolves,
Infest our English seas, devouring all
Our burdened vessels, spoiling our naval flocks.
The merchants do complain, and beg our aid.

PERCY. The merchants are rich enough;   70
Can they not help themselves?

BISH. They can, and may; but how to gain their will,
Requires our countenance and help.

PERCY. When that they find they must, my Lord, they will.
Let them but suffer awhile, and you shall see
They will bestir themselves.

BISH. Lord Percy cannot mean that we should suffer
This disgrace; if so, we are not sovereigns
Of the sea: our right, that Heaven gave
To England, when at the birth of Nature   80
She was seated in the deep, the ocean ceased
His mighty roar, and, fawning, played around
Her snowy feet, and owned his awful queen.
Lord Percy, if the heart is sick, the head
Must be aggrieved; if but one member suffer,
The heart doth fail. You say, my Lord, the merchants
Can, if they will, defend themselves against
These rovers; this is a noble scheme,
Worthy the brave Lord Percy, and as worthy

His generous aid to put it into practice.   90
PERCY. Lord Bishop, what was rash in me, is wise
  In you; I dare not own the plan. 'Tis not
  Mine. Yet will I, if you please,
  Quickly to the Lord Mayor, and work him onward
  To this most glorious voyage; on which cast
  I'll set my whole estate,
  But we will bring these Gallic rovers under.
QUEEN. Thanks, brave Lord Percy; you have the thanks
  Of England's Queen, and will, ere long, of England
                                                   [*Exeunt*

SCENE III

At Crécy. Sir Thomas Dagworth and Lord Audley, meeting

AUDLEY. Good morrow, brave Sir Thomas, the bright morn
  Smiles on our army, and the gallant sun
  Springs from the hills like a young hero
  Into the battle, shaking his golden locks
  Exultingly; this is a promising day.
DAGWORTH. Why, my Lord Audley, I don't know.
  Give me your hand, and now I'll tell you what
  I think you do not know—Edward's afraid of Philip.
AUD. Ha, ha, Sir Thomas! you but joke;
  Did you e'er see him fear? At Blanchetaque,   10
  When almost singly he drove six thousand
  French from the ford, did he fear then?
DAGW. Yes, fear; that made him fight so.
AUD. By the same reason I might say, 'tis fear
  That makes you fight.
DAGW. Mayhap you may; look upon Edward's face—
  No one can say he fears. But when he turns
  His back, then I will say it to his face,
  He is afraid; he makes us all afraid.
  I cannot bear the enemy at my back.   20
  Now here we are at Crécy; where, to-morrow,
  To-morrow we shall know. I say, Lord Audley,
  That Edward runs away from Philip.
AUD. Perhaps you think the Prince too is afraid?
DAGW. No; God forbid! I'm sure he is not—
  He is a young lion. Oh I have seen him fight,

And give command, and lightning has flashed
From his eyes across the field; I have seen him
Shake hands with death, and strike a bargain for
The enemy; he has danced in the field   30
Of battle, like the youth at morris play.
I'm sure he's not afraid, nor Warwick, nor none,
None of us but me; and I am very much afraid.
AUD. Are you afraid too, Sir Thomas?
 I believe that as much as I believe
 The King's afraid; but what are you afraid of?
DAGW. Of having my back laid open; we turn
 Our backs to the fire, till we shall burn our skirts.
AUD. And this, Sir Thomas, you call fear? Your fear
 Is of a different kind then from the King's;   40
 He fears to turn his face, and you to turn your back.
 I do not think, Sir Thomas, you know what fear is.

Enter Sir John Chandos

CHANDOS. Good morrow, Generals; I give you joy.
 Welcome to the fields of Crécy. Here we stop,
 And wait for Philip.
DAGW. I hope so.
AUD. There, Sir Thomas; do you call that fear?
DAGW. I don't know; perhaps he takes it by fits.
 Why noble Chandos, look you here—
 One rotten sheep spoils the whole flock;   50
 And if the bell-wether is tainted, I wish
 The Prince may not catch the distemper too.
CHAND. Distemper, Sir Thomas! what distemper?
 I have not heard.
DAGW. Why, Chandos, you are a wise man,
 I know you understand me; a distemper
 The King caught here in France of running away.
AUD. Sir Thomas, you say, you have caught it too.
DAGW. And so will the whole army; 'tis very catching,
 For when the coward runs, the brave man totters.   60
 Perhaps the air of the country is the cause.
 I feel it coming upon me, so I strive against it;
 You yet are whole, but after a few more
 Retreats we all shall know how to retreat
 Better than fight. To be plain, I think retreating

Too often takes away a soldier's courage.

CHAND. Here comes the King himself; tell him your thoughts
Plainly, Sir Thomas.

DAGW. I've told him before, but his disorder
Makes him deaf.   70

Enter King Edward and Black Prince

KING. Good morrow, Generals; when English courage fails,
Down goes our right to France;
But we are conquerors everywhere; nothing
Can stand our soldiers; each man is worthy
Of a triumph. Such an army of heroes
Ne'er shouted to the heav'ns, nor shook the field.
Edward, my son, thou art
Most happy, having such command; the man
Were base who were not fired to deeds
Above heroic, having such examples.   80

PRINCE. Sire! with respect and deference I look
Upon such noble souls, and wish myself
Worthy the high command that Heaven and you
Have given me. When I have seen the field glow,
And in each countenance the soul of war,
Curbed by the manliest reason, I have been winged
With certain victory; and 'tis my boast,
And shall be still my glory, I was inspired
By these brave troops.

DAGW. Your Grace had better make   90
Them all generals.

KING. Sir Thomas Dagworth, you must have your joke,
And shall, while you can fight as you did at
The ford.

DAGW. I have a small petition to your Majesty.

KING. What can Sir Thomas Dagworth ask, that Edward
Can refuse?

DAGW. I hope your Majesty cannot refuse so great
A trifle; I've gilt your cause with my best blood,
And would again, were I not forbid   100
By him whom I am bound to obey; my hands
Are tied up, my courage shrunk and withered,
My sinews slackened, and my voice scarce heard.
Therefore I beg I may return to England.

KING. I know not what you could have asked, Sir Thomas,
  That I would not have sooner parted with
  Than such a soldier as you have been, and such a friend;
  Nay, I will know the most remote particulars
  Of this your strange petition, that, if I can,
  I still may keep you here.   110

DAGW. Here on the fields of Crécy we are settled,
  Till Philip springs the tim'rous covey again.
  The wolf is hunted down by causeless fear;
  The lion flees, and fear usurps his heart,
  Startled, astonished at the clam'rous cock;
  The eagle, that doth gaze upon the sun,
  Fears the small fire that plays about the fen;
  If, at this moment of their idle fear,
  The dog doth seize the wolf, the forester the lion,
  The negro in the crevice of the rock   120
  Doth seize the soaring eagle, undone by flight
  They tame submit; such the effect flight has
  On noble souls. Now hear its opposite:
  The tim'rous stag starts from the thicket wild;
  The fearful crane springs from the splashy fen;
  The shining snake glides o'er the bending grass.
  The stag turns head! and bays the crying hounds;
  The crane, o'ertaken, fighteth with the hawk;
  The snake doth turn, and bite the padding foot;
  And, if your Majesty's afraid of Philip,   130
  You are more like a lion than a crane.
  Therefore I beg I may return to England.

KING. Sir Thomas, now I understand your mirth,
  Which often plays with wisdom for its pastime,
  And brings good counsel from the breast of laughter,
  I hope you'll stay, and see us fight this battle,
  And reap rich harvest in the fields of Crécy;
  Then go to England, tell them how we fight,
  And set all hearts on fire to be with us.
  Philip is plumed, and thinks we flee from him,   140
  Else he would never dare to attack us. Now,
  Now the quarry's set! and Death doth sport
  In the bright sunshine of this fatal day.

DAGW. Now my heart dances, and I am as light
  As the young bridegroom going to be married.

Now must I to my soldiers, get them ready,
Furbish our armours bright, new plume our helms,
And we will sing, like the young housewives busied
In the dairy; my feet are winged, but not
For flight, an please your grace.　　　　　　　　　150
KING. If all my soldiers are as pleased as you,
'Twill be a gallant thing to fight or die;
Then I can never be afraid of Philip.
DAGW. A raw-boned fellow t'other day passed by me;
I told him to put off his hungry looks;
He answered me, 'I hunger for another battle'.
I saw a little Welshman with a fiery face;
I told him he looked like a candle half
Burned out; he answered, he was 'pig enough
To light another pattle.' Last night beneath　　　160
The moon I walked abroad, when all had pitched
Their tents, and all were still;
I heard a blooming youth singing a song
He had composed, and at each pause he wiped
His dropping eyes. The ditty was, 'If he
Returned victorious, he should wed a maiden
Fairer than snow, and rich as midsummer.'
Another wept, and wished health to his father.
I chid them both, but gave them noble hopes.
These are the minds that glory in the battle,　　　170
And leap and dance to hear the trumpet sound.
KING. Sir Thomas Dagworth, be thou near our person;
Thy heart is richer than the vales of France.
I will not part with such a man as thee.
If Philip came armed in the ribs of death,
And shook his mortal dart against my head,
Thoud'st laugh his fury into nerveless shame!
Go now, for thou art suited to the work,
Throughout the camp; enflame the timorous,
Blow up the sluggish into ardour, and　　　180
Confirm the strong with strength; the weak inspire,
And wing their brows with hope and expectation.
Then to our tent return, and meet to council. [*Exit Dagworth*
CHAND. That man's a hero in his closet, and more
A hero to the servants of his house,
Than to the gaping world; he carries windows

In that enlarged breast of his, that all
May see what's done within.
PRINCE. He is a genuine Englishman, my Chandos,
And hath the spirit of liberty within him.   190
Forgive my prejudice, Sir John; I think
My Englishmen the bravest people on
The face of the earth.
CHAND. Courage, my Lord, proceeds from self-dependence;
Teach man to think he's a free agent,
Give but a slave his liberty, he'll shake
Off sloth, and build himself a hut, and hedge
A spot of ground; this he'll defend; 'tis his
By right of nature. Thus set in action,
He will still move onward to plan conveniences,   200
'Till glory fires his breast to enlarge his castle,
While the poor slave drudges all day, in hope
To rest at night.
KING. O Liberty, how glorious art thou!
I see thee hov'ring o'er my army, with
Thy wide-stretched plumes; I see thee
Lead them on to battle;
I see thee blow thy golden trumpet, while
Thy sons shout the strong shout of victory!
O noble Chandos! think thyself a gardener,   210
My son a vine, which I commit unto
Thy care; prune all extravagant shoots, and guide
Th' ambitious tendrils in the paths of wisdom;
Water him with thy advice, and Heav'n
Rain fresh'ning dew upon his branches. And,
O Edward, my dear son! learn to think lowly of
Thyself, as we may all each prefer other.
'Tis the best policy, and 'tis our duty.   [Exit King Edward
PRINCE. And may our duty, Chandos, be our pleasure—
Now we are alone, Sir John, I will unburden,   220
And breathe my hopes into the burning air,
Where thousand deaths are posting up and down,
Commissioned to this fatal field of Crécy;
Methinks I see them arm my gallant soldiers,
And gird the sword upon each thigh, and fit
Each shining helm, and string each stubborn bow,
And dance to the neighing of our steeds.

Methinks the shout begins, the battle burns;
Methinks I see them perch on English crests,
And roar the wild flame of fierce war upon   230
The thronged enemy! In truth, I am too full;
It is my sin to love the noise of war.
Chandos, thou seest my weakness; strong nature
Will bend or break us; my blood, like a spring-tide,
Does rise so high, to overflow all bounds
Of moderation; while Reason, in his
Frail bark, can see no shore or bound for vast
Ambition. Come, take the helm, my Chandos,
That my full-blown sails overset me not
In the wild tempest; condemn my 'ventrous youth,   240
That plays with danger, as the innocent child,
Unthinking, plays upon the viper's den.
I am a coward, in my reason, Chandos.

CHAND. You are a man, my prince, and a brave man,
If I can judge of actions; but your heat
Is the effect of youth, and want of use;
Use makes the armed field and noisy war
Pass over as a summer cloud, unregarded,
Or but expected as a thing of course.
Age is contemplative; each rolling year   250
Brings forth fruit to the mind's treasure-house;
While vacant youth doth crave and seek about
Within itself, and findeth discontent;
Then, tired of thought, impatient takes the wing,
Seizes the fruits of time, attacks experience,
Roams round vast Nature's forest, where no bounds
Are set, the swiftest may have room, the strongest
Find prey—till, tired at length, sated and tired
With the changing sameness, old variety,
We sit us down, and view our former joys   260
With distaste and dislike.

PRINCE. Then if we must tug for experience,
Let us not fear to beat round Nature's wilds,
And rouse the strongest prey; then if we fall,
We fall with glory. I know the wolf
Is dangerous to fight, not good for food,
Nor is the hide a comely vestment; so
We have our battle for our pains. I know

That youth has need of age to point fit prey,
And oft the stander-by shall steal the fruit   270
Of th' others' labour. This is philosophy;
These are the tricks of the world; but the pure soul
Shall mount on native wings, disdaining
Little sport, and cut a path into the heaven of glory,
Leaving a track of light for men to wonder at.
I'm glad my father does not hear me talk;
You can find friendly excuses for me, Chandos.
But do you not think, Sir John, that if it please
Th' Almighty to stretch out my span of life,
I shall with pleasure view a glorious action,   280
Which my youth mastered?
CHAND. Considerate age, my Lord, views motives,
And not acts. When neither warbling voice
Nor trilling pipe is heard, nor pleasure sits
With trembling age, the voice of Conscience then,
Sweeter than music in a summer's eve,
Shall warble round the snowy head, and keep
Sweet symphony to feathered angels, sitting
As guardians round your chair; then shall the pulse   289
Beat slow, and taste, and touch, and sight, and sound, and smell,
That sing and dance round Reason's fine-wrought throne,
Shall flee away, and leave him all forlorn;
Yet not forlorn if Conscience is his friend.

                                        [*Exeunt*

SCENE IV

Sir Thomas Dagworth's Tent. Dagworth and William his man

DAGWORTH. Bring hither my armour, William;
    Ambition is the growth of ev'ry clime.
WILLIAM. Does it grow in England, Sir?
DAGW. Aye, it grows most in lands most cultivated.
WILL. Then it grows most in France; the vines here
    Are finer than any we have in England.
DAGW. Aye, but the oaks are not.
WILL. What is the tree you mentioned? I don't think
    I ever saw it.
DAGW. Ambition.
WILL. Is it a little creeping root that grows in ditches?

DAGW. Thou dost not understand me, William.
It is a root that grows in every breast;
Ambition is the desire or passion that one man
Has to get before another, in any pursuit after glory;
But I don't think you have any of it.

WILL. Yes, I have; I have a great ambition to know every thing, Sir.

DAGW. But when our first ideas are wrong, what follows must all be wrong of course; 'tis best to know a little, and to know that little aright.

WILL. Then, Sir, I should be glad to know if it was not ambition that brought over our king to France to fight for his right?

DAGW. Though the knowledge of that will not profit thee much, yet I will tell you that it was ambition.

WILL. Then if ambition is a sin, we are all guilty in coming with him, and in fighting for him.

DAGW. Now, William, thou dost thrust the question home; but I must tell you, that guilt being an act of the mind, none are guilty but those whose minds are prompted by that same ambition.

WILL. Now I always thought, that a man might be guilty of doing wrong, without knowing it was wrong.

DAGW. Thou art a natural philosopher, and knowest truth by instinct; while reason runs aground, as we have run our argument. Only remember, William, all have it in their power to know the motives of their own actions, and 'tis a sin to act without some reason.

WILL. And whoever acts without reason, may do a great deal of harm without knowing it.

DAGW. Thou art an endless moralist.

WILL. Now there's a story come into my head, that I will tell your honour, if you'll give me leave.

DAGW. No, William, save it till another time; this is no time for story-telling; but here comes one who is as entertaining as a good story.

Enter Peter Blunt

PETER. Yonder's a musician going to play before the King; it's a new song about the French and English, and the Prince has made the minstrel a squire, and given him I don't know what, and I can't tell whether he don't mention us all one by one; and he is to write another about all us that are to die, that we may be remembered in Old England, for all our blood and bones are in France; and a great deal more that we shall all hear by and by;

and I came to tell your honour, because you love to hear war-songs.

DAGW. And who is the minstrel, Peter, do'st know?

PETER. Oh aye, I forgot to tell that; he has got the same name as Sir John Chandos, that the prince is always with—the wise man, that knows us all as well as your honour, only e'nt so good natured.

DAGW. I thank you, Peter, for your information, but not for your compliment, which is not true; there's as much difference between him and me, as between glittering sand and fruitful mould; or shining glass and a wrought diamond, set in rich gold, and fitted to the finger of an emperor: such is that worthy Chandos.

PETER. I know your honour does not think anything of yourself, but everybody else does.

DAGW. Go, Peter, get you gone; flattery is delicious, even from the lips of a babbler.   [Exit Peter

WILL. I never flatter your honour.

DAGW. I don't know that.

WILL. Why you know, Sir, when we were in England, at the tournament at Windsor, and the Earl of Warwick was tumbled over, you asked me if he did not look well when he fell? and I said, No, he looked very foolish; and you was very angry with me for not flattering you.

DAGW. You mean that I was angry with you for not flattering the Earl of Warwick.   [Exeunt

SCENE V

Sir Thomas Dagworth's Tent. Sir Thomas Dagworth. To him enters Sir Walter Manny

SIR WALTER. Sir Thomas Dagworth, I have been weeping
    Over the men that are to die to-day.

DAGW. Why, brave Sir Walter, you or I may fall.

SIR WALTER. I know this breathing flesh must lie and rot,
    Covered with silence and forgetfulness.
    Death wons in cities' smoke, and in still night,
    When men sleep in their beds, walketh about!
    How many in walled cities lie and groan,
    Turning themselves upon their beds,
    Talking with Death, answering his hard demands!   10

How many walk in darkness; terrors are round
The curtains of their beds; destruction is
Ready at the door! How many sleep
In earth, covered with stones and deathy dust,
Resting in quietness, whose spirits walk
Upon the clouds of Heaven, to die no more!
Yet Death is terrible, though borne on angels' wings!
How terrible then is the field of Death,
Where he doth rend the vault of Heaven,
And shake the gates of Hell!　　　　　　　　　　20
O Dagworth, France is sick! The very sky,
Though sunshine light it, seems to me as pale
As the pale fainting man on his death-bed,
Whose face is shown by light of sickly taper!
It makes me sad and sick at very heart,
Thousands must fall to-day!

DAGW. Thousands of souls must leave this prison-house,
To be exalted to those heavenly fields,
Where songs of triumph, palms of victory,
Where peace, and joy, and love, and calm content　　30
Sit singing in the azure clouds, and strew
Flowers of Heaven's growth over the banquet-table.
Bind ardent hope upon your feet like shoes,
Put on the robe of preparation;
The table is prepared in shining Heaven;
The flowers of immortality are blown.
Let those that fight, fight in good stedfastness,
And those that fall shall rise in victory.

SIR WALTER. I've often seen the burning field of war,
And often heard the dismal clang of arms;　　　　40
But never, till this fatal day of Crécy,
Has my soul fainted with these views of Death!
I seem to be in one great charnel-house,
And seem to scent the rotten carcases!
I seem to hear the dismal yells of Death,
While the black gore drops from his horrid jaws:
Yet I not fear the monster in his pride.
But oh the souls that are to die to-day!

DAGW. Stop, brave Sir Walter; let me drop a tear,
Then let the clarion of war begin.　　　　　　　50
I'll fight and weep, 'tis in my country's cause;

I'll weep and shout for glorious liberty.
Grim War shall laugh and shout, decked in tears,
And blood shall flow like streams across the meadows,
That murmur down their pebbly channels, and
Spend their sweet lives to do their country service.
Then shall England's verdure shoot, her fields shall smile,
Her ships shall sing across the foaming sea,
Her mariners shall use the flute and viol,
And rattling guns, and black and dreary war,   60
Shall be no more.
SIR WALTER. Well; let the trumpet sound, and the drum beat;
Let war stain the blue heavens with bloody banners,
I'll draw my sword, nor ever sheath it up,
'Till England blow the trump of victory,
Or I lay stretched upon the field of Death!

> [*Exeunt*

SCENE VI

*In the Camp. Several of the warriors met at the King's tent with a
minstrel, who sings the following song:*

O sons of Trojan Brutus, clothed in war,
Whose voices are the thunder of the field,
Rolling dark clouds o'er France, muffling the sun
In sickly darkness like a dim eclipse,
Threatening as the red brow of storms, as fire
Burning up nations in your wrath and fury!

Your ancestors came from the fires of Troy,
(Like lions roused by lightning from their dens,
Whose eyes do glare against the stormy fires)
Heated with war, filled with the blood of Greeks,   10
With helmets hewn, and shields covered with gore,
In navies black, broken with wind and tide!

They landed in firm array upon the rocks
Of Albion; they kissed the rocky shore;
'Be thou our mother, and our nurse,' they said,
'Our children's mother; and thou shalt be our grave,
The sepulchre of ancient Troy, from whence
Shall rise cities, and thrones, and arms, and awful powers.'

Our fathers swarm from the ships. Giant voices
Are heard from the hills, the enormous sons　　　　　　20
Of ocean run from rocks and caves: wild men,
Naked and roaring like lions, hurling rocks,
And wielding knotty clubs, like oaks entangled
Thick as a forest, ready for the axe.

Our fathers move in firm array to battle;
The savage monsters rush like roaring fire.
Like as a forest roars with crackling flames,
When the red lightning, borne by furious storms,
Lights on some woody shore; the parched heavens
Rain fire into the molten raging sea!　　　　　　30

The smoking trees are strewn upon the shore,
Spoiled of their verdure! Oh how oft have they
Defied the storm that howled o'er their heads!
Our fathers, sweating, lean on their spears, and view
The mighty dead: giant bodies, streaming blood,
Dread visages, frowning in silent death!

Then Brutus spoke, inspired; our fathers sit
Attentive on the melancholy shore.
Hear ye the voice of Brutus. 'The flowing waves
Of time come rolling o'er my breast,' he said,　　　　　　40
'And my heart labours with futurity.
Our sons shall rule the empire of the sea;

'Their mighty wings shall stretch from east to west;
Their nest is in the sea, but they shall roam
Like eagles for the prey. Nor shall the young
Crave or be heard, for plenty shall bring forth;
Cities shall sing, and vales in rich array
Shall laugh, whose fruitful laps bend down with fulness.

'Our sons shall rise from thrones in joy,
Each one buckling on his armour; morning　　　　　　50
Shall be prevented by their swords' gleaming,
And evening hear their song of victory!
Their towers shall be built upon the rocks;
Their daughters shall sing, surrounded with shining spears!

'Liberty shall stand upon the cliffs of Albion,
Casting her blue eyes over the green ocean;
Or, tow'ring, stand upon the roaring waves,
Stretching her mighty spear o'er distant lands;
While, with her eagle wings, she covereth
Fair Albion's shore, and all her families.'   60

LYRICS OF *c*.1784

Song First by a Shepherd

Welcome, stranger, to this place,
Where Joy doth sit on every bough;
Paleness flies from every face;
We reap not what we do not sow.

Innocence doth like a rose
Bloom on every maiden's cheek;
Honour twines around her brows;
The jewel Health adorns her neck

Song Third by an Old Shepherd

When silver snow decks Sylvio's clothes,
And jewel hangs at shepherd's nose,
We can abide life's pelting storm,
That makes our limbs quake, if our hearts be warm.

Whilst Virtue is our walking-staff,
And Truth a lantern to our path,
We can abide life's pelting storm,
That makes our limbs quake, if our hearts be warm.

Blow, boisterous wind; stern winter, frown.
Innocence is a winter's gown;   10
So clad, we'll abide life's pelting storm,
That makes our limbs quake, if our hearts be warm.

[*The Cynic's First Song*]

I

When old Corruption first begun,
Adorned in yellow vest,
He committed on Flesh a whoredom:
Oh what a wicked beast!

2

From them a callow babe did spring,
And old Corruption smiles,
To think his race should never end,
For now he had a child.

3

He called him Surgery, and fed
The babe with his own milk —   10
For Flesh and he could ne'er agree:
She would not let him suck.

4

And this he always kept in mind,
And formed a crooked knife,
And ran about with bloody hands
To seek his mother's life.

5

And as he ran to seek his mother
He met with a dead woman;
He fell in love and married her,
A deed which is not common.   20

6

She soon grew pregnant, and brought forth
Scurvy and Spotted Fever.
The father grinned and skipped about,
And said, 'I'm made for ever.

7

'For now I have procured these imps,
I'll try experiments.'
With that he tied poor Scurvy down
And stopped up all its vents;

8

And when the child began to swell
He shouted out aloud: 30
'I've found the dropsy out, and soon
Shall do the world more good.'

9

He took up Fever by the neck
And cut out all its spots,
And through the holes which he had made
He first discovered guts.

[*Miss Gittipin's First Song*]

Phoebe dressed like beauty's queen,
Jellicoe in faint pea-green—
Sitting all beneath a grot,
Where the little lambkins trot.

Maidens dancing, loves a-sporting,
All the country folks a-courting,
Susan, Johnny, Bet, and Joe,
Lightly tripping on a row.

Happy people, who can be
In happiness compared with ye?   10
The pilgrim with his crook and hat
Sees your happiness complete.

[*The Cynic's Second Song*]

Hail Matrimony, made of Love!
To thy wide gates how great a drove
On purpose to be yoked do come,
Widows and maids, and youths also,
That lightly trip on beauty's toe,
Or sit on beauty's bum.

Hail, fingerfooted lovely creatures!
The females of our human natures,
Formed to suckle all mankind.
'Tis you that come in time of need;   10
Without you we should never breed,
Or any comfort find.

For if a damsel's blind or lame,
Or Nature's hand has crooked her frame,
Or if she's deaf or is wall-eyed —
Yet if her heart is well inclined,
Some tender lover she shall find
That panteth for a bride.

The universal poultice this,
To cure whatever is amiss   20
In damsel or in widow gay.
It makes them smile, it makes them skip;
Like birds just cured of the pip,
They chirp and hop away.

Then come ye maidens, come ye swains,
Come and be eased of all your pains,
In Matrimony's golden cage.

[*Obtuse Angle's Song*]

To be or not to be
Of great capacity,
Like Sir Isaac Newton,
Or Locke, or Doctor South,
Or Sherlock upon death.
I'd rather be Sutton.

For he did build a house
For aged men and youth,
With walls of brick and stone,
He furnished it within   10
With whatever he could win,
And all his own.

He drew out of the stocks
His money in a box,
And sent his servant
To Green the bricklayer,
And to the carpenter—
He was so fervent.

The chimneys were three score,
The windows many more;   20
And for convenience
He sinks and gutters made,
And all the way he paved
To hinder pestilence.

Was not this a good man,
Whose life was but a span,
Whose name was Sutton,
As Locke, or Doctor South,
Or Sherlock upon Death,
Or Sir Isaac Newton?   30

[*The Lawgiver's Song*]

This city and this country has brought forth many mayors,
To sit in state and give forth laws, out of their old oak chairs,
With face as brown as any nut with drinking of strong ale.
Good English hospitality, oh, then it did not fail!

With scarlet gowns and broad gold lace would make a yeoman
    sweat,
With stockings rolled above their knees, and shoes as black as jet—
With eating beef and drinking beer, oh, they were stout and hale.
Good English hospitality, oh, then it did not fail!

Thus sitting at the table wide, the Mayor and Aldermen
Were fit to give law to the City: each ate as much as ten.   10
The hungry poor entered the hall to eat good beef and ale.
Good English hospitality, oh, then it did not fail!

[*Miss Gittipin's Second Song*]

Leave, oh, leave me to my sorrows;
Here I'll sit and fade away,
Till I'm nothing but a spirit,
And I lose this form of clay.

Then if chance along this forest
Any walk in pathless ways,
Through the gloom he'll see my shadow,
Hear my voice upon the breeze.

All Religions are One (c. 1788)

The voice of one crying in the wilderness

As the true method of knowledge is experiment the true faculty of knowing must be the faculty which experiences. This faculty I treat of.

PRINCIPLE 1

That the Poetic Genius is the true Man, and that the body or outward form of Man is derived from the Poetic Genius. Likewise that the forms of all things are derived from their genius, which by the ancients was called an Angel and Spirit and Demon.

PRINCIPLE 2

As all men are alike in outward form, so (and with the same infinite variety) all are alike in the Poetic Genius.

PRINCIPLE 3

No man can think, write or speak from his heart, but he must intend truth. Thus all sects of philosophy are from the Poetic Genius adapted to the weaknesses of every individual.

PRINCIPLE 4

As none by travelling over known lands can find out the unknown, so from already acquired knowledge Man could not acquire more. Therefore an universal Poetic Genius exists.

PRINCIPLE 5

The religions of all nations are derived from each nation's different reception of the Poetic Genius, which is everywhere called the Spirit of Prophecy.

PRINCIPLE 6

The Jewish and Christian testaments are an original derivation from the Poetic Genius. This is necessary from the confined nature of bodily sensation.

PRINCIPLE 7

As all men are alike (though infinitely various) so all religions—and, as all similars, have one source.

The true Man is the source, he being the Poetic Genius.

There is No Natural Religion (c.1788)

(1)

THE ARGUMENT

Man has no notion of moral fitness but from education. Naturally he is only a natural organ subject to sense.

I

Man cannot naturally perceive but through his natural or bodily organs.

II

Man by his reasoning power can only compare and judge of what he has already perceived.

III

From a perception of only 3 senses or 3 elements none could deduce a fourth or fifth.

IV

None could have other than natural or organic thoughts if he had none but organic perceptions.

V

Man's desires are limited by his perceptions; none can desire what he has not perceived.

VI

The desires and perceptions of Man untaught by anything but organs of sense must be limited to objects of sense.

(2)

I

Man's perceptions are not bounded by organs of perception; he perceives more than sense (though ever so acute) can discover.

II

Reason or the ratio of all we have already known is not the same that it shall be when we know more.

[*The third proposition in this sequence seems not to have survived*]

IV

The bounded is loathed by its possessor. The same dull round even of a universe would soon become a mill with complicated wheels.

V

If the many become the same as the few, when possessed, 'More! More!' is the cry of a mistaken soul. Less than all cannot satisfy Man.

VI

If any could desire what he is incapable of possessing, despair must be his eternal lot.

VII

The desire of Man being infinite the possession is infinite and himself infinite.

APPLICATION

He who sees the infinite in all things sees God. He who sees the ratio only sees himself only.

CONCLUSION

If it were not for the poetic or prophetic character the philosophic and experimental would soon be at the ratio of all things, and stand still, unable to do other than repeat the same dull round over again.

Tiriel (*c.* 1789)

And aged Tiriel stood before the gates of his beautiful palace
With Myratana, once the queen of all the western plains;
But now his eyes were darkened, and his wife fading in death.
They stood before their once delightful palace, and thus the
   voice
Of aged Tiriel arose, that his sons might hear in their gates:

'Accursed race of Tiriel, behold your father.
Come forth and look on her that bore you; come you accursed
   sons!
In my weak arms I here have borne your dying mother.
Come forth, sons of the curse, come forth, see the death of
   Myratana!'

His sons ran from their gates and saw their aged parents stand,   10
And thus the eldest son of Tiriel raised his mighty voice:

'Old man, unworthy to be called the father of Tiriel's race
(For every one of those thy wrinkles, each of those grey hairs,
Are cruel as death, and as obdurate as the devouring pit),
Why should thy sons care for thy curses, thou accursed man?
Were we not slaves till we rebelled? Who cares for Tiriel's
   curse?
His blessing was a cruel curse; his curse may be a blessing.'

He ceased. The aged man raised up his right hand to the
   heavens:
His left supported Myratana shrinking in pangs of death.
The orbs of his large eyes he opened, and thus his voice went
   forth: 20

'Serpents, not sons, wreathing around the bones of Tiriel!
Ye worms of death feasting upon your aged parents' flesh,
Listen and hear your mother's groans. No more accursed sons
She bears; she groans not at the birth of Heuxos or Yuva.
These are the groans of death, ye serpents, these are the
   groans of death.
Nourished with milk, ye serpents, nourished with mother's
   tears and cares,

Look at my eyes, blind as the orbless skull among the stones.
Look at my bald head! Hark, listen, ye serpents! Listen!
What, Myratana? What, my wife? O soul, O spirit, O fire!
What, Myratana, art thou dead? Look here, ye serpents look!   30
The serpents sprung from her own bowels have drained her
    dry as this.
Curse on your ruthless heads, for I will bury her even here.'

So saying be began to dig a grave with his aged hands,
But Heuxos called a son of Zazel to dig their mother a grave:

'Old cruelty, desist, and let us dig a grave for thee.
Thou hast refused our charity, thou hast refused our food,
Thou hast refused our clothes, our beds, our houses for thy
    dwelling,
Choosing to wander like a son of Zazel in the rocks.
Why dost thou curse? Is not the curse now come upon your head?
Was it not you enslaved the sons of Zazel, and they have
    cursed,   40
And now you feel it? Dig a grave and let us bury our mother.'

'There take the body, cursed sons, and may the heavens rain
    wrath
As thick as northern fogs around your gates to choke you up,
That you may lie, as now your mother lies, like dogs cast out,
The stink of your dead carcases annoying man and beast,
Till your white bones are bleached with age for a memorial.
No! your remembrance shall perish; for when your carcases
Lie stinking on the earth the buriers shall arise from the east,
And not a bone of all the sons of Tiriel remain.
Bury your mother; but you cannot bury the curse of Tiriel.'   50

He ceased, and darkling o'er the mountains sought his
    pathless way.

                                    II

He wandered day and night. To him both day and night were
    dark;
The sun he felt, but the bright moon was now a useless globe.
O'er mountains, through vales of woe, the blind and aged man
Wandered, till he that leadeth all led him to the vales of Har;

And Har and Heva like two children sat beneath the oak.
Mnetha, now aged, waited on them, and brought them food
  and clothing,
But they were as the shadow of Har, and as the years forgotten.
Playing with flowers, and running after birds, they spent the
  day,
And in the night like infants slept delighted with infant dreams.   60

Soon as the blind wanderer entered the pleasant gardens of
  Har
They ran weeping like frighted infants for refuge in Mnetha's
  arms.
The blind man felt his way and cried: 'Peace to these open
  doors!
Let no one fear, for poor blind Tiriel hurts none but himself.
Tell me, O friends, where am I now, and in what pleasant
  place?'

'This is the valley of Har,' said Mnetha, 'and this the tent of
  Har.
Who art thou, poor blind man, that takest the name of Tiriel
  on thee?
Tiriel is king of all the west. Who art thou? I am Mnetha,
And this is Har and Heva, trembling like infants by my side'.

'I know Tiriel is king of the west, and there he lives in joy.   70
No matter who I am, O Mnetha, if thou hast any food
Give it to me, for I cannot stay; my journey is far from hence.'

Then Har said: 'O my mother Mnetha, venture not so near
  him,
For he is the king of rotten wood, and of the bones of death.
He wanders without eyes, and passes through thick walls and
  doors.
Thou shalt not smite my mother Mnetha, O thou eyeless man!'

'A wanderer, I beg for food. You see I cannot weep.
I cast away my staff, the kind companion of my travel,
And I kneel down that you may see I am a harmless man.'

He kneeled down, and Mnetha said: 'Come, Har and Heva,
  rise.
                                                                    80
He is an innocent old man, and hungry with his travel.'

Then Har arose, and laid his hand upon old Tiriel's head.

'God bless thy poor bald pate. God bless thy hollow winking
  eyes.
God bless thy shrivelled beard. God bless thy many-wrinkled
  forehead.
Thou hast no teeth, old man; and thus I kiss thy sleek bald
  head.
Heva, come kiss his bald head, for he will not hurt us, Heva.'

Then Heva came, and took old Tiriel in her mother's arms.

'Bless thy poor eyes, old man, and bless the old father of
  Tiriel.
Thou art my Tiriel's old father. I know thee through thy
  wrinkles,
Because thou smellest like the fig tree; thou smellest like ripe
  figs.   90
How didst thou lose thy eyes, old Tiriel? Bless thy wrinkled
  face.'

Mnetha said: 'Come in, aged wanderer; tell us of thy name.
Why shouldest thou conceal thyself from those of thine own
  flesh?'

'I am not of this region,' said Tiriel dissemblingly.
'I am an aged wanderer, once father of a race
Far in the north, but they were wicked and were all
  destroyed,
And I their father sent an outcast. I have told you all;
Ask me no more, I pray, for grief hath sealed my precious
  sight.'

'O Lord,' said Mnetha, 'how I tremble! Are there then more
  people,
More human creatures on this earth, beside the sons of Har?'   100

'No more,' said Tiriel, 'but I, remain on all this globe;
And I remain an outcast. Hast thou anything to drink?'

Then Mnetha gave him milk and fruits, and they sat down
  together.

III

They sat and ate, and Har and Heva smiled on Tiriel.

'Thou art a very old, old man, but I am older than thou.
How came thine hair to leave thy forehead? How came thy
  face so brown?
My hair is very long. My beard doth cover all my breast.
God bless thy piteous face! To count the wrinkles in thy face
Would puzzle Mnetha. Bless thy face, for thou art Tiriel.'

'Tiriel I never saw but once. I sat with him and ate.   110
He was as cheerful as a prince, and gave me entertainment;
But long I stayed not at his palace, for I am forced to wander.'

'What! Wilt thou leave us too?' said Heva. 'Thou shalt not
  leave us too.
For we have many sports to show thee, and many songs to
  sing;
And after dinner we will walk into the cage of Har,
And thou shalt help us to catch birds, and gather them ripe
  cherries.
Then let thy name be Tiriel, and never leave us more.'

'If thou dost go,' said Har, 'I wish thine eyes may see thy
  folly.
My sons have left me; did thine leave thee? Oh, 'twas very
  cruel!'   120

'No, venerable man,' said Tiriel, 'Ask me not such things;
For thou dost make my heart to bleed. My sons were not like
  thine,
But worse. Oh, never ask me more, or I must flee away.'

'Thou shalt not go,' said Heva, 'till thou hast seen our
  singing birds,
And heard Har sing in the great cage, and slept upon our
  fleeces.
Go not, for thou are so like Tiriel that I love thine head—
Though it is wrinkled, like the earth parched with the
  summer heat.'

Then Tiriel rose up from the seat, and said: 'God bless these
  tents.

My journey is o'er rocks and mountains, not in pleasant vales.
I must not sleep nor rest, because of madness and dismay.'

And Mnetha said: 'Thou must not go to wander dark,
   alone,   130
But dwell with us and let us be to thee instead of eyes;
And I will bring thee food, old man, till death shall call thee
   hence.'

Then Tiriel frowned, and answered: 'Did I not command
   you, saying
Madness and deep dismay possess the heart of the blind
   man,
The wanderer who seeks the woods leaning upon his staff?'

Then Mnetha trembling at his frowns led him to the tent
   door,
And gave to him his staff and blessed him. He went on his way.

But Har and Heva stood and watched him till he entered the
   wood,
And then they went and wept to Mnetha; but they soon
   forgot their tears.

IV

Over the weary hills the blind man took his lonely way.   140
To him the day and night alike was dark and desolate.
But far he had not gone when Ijim, from his woods come
   down,
Met him at entrance of the forest in a dark and lonely way.

'Who art thou, eyeless wretch, that thus obstruct'st the lion's
   path?
Ijim shall rend thy feeble joints, thou tempter of dark Ijim.
Thou hast the form of Tiriel, but I know thee well enough.
Stand from my path, foul fiend. Is this the last of thy deceits:
To be a hypocrite, and stand in shape of a blind beggar?'

The blind man heard his brother's voice, and kneeled down
   on his knee.
'O brother Ijim—if it is thy voice that speaks to me—   150

Smite not thy brother Tiriel, though weary of his life.
My sons have smitten me already, and if thou smitest me
The curse that rolls over their heads will rest itself on thine.
'Tis now seven years since in my palace I beheld thy face.'

'Come, thou dark fiend, I dare thy cunning! Know that Ijim
   scorns
To smite thee in the form of helpless age and eyeless policy.
Rise up, for I discern thee, and I dare thy eloquent tongue!
Come, I will lead thee on thy way, and use thee as a scoff.'

'O brother Ijim, thou beholdest wretched Tiriel.
Kiss me, my brother, and then leave me to wander desolate.'   160

'No, artful fiend; but I will lead thee. Dost thou want to go?
Reply not, lest I bind thee with the green flags of the brook.
Ay, now thou art discovered I will use thee like a slave.'

When Tiriel heard the words of Ijim he sought not to reply.
He knew 'twas vain, for Ijim's words were as the voice of fate.

And they went on together, over hills, through woody dales,
Blind to the pleasures of the sight, and deaf to warbling birds.
All day they walked, and all the night beneath the pleasant
   moon,
Westwardly journeying, till Tiriel grew weary with his travel.

'O Ijim, I am faint and weary, for my knees forbid   170
To bear me further. Urge me not, lest I should die with travel.
A little rest I crave, a little water from a brook,
Or I shall soon discover that I am a mortal man,
And you will lose your once-loved Tiriel. Alas, how faint I
   am!'

'Impudent fiend,' said Ijim, 'Hold thy glib and eloquent
   tongue!
Tiriel is a king, and thou the tempter of dark Ijim.
Drink of this running brook, and I will bear thee on my
   shoulders.'

He drank, and Ijim raised him up and bore him on his
   shoulders.

All day he bore him and, when evening drew her solemn
    curtain,
Entered the gates of Tiriel's palace, and stood and called
    aloud: 180

'Heuxos, come forth! I here have brought the fiend that
    troubles Ijim.
Look! Know'st thou aught of this grey beard, or of these
    blinded eyes?'

Heuxos and Lotho ran forth at the sound of Ijim's voice,
And saw their aged father borne upon his mighty shoulders.
Their eloquent tongues were dumb, and sweat stood on
    their trembling limbs.
They knew 'twas vain to strive with Ijim; they bowed and
    silent stood.

'What, Heuxos! Call thy father, for I mean to sport tonight.
This is the hypocrite that sometimes roars a dreadful lion.
Then I have rent his limbs, and left him rotting in the forest
For birds to eat; but I have scarce departed from the place   190
But like a tiger he would come, and so I rent him too.
Then like a river he would seek to drown me in his waves,
But soon I buffeted the torrent; anon like to a cloud
Fraught with the swords of lightning, but I braved the
    vengeance too.

Then he would creep like a bright serpent, till around my
    neck,
While I was sleeping, he would twine; I squeezed his
    pois'nous soul.
Then, like a toad or like a newt, would whisper in my ears,
Or like a rock stood in my way, or like a pois'nous shrub.
At last I caught him in the form of Tiriel, blind and old,
And so I'll keep him. Fetch your father, fetch forth
    Myratana!'   200

They stood confounded, and thus Tiriel raised his silver
    voice:

'Serpents, not sons, why do you stand? Fetch hither Tiriel,
Fetch hither Myratana; and delight yourselves with scoffs.

For poor blind Tiriel is returned, and this much injured head
Is ready for your bitter taunts. Come forth, sons of the curse!'

Meantime the other sons of Tiriel ran around their father.
Confounded at the terrible strength of Ijim, they knew 'twas
    vain;
Both spear and shield were useless, and the coat of iron mail.
When Ijim stretched his mighty arm the arrow from his limbs
Rebounded, and the piercing sword broke on his naked flesh.   210

'Then is it true, Heuxos, that thou hast turned thy aged
    parent
To be the sport of wintry winds?' said Ijim. 'Is this true?
It is a lie, and I am like the tree torn by the wind.
Thou eyeless fiend, and you dissemblers! Is this Tiriel's
    house?
It is as false as Matha, and as dark as vacant Orcus.
Escape, ye fiends, for Ijim will not lift his hand against ye.'

So saying, Ijim gloomy turned his back, and silent sought
The secret forests, and all night wandered in desolate ways.

V

And aged Tiriel stood and said: 'Where does the thunder
    sleep?
Where doth he hide his terrible head? And his swift and fiery
    daughters,   220
Where do they shroud their fiery wings and the terrors of
    their hair?
Earth, thus I stamp thy bosom. Rouse the earthquake from
    his den,
To raise his dark and burning visage through the cleaving
    ground,
To thrust these towers with his shoulders. Let his fiery dogs
Rise from the centre, belching flames and roarings, dark
    smoke.
Where art thou, pestilence that bathest in fogs and standing
    lakes?
Rise up thy sluggish limbs, and let the loathsomest of poisons
Drop from thy garments as thou walkest wrapped in yellow
    clouds.

Here take thy seat, in this wide court; let it be strewn with
     dead,
And sit and smile upon these cursed sons of Tiriel.   230
Thunder and fire and pestilence, hear you not Tiriel's
     curse?'

He ceased; the heaving clouds confused rolled round the
     lofty towers,
Discharging their enormous voices. At the father's curse
The earth trembled, fires belched from the yawning clefts,
And when the shaking ceased a fog possessed the accursed
     clime.

The cry was great in Tiriel's palace. His five daughters ran
And caught him by the garments, weeping with cries of bitter
     woe.

'Ay, now you feel the curse, you cry; but may all ears be deaf
As Tiriel's, and all eyes as blind as Tiriel's to your woes!
May never stars shine on your roofs, may never sun nor
     moon   240
Visit you, but eternal fogs hover around your walls!
Hela, my youngest daughter, you shall lead me from this
     place,
And let the curse fall on the rest and wrap them up together!'

He ceased, and Hela led her father from the noisome place.
In haste they fled, while all the sons and daughters of Tiriel,
Chained in thick darkness, uttered cries of mourning all the
     night.
And in the morning, lo, an hundred men in ghastly death,
The four daughters stretched on the marble pavement, silent
     all,
Fall'n by the pestilence. The rest moped round in guilty
     fears;
And all the children in their beds were cut off in one night.   250
Thirty of Tiriel's sons remained to wither in the palace:
Desolate, loathed, dumb, astonished, waiting for black death.

                                    VI

And Hela led her father through the silent of the night,
Astonished, silent, till the morning beams began to spring.

'Now, Hela, I can go with pleasure and dwell with Har and
Heva,
Now that the curse shall clean devour all those guilty sons.
This is the right and ready way; I know it by the sound
That our feet make. Remember, Hela, I have saved thee
from death.
Then be obedient to thy father, for the curse is taken off
thee.
I dwelt with Myratana five years in the desolate rock,   260
And all that time we waited for the fire to fall from heaven,
Or for the torrents of the sea to overwhelm you all.
But now my wife is dead and all the time of grace is past.
You see the parents' curse. Now lead me where I have
commanded.'

'O leagued with evil spirits, thou accursed man of sin!
True, I was born thy slave. Who asked thee to save me from
death?
'Twas for thyself, thou cruel, because thou wantest eyes.'

'True, Hela: this is the desert of all those cruel ones.
Is Tiriel cruel? Look! His daughter—and his youngest
daughter—
Laughs at affection, glories in rebellion, scoffs at love.   270
I have not eat these two days. Lead me to Har and Heva's
tent,
Or I will wrap thee up in such a terrible father's curse
That thou shalt feel worms in thy marrow creeping through
thy bones.
Yet thou shalt lead me. Lead me, I command, to Har and
Heva.'

'O cruel! O destroyer! O consumer! O avenger!
To Har and Heva I will lead thee then. Would that they
would curse!
Then would they curse as thou hast cursed. But they are not
like thee.
Oh, they are holy and forgiving, filled with loving mercy,
Forgetting the offences of their most rebellious children!
Or else thou wouldest not have lived to curse thy helpless
children.'   280

'Look on my eyes, Hela, and see, for thou hast eyes to see.
The tears swell from my stony fountains; wherefore do I
   weep?
Wherefore from my blind orbs art thou not seized with
   pois'nous stings?
Laugh, serpent, youngest venomous reptile of the flesh of
   Tiriel,
Laugh! For thy father Tiriel shall give thee cause to laugh,
Unless thou lead me to the tent of Har, child of the curse.'

'Silence thy evil tongue, thou murderer of thy helpless
   children!
I lead thee to the tent of Har: not that I mind thy curse,
But that I feel they will curse thee, and hang upon thy bones
Fell shaking agonies, and in each wrinkle of that face   290
Plant worms of death, to feast upon the tongue of terrible
   curses.'

'Hela, my daughter, listen! Thou art the daughter of Tiriel.
Thy father calls. Thy father lifts his hand unto the heavens,
For thou hast laughed at my tears, and cursed thy aged
   father.
Let snakes rise from thy bedded locks and laugh among thy
   curls!'

He ceased; her dark hair upright stood, while snakes
   enfolded round
Her madding brows. Her shrieks appalled the soul of Tiriel.

'What have I done, Hela, my daughter? Fear'st thou now the
   curse,
Or wherefore dost thou cry? Ah, wretch to curse thy aged
   father!
Lead me to Har and Heva, and the curse of Tiriel   300
Shall fail. If thou refuse, howl in the desolate mountains!'

VII

She howling led him over mountains and through frighted
   vales,
Till to the caves of Zazel they approached at eventide.

Forth from their caves old Zazel and his sons ran, when they
  saw
Their tyrant prince blind, and his daughter howling and
  leading him.

They laughed and mocked. Some threw dirt and stones as
  they passed by.
But when Tiriel turned around and raised his awful voice
Some fled away, but Zazel stood still and thus began:
'Bald tyrant, wrinkled cunning, listen to Zazel's chains!
'Twas thou that chained thy brother Zazel. Where are now
  thine eyes?   310
Shout, beautiful daughter of Tiriel! Thou singest a sweet
  song.
Where are you going? Come and eat some roots and drink
  some water.
Thy crown is bald, old man; the sun will dry thy brains away,
And thou wilt be as foolish as thy foolish brother Zazel.'

The blind man heard, and smote his breast and trembling
  passed on.
They threw dirt after them, till to the covert of a wood
The howling maiden led her father, where wild beasts resort,
Hoping to end her woes; but from her cries the tigers fled.
All night they wandered through the wood, and when the sun
  arose
They entered on the mountains of Har. At noon the happy
  tents   320
Were frighted by the dismal cries of Hela on the mountains,

But Har and Heva slept, fearless as babes on loving breasts.
Mnetha awoke; she ran and stood at the tent door, and saw
The aged wanderer led towards the tents. She took her bow
And chose her arrows, then advanced to meet the terrible
  pair.

VIII

And Mnetha hasted and met them at the gate of the lower
  garden.

'Stand still, or from my bow receive a sharp and winged
  death!'

Then Tiriel stood, saying: 'What soft voice threatens such
    bitter things?
Lead me to Har and Heva. I am Tiriel, King of the west.'

And Mnetha led them to the tent of Har, and Har and Heva
Ran to the door. When Tiriel felt the ankles of aged Har
He said: 'O weak mistaken father of a lawless race!
Thy laws O Har, and Tiriel's wisdom, end together in a
    curse.
Why is one law given to the lion and the patient ox,
And why men bound beneath the heavens in a reptile form:
A worm of sixty winters creeping on the dusky ground?
The child springs from the womb, the father ready stands to
    form
The infant head, while the mother idle plays with her dog on
    her couch.
The young bosom is cold for lack of mother's nourishment,
    and milk
Is cut off from the weeping mouth, with difficulty and pain   340
The little lids are lifted and the little nostrils opened.
The father forms a whip to rouse the sluggish senses to act,
And scourges off all youthful fancies from the newborn man.
And when the drone has reached his crawling length
Black berries appear that poison all around him. Such was
    Tiriel:
Compelled to pray repugnant, and to humble the immortal
    spirit—
Till I am subtle as a serpent in a paradise,
Consuming all, both flowers and fruits, insects and warbling
    birds.
And now my paradise is fall'n, and a drear sandy plain
Returns my thirsty hissings in a curse on thee, O Har,   350
Mistaken father of a lawless race. My voice is past.'

He ceased, outstretched at Har and Heva's feet in awful
death.

From the annotations to Emanuel Swedenborg's
Wisdom of Angels Concerning Divine Love
and Divine Wisdom (*c.*1789)

Understanding or thought is not natural to Man. It is acquired by
means of suffering and distress i.e. experience. Will, desire, love,
rage, envy, and all other affections are natural, but understanding
is acquired.

Man can have no idea of any thing greater than Man as a cup
cannot contain more than its capaciousness.
    But God is a man not because he is so perceived by Man but
because he is the creator of Man.

Think of a white cloud as being holy—you cannot love it. But think
of a holy man within the cloud—love springs up in your thought.
For to think of holiness distinct from Man is impossible to the
affections. Thought alone can make monsters, but the affections
cannot.

The Book of Thel (*c.*1789)

THEL'S MOTTO

> Does the eagle know what is in the pit?
> Or wilt thou go ask the mole?
> Can wisdom be put in a silver rod,
> Or love in a golden bowl?

I

The daughters of Mne Seraphim led round their sunny flocks,
All but the youngest. She in paleness sought the secret air,
To fade away like morning beauty from her mortal day.
Down by the river of Adona her soft voice is heard,
And thus her gentle lamentation falls like morning dew:

'O life of this our spring, why fades the lotus of the water?   10

Why fade these children of the spring, born but to smile and
    fall?
Ah! Thel is like a wat'ry bow, and like a parting cloud,
Like a reflection in a glass, like shadows in the water,
Like dreams of infants, like a smile upon an infant's face,
Like the dove's voice, like transient day, like music in the air.
Ah! gentle may I lay me down, and gentle rest my head,
And gentle sleep the sleep of death, and gentle hear the voice
Of him that walketh in the garden in the evening time.'

The Lily of the valley breathing in the humble grass
Answered the lovely maid, and said: 'I am a wat'ry weed,   20
And I am very small, and love to dwell in lowly vales:
So weak, the gilded butterfly scarce perches on my head.
Yet I am visited from heaven, and he that smiles on all
Walks in the valley, and each morn over me spreads his hand,
Saying: "Rejoice, thou humble grass, thou new-born lily
    flower,
Thou gentle maid of silent valleys and of modest brooks;
For thou shalt be clothed in light and fed with morning manna,
Till summer's heat melts thee beside the fountains and the
    springs,
To flourish in eternal vales." Then why should Thel complain?
Why should the mistress of the vales of Har utter a sigh?'   30

She ceased and smiled in tears, then sat down in her silver
    shrine.
Thel answered: 'O thou little virgin of the peaceful valley,
Giving to those that cannot crave, the voiceless, the o'ertired—
Thy breath doth nourish the innocent lamb; he smells thy
    milky garments;
He crops thy flowers, while thou sittest smiling in his face,
Wiping his mild and meekin mouth from all contagious taints.
Thy wine doth purify the golden honey; thy perfume,
Which thou dost scatter on every little blade of grass that
    springs,
Revives the milked cow and tames the fire-breathing steed.
But Thel is like a faint cloud kindled at the rising sun;   40
I vanish from my pearly throne, and who shall find my place?'

'Queen of the vales', the Lily answered, 'ask the tender cloud,
And it shall tell thee why it glitters in the morning sky,

And why it scatters its bright beauty through the humid air.
Descend, O little Cloud, and hover before the eyes of Thel.'

The Cloud descended, and the Lily bowed her modest head,
And went to mind her numerous charge among the verdant
  grass.

II

'O little Cloud', the virgin said, 'I charge thee, tell to me
Why thou complainest not, when in one hour thou fade
  away—
Then we shall seek thee but not find. Ah! Thel is like to thee: 50
I pass away. Yet I complain, and no one hears my voice.'

The Cloud then showed his golden head, and his bright form
  emerged,
Hovering and glittering on the air before the face of Thel:

'O virgin, know'st thou not our steeds drink of the golden
  springs
Where Luvah doth renew his horses? Look'st thou on my
  youth,
And fearest thou because I vanish and am seen no more,
Nothing remains? O maid, I tell thee, when I pass away
It is to tenfold life, to love, to peace, and raptures holy.
Unseen descending weigh my light wings upon balmy flowers,
And court the fair-eyed dew to take me to her shining tent.   60
The weeping virgin trembling kneels before the risen sun,
Till we arise linked in a golden band and never part,
But walk united, bearing food to all our tender flowers.'

'Dost thou, O Little Cloud? I fear that I am not like thee;
For I walk through the vales of Har, and smell the sweetest
  flowers,
But I feed not the little flowers. I hear the warbling birds,
But I feed not the warbling birds; they fly and seek their food.
But Thel delights in these no more, because I fade away,
And all shall say: "Without a use this shining woman lived;
Or did she only live to be at death the food of worms?"'   70

The Cloud reclined upon his airy throne and answered thus:

'Then if thou art the food of worms, O virgin of the skies,
How great thy use, how great thy blessing! Every thing that
  lives
Lives not alone, nor for itself. Fear not, and I will call
The weak worm from its lowly bed, and thou shalt hear its
  voice.
Come forth, Worm of the silent valley, to thy pensive queen.'

The helpless Worm arose, and sat upon the Lily's leaf,
And the bright Cloud sailed on to find his partner in the vale.

III

Then Thel astonished viewed the Worm upon its dewy bed.

'Art thou a Worm? Image of weakness, art thou but a Worm?   80
I see thee like an infant wrapped in the Lily's leaf.
Ah, weep not little voice! Thou canst not speak, but thou canst
  weep.
Is this a Worm? I see thee lay helpless and naked, weeping,
And none to answer, none to cherish thee with mother's
  smiles.'

The Clod of Clay heard the Worm's voice and raised her
  pitying head;
She bowed over the weeping infant and her life exhaled
In milky fondness: then on Thel she fixed her humble eyes.

'O beauty of the vales of Har, we live not for ourselves.
Thou seest me, the meanest thing, and so I am indeed;
My bosom of itself is cold, and of itself is dark.   90
But he that loves the lowly pours his oil upon my head,
And kisses me, and binds his nuptial bands around my breast,
And says: "Thou mother of my children, I have loved thee,
And I have given thee a crown that none can take away".
But how this is, sweet maid, I know not, and I cannot know;
I ponder, and I cannot ponder; yet I live and love.'

The daughter of beauty wiped her pitying tears with her white
  veil
And said: 'Alas! I knew not this, and therefore did I weep.
That God would love a worm I knew, and punish the evil foot

That wilful bruised its helpless form. But that he cherished it   100
With milk and oil I never knew, and therefore did I weep;
And I complained in the mild air, because I fade away,
And lay me down in thy cold bed, and leave my shining lot.'

'Queen of the vales', the matron Clay answered, 'I heard thy
    sighs,
And all thy moans flew o'er my roof, but I have called them
    down.
Wilt thou, O Queen, enter my house? 'Tis given thee to enter
And to return. Fear nothing; enter with thy virgin feet.'

IV

The eternal gates' terrific porter lifted the northern bar.
Thel entered in and saw the secrets of the land unknown.
She saw the couches of the dead, and where the fibrous roots   110
Of every heart on earth infixes deep its restless twists:
A land of sorrows and of tears, where never smile was seen.

She wandered in the land of clouds, through valleys dark,
    list'ning
Dolours and lamentations. Waiting oft beside a dewy grave
She stood in silence, list'ning to the voices of the ground,
Till to her own grave plot she came, and there she sat down,
And heard this voice of sorrow breathed from the hollow pit:

'Why cannot the ear be closed to its own destruction,
Or the glist'ning eye to the poison of a smile?
Why are the eyelids stored with arrows ready drawn,   120
Where a thousand fighting men in ambush lie,
Or an eye of gifts and graces, show'ring fruits and coined
    gold?
Why a tongue impressed with honey from every wind?
Why an ear a whirlpool fierce to draw creations in?
Why a nostril wide inhaling terror, trembling and affright?
Why a tender curb upon the youthful burning boy?
Why a little curtain of flesh on the bed of our desire?'
The virgin started from her seat, and with a shriek
Fled back unhindered till she came into the vales of Har.

THE END

SONGS OF INNOCENCE (1789)

Introduction

Piping down the valleys wild,
Piping songs of pleasant glee,
On a cloud I saw a child,
And he laughing said to me:

'Pipe a song about a lamb.'
So I piped with merry cheer.
'Piper, pipe that song again.'
So I piped; he wept to hear.

'Drop thy pipe, thy happy pipe;
Sing thy songs of happy cheer.'   10
So I sung the same again,
While he wept with joy to hear.

'Piper sit thee down and write
In a book that all may read—'
So he vanished from my sight.
And I plucked a hollow reed,

And I made a rural pen,
And I stained the water clear,
And I wrote my happy songs
Every child may joy to hear.   20

A Dream

Once a dream did weave a shade
O'er my angel-guarded bed,
That an emmet lost its way
Where on grass methought I lay.

Troubled, wildered and forlorn,
Dark, benighted, travel-worn,
Over many a tangled spray
All heart-broke I heard her say:

'Oh my children! Do they cry?
Do they hear their father sigh?   10
Now they look abroad to see,
Now return and weep for me.'

Pitying I dropped a tear;
But I saw a glow-worm near,
Who replied: 'What wailing wight
Calls the watchman of the night?

'I am set to light the ground,
While the beetle goes his round.
Follow now the beetle's hum.
Little wanderer hie thee home.'   20

The Little Girl Lost

In futurity
I prophetic see
That the earth from sleep
(Grave the sentence deep)

Shall arise and seek
For her maker meek,
And the desert wild
Become a garden mild.

In the southern clime,
Where the summer's prime   10
Never fades away,
Lovely Lyca lay.

Seven summers old
Lovely Lyca told;
She had wandered long,
Hearing wild birds' song.

'Sweet sleep come to me
Underneath this tree;
Do father, mother weep?
Where can Lyca sleep?   20

'Lost in desert wild
Is your little child.
How can Lyca sleep,
If her mother weep?

'If her heart does ache,
Then let Lyca wake;
If my mother sleep,
Lyca shall not weep.

'Frowning, frowning night,
O'er this desert bright,   30
Let thy moon arise
While I close my eyes.'

Sleeping Lyca lay,
While the beasts of prey,
Come from caverns deep,
Viewed the maid asleep.

The kingly lion stood
And the virgin viewed,
Then he gambolled round
O'er the hallowed ground.   40

Leopards, tigers play,
Round her as she lay,
While the lion old
Bowed his mane of gold,

And her bosom lick,
And upon her neck;
From his eyes of flame
Ruby tears there came;

While the lioness
Loosed her slender dress   50
And naked they conveyed
To caves the sleeping maid.

The Little Girl Found

All the night in woe
Lyca's parents go,
Over valleys deep
While the deserts weep.

Tired and woe-begone,
Hoarse with making moan,
Arm in arm seven days
They traced the desert ways.

Seven nights they sleep
Among shadows deep,   10
And dream they see their child
Starved in desert wild.

Pale through pathless ways
The fancied image strays,
Famished, weeping, weak,
With hollow piteous shriek.

Rising from unrest,
The trembling woman pressed
With feet of weary woe;
She could no further go.   20

In his arms he bore
Her, armed with sorrow sore,
Till before their way
A couching lion lay.

Turning back was vain.
Soon his heavy mane
Bore them to the ground;
Then he stalked around,

Smelling to his prey;
But their fears allay   30
When he licks their hands,
And silent by them stands.

They look upon his eyes,
Filled with deep surprise,
And wondering behold
A spirit armed in gold.

On his head a crown,
On his shoulders down
Flowed his golden hair.
Gone was all their care.   40

'Follow me', he said,
'Weep not for the maid;
In my palace deep,
Lyca lies asleep.'

Then they followed
Where the vision led,
And saw their sleeping child,
Among tigers wild.

To this day they dwell
In a lonely dell,   50
Nor fear the wolvish howl,
Nor the lion's growl.

The Blossom

Merry, merry sparrow,
Under leaves so green,
A happy blossom
Sees you swift as arrow
Seek your cradle narrow
Near my bosom.

Pretty, pretty robin,
Under leaves so green,
A happy blossom
Hears you sobbing, sobbing,   10
Pretty, pretty robin
Near my bosom.

The Lamb

Little Lamb who made thee?
　Dost thou know who made thee?
Gave thee life and bid thee feed
By the stream and o'er the mead;
Gave thee clothing of delight,
Softest clothing woolly bright;
Gave thee such a tender voice,
Making all the vales rejoice.
　Little Lamb who made thee?
　Dost thou know who made thee?　　　　10

Little Lamb I'll tell thee,
　Little Lamb I'll tell thee:
He is called by thy name,
For he calls himself a lamb.
He is meek and he is mild;
He became a little child.
I a child and thou a lamb,
We are called by his name.
　Little Lamb God bless thee.
　Little Lamb God bless thee.　　　　20

The Shepherd

How sweet is the shepherd's sweet lot!
From the morn to the evening he strays;
He shall follow his sheep all the day,
And his tongue shall be filled with praise.

For he hears the lamb's innocent call,
And he hears the ewe's tender reply.
He is watchful, while they are in peace,
For they know when their shepherd is nigh.

Infant Joy

'I have no name;
I am but two days old'.
What shall I call thee?
'I happy am;
Joy is my name.'
Sweet joy befall thee!

Pretty joy!
Sweet joy but two days old,
Sweet joy I call thee.
Thou dost smile;   10
I sing the while.
Sweet joy befall thee.

On Another's Sorrow

Can I see another's woe,
And not be in sorrow too?
Can I see another's grief
And not seek for kind relief?

Can I see a falling tear,
And not feel my sorrow's share?
Can a father see his child
Weep, nor be with sorrow filled?

Can a mother sit, and hear
An infant groan, an infant fear?   10
No, no, never can it be.
Never, never can it be.

And can he who smiles on all
Hear the wren with sorrows small,
Hear the small bird's grief and care,
Hear the woes that infants bear—

And not sit beside the nest,
Pouring pity in their breast;
And not sit the cradle near
Weeping tear on infant's tear; 20

And not sit both night and day,
Wiping all our tears away?
Oh no! never can it be.
Never, never can it be.

He doth give his joy to all.
He becomes an infant small.
He becomes a man of woe.
He doth feel the sorrow too.

Think not thou canst sigh a sigh,
And thy maker is not by. 30
Think not thou canst weep a tear,
And thy maker is not near.

Oh! he gives to us his joy,
That our grief he may destroy,
Till our grief is fled and gone
He doth sit by us and moan.

Spring

Sound the flute!
Now it's mute.
Birds delight
Day and night.
Nightingale
In the dale,
Lark in sky,
Merrily,
Merrily, merrily to welcome in the year.

Little boy   10
Full of joy,
Little girl
Sweet and small.
Cock does crow,
So do you.
Merry voice,
Infant noise,
Merrily, merrily to welcome in the year.

Little lamb
Here I am   20
Come and lick
My white neck.
Let me pull
Your soft wool.
Let me kiss
Your soft face,
Merrily, merrily we welcome in the year.

The Schoolboy

I love to rise in a summer morn,
When the birds sing on every tree;
The distant huntsman winds his horn,
And the skylark sings with me.
Oh! what sweet company.

But to go to school in a summer morn,
Oh! it drives all joy away;
Under a cruel eye outworn,
The little ones spend the day
In sighing and dismay.   10

Ah! then at times I drooping sit,
And spend many an anxious hour,
Nor in my book can I take delight,
Nor sit in learning's bower,
Worn through with the dreary shower.

How can the bird that is born for joy
Sit in a cage and sing?
How can a child when fears annoy
But droop his tender wing,
And forget his youthful spring?   20

O father and mother! if buds are nipped,
And blossoms blown away,
And if the tender plants are stripped
Of their joy in the springing day,
By sorrow and care's dismay,

How shall the summer arise in joy,
Or the summer fruits appear?
Or how shall we gather what griefs destroy,
Or bless the mellowing year,
When the blasts of winter appear?   30

Laughing Song

When the green woods laugh with the voice of joy
And the dimpling stream runs laughing by,
When the air does laugh with our merry wit
And the green hill laughs with the noise of it,

When the meadows laugh with lively green
And the grasshopper laughs in the merry scene,
When Mary and Susan and Emily
With their sweet round mouths sing 'Ha, Ha, He,'

When the painted birds laugh in the shade
Where our table with cherries and nuts is spread—   10
Come live and be merry and join with me,
To sing the sweet chorus of 'Ha, Ha, He.'

The Little Black Boy

My mother bore me in the southern wild,
And I am black, but oh! my soul is white.
White as an angel is the English child;
But I am black as if bereaved of light.

My mother taught me underneath a tree,
And sitting down before the heat of day
She took me on her lap and kissed me,
And pointing to the east began to say:

'Look on the rising sun! There God does live,
And gives his light and gives his heat away;   10
And flowers and trees and beasts and men receive
Comfort in morning, joy in the noon day.

'And we are put on earth a little space,
That we may learn to bear the beams of love;
And these black bodies and this sun-burnt face
Is but a cloud, and like a shady grove.

'For when our souls have learned the heat to bear
The cloud will vanish; we shall hear his voice,
Saying: "Come out from the grove my love and care,
And round my golden tent like lambs rejoice."'   20

Thus did my mother say and kissed me,
And thus I say to little English boy.
When I from black and he from white cloud free,
And round the tent of God like lambs we joy,

I'll shade him from the heat till he can bear
To lean in joy upon our father's knee,
And then I'll stand and stroke his silver hair
And be like him, and he will then love me.

The Voice of the Ancient Bard

Youth of delight come hither
And see the opening morn,
Image of truth new-born.
Doubt is fled and clouds of reason,
Dark disputes and artful teasing.
Folly is an endless maze;
Tangled roots perplex her ways.
How many have fallen there!
They stumble all night over bones of the dead,
And feel they know not what but care,   10
And wish to lead others when they should be led.

The Echoing Green

The sun does arise,
And make happy the skies.
The merry bells ring
To welcome the spring.
The skylark and thrush,
The birds of the bush,
Sing louder around,
To the bells' cheerful sound,
While our sports shall be seen
On the echoing green.   10

Old John with white hair
Does laugh away care,
Sitting under the oak,
Among the old folk.
They laugh at our play,
And soon they all say:
'Such, such were the joys
When we all, girls and boys,
In our youth-time were seen
On the echoing green.'   20

Till the little ones weary
No more can be merry;
The sun does descend,
And our sports have an end.
Round the laps of their mother
Many sisters and brothers,
Like birds in their nest,
Are ready for rest;
And sport no more seen
On the darkening green.   30

Nurse's Song

When the voices of children are heard on the green
And laughing is heard on the hill,
My heart is at rest within my breast
And everything else is still.

'Then come home my children: the sun is gone down
And the dews of night arise.
Come, come leave off play and let us away,
Till the morning appears in the skies.'

'No, no let us play, for it is yet day
And we cannot go to sleep.   10
Besides, in the sky the little birds fly,
And the hills are all covered with sheep.'

'Well, well go and play till the light fades away,
And then go home to bed.'
The little ones leaped and shouted and laughed
And all the hills echoed.

Holy Thursday

'Twas on a Holy Thursday, their innocent faces clean,
The children walking two and two in red and blue and green,
Grey headed beadles walked before with wands as white as
    snow;
Till into the high dome of Paul's they like Thames waters flow.

Oh what a multitude they seemed, these flowers of London
    town.
Seated in companies they sit, with radiance all their own.
The hum of multitudes was there, but multitudes of lambs:
Thousands of little boys and girls raising their innocent hands.

Now like a mighty wind they raise to Heaven the voice of song,
Or like harmonious thunderings the seats of Heaven among.   10
Beneath them sit the aged men, wise guardians of the poor.
Then cherish pity, lest you drive an angel from your door.

The Divine Image

To Mercy, Pity, Peace and Love
All pray in their distress,
And to these virtues of delight
Return their thankfulness.

For Mercy, Pity, Peace and Love
Is God our father dear,
And Mercy, Pity, Peace and Love
Is Man his child and care.

For Mercy has a human heart,
Pity a human face,   10
And Love the human form divine,
And Peace the human dress.

Then every man of every clime
That prays in his distress,
Prays to the human form divine:
Love, Mercy, Pity, Peace.

And all must love the human form,
In heathen, Turk or Jew.
Where Mercy, Love and Pity dwell,
There God is dwelling too.   20

The Chimney-Sweeper

When my mother died I was very young,
And my father sold me while yet my tongue
Could scarcely cry, 'weep weep weep weep'.
So your chimneys I sweep and in soot I sleep.

There's little Tom Dacre, who cried when his head,
That curled like a lamb's back, was shaved, so I said:
'Hush Tom, never mind it, for when your head's bare,
You know that the soot cannot spoil your white hair.'

And so he was quiet, and that very night,
As Tom was a-sleeping, he had such a sight: 10
That thousands of sweepers, Dick, Joe, Ned and Jack,
Were all of them locked up in coffins of black,

And by came an angel who had a bright key,
And he opened the coffins and set them all free.
Then down a green plain leaping, laughing they run,
And wash in a river and shine in the sun.

Then naked and white, all their bags left behind,
They rise upon clouds, and sport in the wind.
And the angel told Tom if he'd be a good boy,
He'd have God for his father and never want joy.   20

And so Tom awoke, and we rose in the dark,
And got with our bags and our brushes to work.
Though the morning was cold, Tom was happy and warm.
So if all do their duty, they need not fear harm.

A Cradle Song

Sweet dreams, form a shade
O'er my lovely infant's head,
Sweet dreams of pleasant streams,
By happy, silent, moony beams.

Sweet sleep, with soft down
Weave thy brows an infant crown.
Sweet sleep, angel mild,
Hover o'er my happy child.

Sweet smiles in the night,
Hover over my delight.   10
Sweet smiles, mother's smiles,
All the livelong night beguiles

Sweet moans, dovelike sighs,
Chase not slumber from thy eyes.
Sweet moans, sweeter smiles,
All the dovelike moans beguiles.

Sleep, sleep happy child.
All creation slept and smiled.
Sleep, sleep, happy sleep,
While o'er thee thy mother weep.   20

Sweet babe, in thy face,
Holy image I can trace.
Sweet babe, once like thee
Thy maker lay, and wept for me,

Wept for me, for thee, for all,
When he was an infant small.
Thou his image ever see,
Heavenly face that smiles on thee,

Smiles on thee, on me, on all,
Who became an infant small,
Infant smiles are his own smiles;
Heaven and earth to peace beguiles.

30

The Little Boy Lost

'Father, father where are you going?
Oh do not walk so fast.
Speak father, speak to your little boy,
Or else I shall be lost.'

The night was dark, no father was there,
The child was wet with dew.
The mire was deep, and the child did weep,
And away the vapour flew.

The Little Boy Found

The little boy lost in the lonely fen,
Led by the wand'ring light,
Began to cry, but God ever nigh
Appeared like his father in white.

He kissed the child and by the hand led,
And to his mother brought,
Who in sorrow pale through the lonely dale
Her little boy weeping sought.

Night

The sun descending in the west,
The evening star does shine.
The birds are silent in their nest,
And I must seek for mine.
The moon, like a flower
In heaven's high bower,
With silent delight
Sits and smiles on the night.

Farewell green fields and happy groves,
Where flocks have took delight;   10
Where lambs have nibbled, silent moves
The feet of angels bright.
Unseen they pour blessing,
And joy without ceasing,
On each bud and blossom,
And each sleeping bosom.

They look in every thoughtless nest,
Where birds are covered warm;
They visit caves of every beast,
To keep them all from harm.   20
If they see any weeping
That should have been sleeping,
They pour sleep on their head
And sit down by their bed.

When wolves and tigers howl for prey
They pitying stand and weep,
Seeking to drive their thirst away,
And keep them from the sheep.
But if they rush dreadful,
The angels most heedful,   30
Receive each mild spirit,
New worlds to inherit.

And there the lion's ruddy eyes
Shall flow with tears of gold,
And pitying the tender cries
And walking round the fold,
Saying: 'Wrath by his meekness,
And by his health sickness,
Is driven away
From our immortal day.   40

'And now beside thee, bleating lamb,
I can lie down and sleep,
Or think on him who bore thy name,
Graze after thee and weep.
For washed in life's river,
My bright mane for ever
Shall shine like the gold,
As I guard o'er the fold.'

The Marriage of Heaven and Hell (1790)

THE ARGUMENT

Rintrah roars and shakes his fires in the burdened air;
Hungry clouds swag on the deep.

Once meek, and in a perilous path,
The just man kept his course along
The vale of death.
Roses are planted where thorns grow,
And on the barren heath
Sing the honey bees.

Then the perilous path was planted,
And a river and a spring   10
On every cliff and tomb,
And on the bleached bones
Red clay brought forth.

Till the villain left the paths of ease
To walk in perilous paths, and drive
The just man into barren climes.

Now the sneaking serpent walks
In mild humility,
And the just man rages in the wilds
Where lions roam.   20

Rintrah roars and shakes his fires in the burdened air;
Hungry clouds swag on the deep.

As a new Heaven is begun, and it is now thirty-three years since
its advent, the eternal Hell revives. And lo! Swedenborg is the angel
sitting at the tomb; his writings are the linen clothes folded up. Now
is the dominion of Edom, and the return of Adam into Paradise;
see Isaiah xxxiv and xxxv.

Without contraries is no progression. Attraction and repulsion,
reason and energy, love and hate, are necessary to human existence.

From these contraries spring what the religious call Good and
Evil. Good is the passive that obeys reason, Evil is the active
springing from energy.

Good is Heaven. Evil is Hell.

THE VOICE OF THE DEVIL

All bibles or sacred codes have been the causes of the following errors:

1. That Man has two real existing principles, viz, a body and a soul.

2. That energy, called Evil, is alone from the body, and that reason, called Good, is alone from the soul.

3. That God will torment Man in eternity for following his energies.

But the following contraries to these are true:

1. Man has no body distinct from his soul, for that called body is a portion of soul discerned by the five senses, the chief inlets of soul in this age.

2. Energy is the only life and is from the body, and reason is the bound or outward circumference of energy.

3. Energy is eternal delight.

Those who restrain desire do so because theirs is weak enough to be restrained; and the restrainer, or reason, usurps its place and governs the unwilling.

And being restrained it by degrees becomes passive, till it is only the shadow of desire.

The history of this is written in *Paradise Lost*, and the governor, or reason, is called Messiah.

And the original archangel, or possessor of the command of the heavenly host, is called the Devil or Satan, and his children are called Sin and Death.

But in the *Book of Job* Milton's Messiah is called Satan.

For this history has been adopted by both parties.

It indeed appeared to reason as if desire was cast out, but the Devil's account is that the Messiah fell, and formed a heaven of what he stole from the abyss.

This is shown in the Gospel, where he prays to the Father to send the comforter, or desire, that reason may have ideas to build on, the Jehovah of the Bible being no other than he who dwells in flaming fire. Know that after Christ's death he became Jehovah.

But in Milton the Father is destiny, the Son a ratio of the five senses, and the Holy Ghost vacuum!

Note. The reason Milton wrote in fetters when he wrote of angels and God, and at liberty when of devils and Hell, is because he was a true poet, and of the Devil's party without knowing it.

A MEMORABLE FANCY

As I was walking among the fires of Hell, delighted with the enjoyments of genius, which to angels look like torment and insanity, I collected some of their proverbs, thinking that, as the sayings used in a nation mark its character, so the proverbs of Hell show the nature of infernal wisdom better than any description of buildings or garments.

When I came home, on the abyss of the five senses, where a flat-sided steep frowns over the present world, I saw a mighty devil folded in black clouds, hovering on the sides of the rock. With corroding fires he wrote the following sentence now perceived by the minds of men, and read by them on earth:

> How do you know but ev'ry bird that cuts the airy way
> Is an immense world of delight, closed by your senses five?

PROVERBS OF HELL

In seed time learn, in harvest teach, in winter enjoy.
Drive your cart and your plough over the bones of the dead.
The road of excess leads to the palace of wisdom.
Prudence is a rich ugly old maid courted by incapacity.
He who desires but acts not breeds pestilence.
The cut worm forgives the plough.
Dip him in the river who loves water.
A fool sees not the same tree that a wise man sees.
He whose face gives no light shall never become a star.
Eternity is in love with the productions of time.
The busy bee has no time for sorrow.
The hours of folly are measured by the clock, but of wisdom no clock can measure.
All wholesome food is caught without a net or a trap.
Bring out number, weight and measure in a year of dearth.
No bird soars too high, if he soars with his own wings.
A dead body revenges not injuries.
The most sublime act is to set another before you.
If the fool would persist in his folly he would become wise.
Folly is the cloak of knavery.
Shame is pride's cloak.
Prisons are built with stones of law, brothels with bricks of religion.

The pride of the peacock is the glory of God.

The lust of the goat is the bounty of God.

The wrath of the lion is the wisdom of God.

The nakedness of Woman is the work of God.

Excess of sorrow laughs. Excess of joy weeps.

The roaring of lions, the howling of wolves, the raging of the stormy sea, and the destructive sword are portions of eternity too great for the eye of Man.

The fox condemns the trap, not himself.

Joys impregnate. Sorrows bring forth.

Let Man wear the fell of the lion, Woman the fleece of the sheep.

The bird a nest, the spider a web, Man friendship.

The selfish smiling fool and the sullen frowning fool shall be both thought wise, that they may be a rod.

What is now proved was once only imagined.

The rat, the mouse, the fox, the rabbit, watch the roots. The lion, the tiger, the horse, the elephant, watch the fruits.

The cistern contains; the fountain overflows.

One thought fills immensity.

Always be ready to speak your mind, and a base man will avoid you.

Everything possible to be believed is an image of truth.

The eagle never lost so much time as when he submitted to learn of the crow.

The fox provides for himself, but God provides for the lion.

Think in the morning; act in the noon; eat in the evening; sleep in the night.

He who has suffered you to impose on him, knows you.

As the plough follows words, so God rewards prayers.

The tigers of wrath are wiser than the horses of instruction.

Expect poison from the standing water.

You never know what is enough unless you know what is more than enough.

Listen to the fool's reproach! It is a kingly title!

The eyes of fire, the nostrils of air, the mouth of water, the beard of earth.

The weak in courage is strong in cunning.

The apple tree never asks the beech how he shall grow, nor the lion the horse, how he shall take his prey.

The thankful receiver bears a plentiful harvest.

If others had not been foolish, we should be so.

The soul of sweet delight can never be defiled.

When thou seest an eagle, thou seest a portion of genius; lift up thy head!

As the caterpillar chooses the fairest leaves to lay her eggs on, so the priest lays his curse on the fairest joys.

To create a little flower is the labour of ages.

Damn braces. Bless relaxes.

The best wine is the oldest. The best water the newest.

Prayers plough not! Praises reap not!

Joys laugh not! Sorrows weep not!

The head Sublime, the heart Pathos, the genitals Beauty, the hands and feet Proportion.

As the air to a bird or the sea to a fish, so is contempt to the contemptible.

The crow wished everything was black; the owl, that everything was white.

Exuberance is beauty.

If the lion was advised by the fox, he would be cunning.

Improvement makes straight roads, but the crooked roads without improvement are roads of genius.

Sooner murder an infant in its cradle than nurse unacted desires.

Where Man is not, Nature is barren.

Truth can never be told so as to be understood, and not be believed.

Enough! Or too much!

The ancient poets animated all sensible objects with gods or geniuses, calling them by the names, and adorning them with the properties of woods, rivers, mountains, lakes, cities, nations, and whatever their enlarged and numerous senses could perceive.

And particularly they studied the genius of each city and country, placing it under its mental deity.

Till a system was formed, which some took advantage of and enslaved the vulgar by attempting to realise or abstract the mental deities from their objects. Thus began priesthood: choosing forms of worship from poetic tales.

And at length they pronounced that the gods had ordered such things.

Thus men forgot that all deities reside in the human breast.

A MEMORABLE FANCY

The prophets Isaiah and Ezekiel dined with me, and I asked them how they dared so roundly to assert that God spake to them; and whether they did not think at the time that they would be misunderstood, and so be the cause of imposition.

Isaiah answered: 'I saw no God, nor heard any, in a finite organical perception; but my senses discovered the infinite in everything, and as I was then persuaded, and remain confirmed, that the voice of honest indignation is the voice of God, I cared not for consequences but wrote.'

Then I asked: 'Does a firm persuasion that a thing is so, make it so?'

He replied: 'All poets believe that it does, and in ages of imagination the firm persuasion removed mountains; but many are not capable of a firm persuasion of anything.'

Then Ezekiel said: 'The philosophy of the east taught the first principles of human perception. Some nations held one principle for the origin and some another. We of Israel taught that the Poetic Genius (as you now call it) was the first principle, and all the others merely derivative—which was the cause of our despising the priests and philosophers of other countries, and prophesying that all gods would at last be proved to originate in ours and to be the tributaries of the Poetic Genius. It was this that our great poet King David desired so fervently and invoked so pathetic'ly, saying by this he conquers enemies and governs kingdoms. And we so loved our god, that we cursed in his name all the deities of surrounding nations, and asserted that they had rebelled. From these opinions the vulgar came to think that all nations would at last be subject to the Jews.

'This,' said he, 'like all firm persuasions, is come to pass, for all nations believe the Jews' code and worship the Jews' god, and what greater subjection can be?'

I heard this with some wonder, and must confess my own conviction. After dinner I asked Isaiah to favour the world with his lost works; he said none of equal value was lost. Ezekiel said the same of his.

I also asked Isaiah what made him go naked and barefoot for three years. He answered: 'The same that made our friend Diogenes the Grecian.'

I then asked Ezekiel why he ate dung, and lay so long on his right and left side. He answered, 'The desire of raising other men into a perception of the infinite. This the North American tribes practise, and is he honest who resists his genius or conscience only for the sake of present ease or gratification?'

The ancient tradition that the world will be consumed in fire at the end of six thousand years is true, as I have heard from Hell.

For the cherub with his flaming sword is hereby commanded to leave his guard at the Tree of Life, and when he does the whole creation will be consumed, and appear infinite and holy, whereas it now appears finite and corrupt.

This will come to pass by an improvement of sensual enjoyment.

But first the notion that Man has a body distinct from his soul is to be expunged. This I shall do by printing in the infernal method by corrosives, which in Hell are salutary and medicinal, melting apparent surfaces away, and displaying the infinite which was hid.

If the doors of perception were cleansed everything would appear to Man as it is: infinite.

For Man has closed himself up, till he sees all things through narrow chinks of his cavern.

A MEMORABLE FANCY

I was in a printing-house in Hell and saw the method in which knowledge is transmitted from generation to generation.

In the first chamber was a dragon-man, clearing away the rubbish from a cave's mouth; within, a number of dragons were hollowing the cave.

In the second chamber was a viper folding round the rock and the cave, and others adorning it with gold, silver and precious stones.

In the third chamber was an eagle with wings and feathers of air; he caused the inside of the cave to be infinite. Around were numbers of eagle-like men, who built palaces in the immense cliffs.

In the fourth chamber were lions of flaming fire, raging around and melting the metals into living fluids.

In the fifth chamber were unnamed forms, which cast the metals into the expanse.

There they were received by men who occupied the sixth chamber, and took the forms of books and were arranged in libraries.

The giants who formed this world into its sensual existence, and now seem to live in it in chains, are in truth the causes of its life and the sources of all activity; but the chains are the cunning of weak and tame minds, which have power to resist energy, according to the proverb: 'The weak in courage is strong in cunning'.

Thus one portion of being is the Prolific, the other, the Devouring. To the devourer it seems as if the producer was in his chains, but it is not so; he only takes portions of existence and fancies that the whole.

But the Prolific would cease to be prolific unless the devourer as a sea received the excess of his delights.

Some will say: 'Is not God alone the Prolific?' I answer: 'God only acts and is in existing beings or men.'

These two classes of men are always upon earth, and they should be enemies; whoever tries to reconcile them seeks to destroy existence.

Religion is an endeavour to reconcile the two.

Note. Jesus Christ did not wish to unite but to separate them, as in the parable of sheep and goats! And he says, 'I came not to send peace, but a sword.'

Messiah or Satan or Tempter was formerly thought to be one of the antediluvians who are our energies.

A MEMORABLE FANCY

An angel came to me and said: 'O pitiable foolish young man! Oh, horrible! Oh, dreadful state! Consider the hot burning dungeon thou art preparing for thyself to all eternity, to which thou art going in such career.'

I said: 'Perhaps you will be willing to show me my eternal lot, and we will contemplate together upon it, and see whether your lot or mine is most desirable.'

So he took me through a stable and through a church and down into the church vault, at the end of which was a mill. Through the mill we went, and came to a cave. Down the winding cavern we groped our tedious way, till a void boundless as a nether sky appeared beneath us, and we held by the roots of trees and hung over this immensity. But I said: 'If you please we will commit ourselves to this void, and see whether providence is here also. If you will not, I will!' But he answered: 'Do not presume, O young man; but as we here remain, behold thy lot which will soon appear when the darkness passes away.'

So I remained with him sitting in the twisted root of an oak. He was suspended in a fungus which hung with the head downward into the deep.

By degrees we beheld the infinite abyss, fiery as the smoke of a burning city. Beneath us at an immense distance was the sun, black but shining. Round it were fiery tracks on which revolved vast spiders, crawling after their prey, which flew or rather swum in the infinite deep, in the most terrific shapes of animals sprung from corruption; and the air was full of them, and seemed composed of them. These are devils, and are called Powers of the Air. I now asked my companion which was my eternal lot. He said: 'Between the black and white spiders'.

But now, from between the black and white spiders, a cloud and fire burst and rolled through the deep, black'ning all beneath, so that the nether deep grew black as a sea, and rolled with a terrible noise. Beneath us was nothing now to be seen but a black tempest, till looking east between the clouds and the waves, we saw a cataract of blood mixed with fire, and not many stones' throw from us appeared and sunk again the scaly fold of a monstrous serpent. At last to the east, distant about three degrees, appeared a fiery crest above the waves. Slowly it reared like a ridge of golden rocks, till we discovered two globes of crimson fire, from which the sea fled away in clouds of smoke; and now we saw it was the head of Leviathan. His forehead was divided into streaks of green and purple like those on a tiger's forehead. Soon we saw his mouth and red gills hang just above the raging foam, tingeing the black deep with beams of blood, advancing toward us with all the fury of a spiritual existence.

My friend the angel climbed up from his station into the mill. I remained alone, and then this appearance was no more, but I found myself sitting on a pleasant bank beside the river by moonlight, hearing a harper who sung to the harp; and his theme was: 'The man who never alters his opinion is like standing water, and breeds reptiles of the mind'.

But I arose, and sought for the mill, and there I found my angel, who, surprised, asked me how I escaped.

I answered: 'All that we saw was owing to your metaphysics; for when you ran away, I found myself on a bank by moonlight hearing a harper. But now we have seen my eternal lot, shall I show you yours?' He laughed at my proposal; but I by force suddenly caught him in my arms, and flew westerly through the night, till we were elevated above the earth's shadow. Then I flung myself with him directly into the body of the sun. Here I clothed myself in white, and taking in my hand Swedenborg's volumes sunk from the glorious clime, and passed all the planets till we came to Saturn. Here I stayed to rest and then leaped into the void between Saturn and the fixed stars.

'Here', said I, 'is your lot, in this space, if space it may be called.' Soon we saw the stable and the church, and I took him to the altar and opened the Bible, and lo! it was a deep pit, into which I descended, driving the angel before me. Soon we saw seven houses of brick. One we entered; in it were a number of monkeys, baboons, and all of that species, chained by the middle, grinning and snatching at one another, but withheld by the shortness of their chains. However I saw that they sometimes grew numerous, and then the weak were caught by the strong and, with a grinning aspect, first coupled with them and then devoured, by plucking off first one limb and then another till the body was left a helpless trunk. This after grinning and kissing it with seeming fondness they devoured too; and here and there I saw one savourily picking the flesh off of his own tail. As the stench terribly annoyed us both we went into the mill, and I in my hand brought the skeleton of a body, which in the mill was Aristotle's *Analytics*.

So the angel said: 'Thy fantasy has imposed upon me and thou oughtest to be ashamed.'

I answered: 'We impose on one another, and it is but lost time to converse with you whose works are only Analytics.'

OPPOSITION IS TRUE FRIENDSHIP

I have always found that angels have the vanity to speak of themselves as the only wise; this they do with a confident insolence sprouting from systematic reasoning.

Thus Swedenborg boasts that what he writes is new, though it is only the contents or index of already-published books.

A man carried a monkey about for a show, and because he was a little wiser than the monkey, grew vain, and conceived himself as much wiser than seven men. It is so with Swedenborg; he shows the folly of churches and exposes hypocrites, till he imagines that all are religious, and himself the single one on earth that ever broke a net.

Now hear a plain fact: Swedenborg has not written one new truth. Now hear another: he has written all the old falsehoods.

And now hear the reason: he conversed with angels, who are all religious, and conversed not with devils who all hate religion, for he was incapable through his conceited notions.

Thus Swedenborg's writings are a recapitulation of all superficial opinions and an analysis of the more sublime, but no further.

Have now another plain fact: any man of mechanical talents may from the writings of Paracelsus or Jacob Behmen produce ten thousand volumes of equal value with Swedenborg's, and from those of Dante or Shakespeare an infinite number.

But when he has done this, let him not say that he knows better than his master, for he only holds a candle in sunshine.

A MEMORABLE FANCY

Once I saw a devil in a flame of fire, who arose before an angel that sat on a cloud, and the devil uttered these words:

'The worship of God is honouring his gifts in other men, each according to his genius, and loving the greatest men best. Those who envy or calumniate great men hate God, for there is no other God.'

The angel, hearing this, became almost blue, but mastering himself he grew yellow, and at last white pink and smiling, and then replied:

'Thou idolater, is not God one, and is not he visible in Jesus Christ? And has not Jesus Christ given his sanction to the law of ten commandments; and are not all other men fools, sinners, and nothings?'

The devil answered: 'Bray a fool in a mortar with wheat, yet shall not his folly be beaten out of him. If Jesus Christ is the greatest man, you ought to love him in the greatest degree. Now hear how he has given his sanction to the law of ten commandments: did he not mock at the sabbath, and so mock the sabbath's god? murder those who were murdered because of him? turn away the law from the woman taken in adultery? steal the labour of others to support him? bear false witness when he omitted making a defence before Pilate? covet when he prayed for his disciples, and when he bid them shake off the dust of their feet against such as refused to lodge them? I tell you, no virtue can exist without breaking these ten commandments. Jesus was all virtue, and acted from impulse, not from rules.'

When he had so spoken I beheld the angel, who stretched out

his arms, embracing the flame of fire, and he was consumed and arose, as Elijah.

Note. This angel, who is now become a devil, is my particular friend. We often read the Bible together in its infernal or diabolical sense, which the world shall have if they behave well.

I have also the Bible of Hell, which the world shall have whether they will or no.

One law for the lion and ox is oppression.

A SONG OF LIBERTY

1. The Eternal Female groaned! It was heard over all the earth.

2. Albion's coast is sick, silent; the American meadows faint.

3. Shadows of prophecy shiver along by the lakes and the rivers, and mutter across the ocean. France, rend down thy dungeon;

4. Golden Spain, burst the barriers of old Rome;

5. Cast thy keys, O Rome, into the deep, down falling, even to eternity down falling—

6. And weep!

7. In her trembling hands she took the new-born terror, howling.

8. On those infinite mountains of light, now barred out by the Atlantic sea, the new-born fire stood before the starry king!

9. Flagged with grey-browed snows and thunderous visages, the jealous wings waved over the deep.

10. The speary hand burned aloft, unbuckled was the shield, forth went the hand of jealousy among the flaming hair, and hurled the new-born wonder through the starry night.

11. The fire, the fire, is falling!

12. Look up! Look up! O citizen of London, enlarge thy countenance! O Jew, leave counting gold! Return to thy oil and wine, O African, black African! (Go, winged thought, widen his forehead.)

13. The fiery limbs, the flaming hair shot like the sinking sun into the western sea.

14. Waked from his eternal sleep, the hoary element roaring fled away.

15. Down rushed, beating his wings in vain, the jealous king: his grey browed counsellors, thunderous warriors, curled veterans among helms, and shields, and chariots, horses, elephants, banners, castles, slings and rocks.

16. Falling, rushing, ruining! Buried in the ruins, on Urthona's dens.

17. All night beneath the ruins; then, their sullen flames faded, emerge round the gloomy king.

18. With thunder and fire, leading his starry hosts through the waste wilderness, he promulgates his ten commands, glancing his beamy eyelids over the deep in dark dismay,

19. Where the son of fire in his eastern cloud, while the morning plumes her golden breast,

20. Spurning the clouds written with curses, stamps the stony law to dust, loosing the eternal horses from the dens of night, crying: Empire is no more! And now the lion and wolf shall cease.

CHORUS

Let the priests of the raven of dawn no longer, in deadly black, with hoarse note curse the sons of joy. Nor his accepted brethren whom, tyrant, he calls free, lay the bound or build the roof. Nor pale religious lechery call that virginity that wishes but acts not.

For everything that lives is holy.

Visions of the Daughters of Albion (1793)

The eye sees more than the heart knows.

THE ARGUMENT

I loved Theotormon,
And I was not ashamed.
I trembled in my virgin fears,
And I hid in Leutha's vale!

I plucked Leutha's flower,
And I rose up from the vale;
But the terrible thunders tore
My virgin mantle in twain.

VISIONS

Enslaved, the daughters of Albion weep a trembling lamentation
Upon their mountains, in their valleys sighs toward America.   10

For the soft soul of America, Oothoon, wandered in woe
Along the vales of Leutha, seeking flowers to comfort her;
And thus she spoke to the bright marigold of Leutha's vale:

'Art thou a flower? Art thou a nymph? I see thee now a flower,
Now a nymph! I dare not pluck thee from thy dewy bed!'

The golden nymph replied: 'Pluck thou my flower, Oothoon
   the mild.
Another flower shall spring, because the soul of sweet delight
Can never pass away.' She ceased and closed her golden
   shrine.

Then Oothoon plucked the flower, saying, 'I pluck thee from
   thy bed,
Sweet flower, and put thee here to glow between my breasts,   20
And thus I turn my face to where my whole soul seeks.'

Over the waves she went in winged exulting swift delight,
And over Theotormon's reign took her impetuous course. .

Bromion rent her with his thunders; on his stormy bed
Lay the faint maid, and soon her woes appalled his thunders
   hoarse.

Bromion spoke: 'Behold this harlot here on Bromion's bed,
And let the jealous dolphins sport around the lovely maid.
Thy soft American plains are mine, and mine thy north and
   south.
Stamped with my signet are the swarthy children of the sun;
They are obedient, they resist not, they obey the scourge;   30
Their daughters worship terrors and obey the violent.
Now thou may'st marry Bromion's harlot, and protect the child
Of Bromion's rage that Oothoon shall put forth in nine moons
   time.'

Then storms rent Theotormon's limbs; he rolled his waves
   around
And folded his black jealous waters round the adulterate pair.
Bound back to back in Bromion's caves, terror and meekness
   dwell.

At entrance Theotormon sits, wearing the threshold hard
With secret tears; beneath him sound like waves on a desert
   shore
The voice of slaves beneath the sun, the children bought with
   money,
That shiver in religious caves beneath the burning fires   40
Of lust, that belch incessant from the summits of the earth.

Oothoon weeps not; she cannot weep! Her tears are locked
   up;
But she can howl incessant, writhing her soft snowy limbs,
And calling Theotormon's eagles to prey upon her flesh.

'I call with holy voice! Kings of the sounding air,
Rend away this defiled bosom that I may reflect
The image of Theotormon on my pure transparent breast.'
The eagles at her call descend and rend their bleeding prey.
Theotormon severely smiles; her soul reflects the smile;   50
As the clear spring mudded with feet of beasts grows pure and
   smiles.

The daughters of Albion hear her woes, and echo back her
   sighs.

'Why does my Theotormon sit weeping upon the threshold,
And Oothoon hovers by his side, persuading him in vain?
I cry: "Arise, O Theotormon, for the village dog
Barks at the breaking day; the nightingale has done lamenting;
The lark does rustle in the ripe corn, and the eagle returns
From nightly prey and lifts his golden beak to the pure east,
Shaking the dust from his immortal pinions to awake.
The sun that sleeps too long. Arise my Theotormon; I am
   pure,
Because the night is gone that closed me in its deadly black."   60
They told me that the night and day were all that I could see;
They told me that I had five senses to enclose me up,
And they enclosed my infinite brain into a narrow circle,
And sunk my heart into the abyss, a red round globe
   hot-burning,
Till all from life I was obliterated and erased.
Instead of morn arises a bright shadow, like an eye

In the eastern cloud; instead of night a sickly charnel-house,
That Theotormon hears me not! To him the night and morn
Are both alike: a night of sighs, a morning of fresh tears—
And none but Bromion can hear my lamentations.   70

'With what sense is it that the chicken shuns the ravenous
    hawk?
With what sense does the tame pigeon measure out the
    expanse?
With what sense does the bee form cells? Have not the mouse
    and frog
Eyes and ears and sense of touch? Yet are their habitations
And their pursuits as different as their forms and as their joys!
Ask the wild ass why he refuses burdens, and the meek camel
Why he loves Man. Is it because of eye, ear, mouth or skin,
Or breathing nostrils? No; for these the wolf and tiger have.
Ask the blind worm the secrets of the grave, and why her
    spires
Love to curl round the bones of death; and ask the rav'nous
    snake   80
Where she gets poison, and the winged eagle why he loves the
    sun—
And then tell me the thoughts of Man that have been hid of old.

'Silent I hover all the night, and all day could be silent,
If Theotormon once would turn his loved eyes upon me.
How can I be defiled when I reflect thy image pure?
Sweetest the fruit that the worm feeds on, and the soul preyed
    on by woe,
The new-washed lamb tinged with the village smoke, and the
    bright swan
By the red earth of our immortal river. I bathe my wings,
And I am white and pure to hover round Theotormon's
    breast.'

Then Theotormon broke his silence, and he answered: 90

'Tell me what is the night or day to one o'erflowed with woe?
Tell me what is a thought, and of what substance is it made?
Tell me what is a joy, and in what gardens do joys grow?
And in what rivers swim the sorrows, and upon what
    mountains

Wave shadows of discontent? And in what houses dwell the
  wretched
Drunken with woe, forgotten and shut up from cold despair?

'Tell me where dwell the thoughts forgotten till thou call
  them forth?
Tell me where dwell the joys of old, and where the ancient
  loves?
And when will they renew again and the night of oblivion
  past?
That I might traverse times and spaces far remote, and bring   100
Comforts into a present sorrow and a night of pain.
Where goest thou, O thought? To what remote land is thy
  flight?
If thou returnest to the present moment of affliction
Wilt thou bring comforts on thy wings, and dews and honey
  and balm,
Or poison from the desert wilds, from the eyes of the envier?'

Then Bromion said, and shook the cavern with his
  lamentation:

'Thou knowest that the ancient trees seen by thine eyes have
  fruit,
But knowest thou that trees and fruits flourish upon the earth
To gratify senses unknown? Trees, beasts and birds
  unknown—
Unknown, not unperceived: spread in the infinite microscope,   110
In places yet unvisited by the voyager, and in worlds
Over another kind of seas, and in atmospheres unknown.
Ah! are there other wars, beside the wars of sword and fire?
And are there other sorrows, beside the sorrows of poverty?
And are there other joys, beside the joys of riches and ease?
And is there not one law for both the lion and the ox?
And is there not eternal fire, and eternal chains,
To bind the phantoms of existence from eternal life?'

Then Oothoon waited silent all the day, and all the night,
But when the morn arose, her lamentation renewed.   120
The daughters of Albion hear her woes, and echo back her
  sighs.

'O Urizen! Creator of men. Mistaken demon of Heaven:
Thy joys are tears, thy labour vain, to form men to thine
　　image.
How can one joy absorb another? Are not different joys
Holy, eternal, infinite! And each joy is a love.

'Does not the great mouth laugh at a gift, and the narrow
　　eyelids mock
At the labour that is above payment? And wilt thou take the ape
For thy counsellor, or the dog for a schoolmaster to thy
　　children?
Does he who contemns poverty, and he who turns with
　　abhorrence
From usury, feel the same passion or are they moved alike?   130
How can the giver of gifts experience the delights of the
　　merchant,
How the industrious citizen the pains of the husbandman?
How different far the fat-fed hireling with hollow drum,
Who buys whole cornfields into wastes and sings upon the
　　heath!
How different their eye and ear! How different the world to
　　them!
With what sense does the parson claim the labour of the
　　farmer?
What are his nets and gins and traps, and how does he
　　surround him
With cold floods of abstraction and with forests of solitude,
To build him castles and high spires, where kings and priests
　　may dwell?
Till she who burns with youth, and knows no fixed lot, is
　　bound   140
In spells of law to one she loathes. And must she drag the
　　chain
Of life in weary lust? Must chilling murderous thoughts
　　obscure
The clear heaven of her eternal spring?—to bear the wintry
　　rage
Of a harsh terror, driv'n to madness, bound to hold a rod
Over her shrinking shoulders all the day—and all the night
To turn the wheel of false desire, and iongings that wake her
　　womb

To the abhorred birth of cherubs in the human form,
That live a pestilence and die a meteor and are no more?
Till the child dwell with one he hates, and do the deed he
    loathes.
And the impure scourge force his seed into its unripe birth   150
Ere yet his eyelids can behold the arrows of the day.
Does the whale worship at thy footsteps as the hungry dog,
Or does he scent the mountain prey, because his nostrils
    wide
Draw in the ocean? Does his eye discern the flying cloud
As the raven's eye, or does he measure the expanse like the
    vulture?
Does the still spider view the cliffs where eagles hide their
    young?
Or does the fly rejoice, because the harvest is brought in?
Does not the eagle scorn the earth and despise the treasures
    beneath?
But the mole knoweth what is there, and the worm shall tell
    it thee.
Does not the worm erect a pillar in the mouldering
    churchyard,   160
And a palace of eternity in the jaws of the hungry grave?
Over his porch these words are written: "Take thy bliss,
    O Man!
And sweet shall be thy taste; and sweet thy infant joys
    renew!"

'Infancy, fearless, lustful, happy! nestling for delight
In laps of pleasure. Innocence! honest, open, seeking
The vigorous joys of morning light, open to virgin bliss.
Who taught thee modesty, subtle modesty, child of night and
    sleep?
When thou awakest, wilt thou dissemble all thy secret joys,
Or wert thou not awake when all this mystery was disclosed?
Then com'st thou forth a modest virgin, knowing to
    dissemble,   170
With nets found under thy night pillow to catch virgin joy,
And brand it with the name of whore, and sell it in the night,
In silence, ev'n without a whisper, and in seeming sleep.
Religious dreams and holy vespers light thy smoky fires:
Once were thy fires lighted by the eyes of honest morn.

And does my Theotormon seek this hypocrite modesty,
This knowing, artful, secret, fearful, cautious, trembling
    hypocrite?
Then is Oothoon a whore indeed! And all the virgin joys
Of life are harlots; and Theotormon is a sick man's dream;
And Oothoon is the crafty slave of selfish holiness.   180

'But Oothoon is not so: a virgin filled with virgin fancies,
Open to joy and to delight wherever beauty appears.
If in the morning sun I find it, there my eyes are fixed
In happy copulation; if in evening mild, wearied with work,
Sit on a bank and draw the pleasures of this freeborn joy.

'The moment of desire! The moment of desire! The virgin
That pines for man shall awaken her womb to enormous joys
In the secret shadows of her chamber. The youth shut up
    from
The lustful joy shall forget to generate, and create an
    amorous image
In the shadows of his curtains and in the folds of his silent
    pillow.   190
Are not these the places of religion, the rewards of
    continence,
The self-enjoyings of self-denial? Why dost thou seek
    religion?
Is it because acts are not lovely that thou seekest solitude,
Where the horrible darkness is impressed with reflections of
    desire?

'Father of jealousy, be thou accursed from the earth!
Why hast thou taught my Theotormon this accursed thing?
Till beauty fades from off my shoulders, darkened and cast
    out,
A solitary wailing on the margin of non-entity.

'I cry, Love! Love! Love! Happy, happy Love! Free as the
    mountain wind!
Can that be Love that drinks another as a sponge drinks
    water,   200
That clouds with jealousy his nights, with weepings all the
    day—

To spin a web of age around him, grey and hoary, dark,
Till his eyes sicken at the fruit that hangs before his sight?
Such is self-love that envies all! A creeping skeleton
With lamplike eyes watching around the frozen marriage
　　bed.

'But silken nets and traps of adamant will Oothoon spread,
And catch for thee girls of mild silver or of furious gold.
I'll lie beside thee on a bank and view their wanton play
In lovely copulation, bliss on bliss with Theotormon.
Red as the rosy morning, lustful as the first-born beam,   210
Oothoon shall view his dear delight, nor e'er with jealous
　　cloud
Come in the heaven of generous love, nor selfish blightings
　　bring.

'Does the sun walk in glorious raiment on the secret floor
Where the cold miser spreads his gold? Or does the bright
　　cloud drop
On his stone threshold? Does his eye behold the beam that
　　brings
Expansion to the eye of pity? Or will he bind himself
Beside the ox to thy hard furrow? Does not that mild beam
　　blot
The bat, the owl, the glowing tiger, and the king of night?
The sea-fowl takes the wintry blast for a cov'ring to her
　　limbs,
And the wild snake the pestilence to adorn him with gems
　　and gold;   220
And trees and birds and beasts and men behold their eternal
　　joy.
Arise, you little glancing wings, and sing your infant joy!
Arise and drink your bliss; for everything that lives is holy!'

Thus every morning wails Oothoon; but Theotormon sits
Upon the margined ocean, conversing with shadows dire.

The daughters of Albion hear her woes, and echo back her
　　sighs.

THE END

America, a Prophecy (1793)

The shadowy daughter of Urthona stood before red Orc,
When fourteen suns had faintly journeyed o'er his dark abode.
His food she brought in iron baskets, his drink in cups of iron.
Crowned with a helmet and dark hair the nameless female
    stood;
A quiver with its burning stores, a bow like that of night
When pestilence is shot from heaven—no other arms she
    need.
Invulnerable though naked (save where clouds roll round her
    loins
Their awful folds in the dark air) silent she stood as night.
For never from her iron tongue could voice or sound arise,
But dumb till that dread day when Orc essayed his fierce
    embrace.   10

'Dark virgin,' said the hairy youth, 'thy father stern abhorred
Rivets my tenfold chains, while still on high my spirit soars.
Sometimes an eagle screaming in the sky, sometimes a lion
Stalking upon the mountains, and sometimes a whale I lash
The raging fathomless abyss; anon a serpent folding
Around the pillars of Urthona, and round thy dark limbs,
On the Canadian wilds I fold. Feeble my spirit folds,
For chained beneath I rend these caverns. When thou bringest
    food
I howl my joy, and my red eyes seek to behold thy face.
In vain! These clouds roll to and fro, and hide thee from my
    sight.'   20

Silent as despairing love, and strong as jealousy,
The hairy shoulders rend the links; free are the wrists of fire.
Round the terrific loins he seized the panting struggling
    womb;
It joyed. She put aside her clouds and smiled her first-born
    smile,
As when a black cloud shows its lightnings to the silent deep.

Soon as she saw the terrible boy, then burst the virgin cry:

'I know thee, I have found thee, and I will not let thee go.
Thou art the image of God who dwells in darkness of Africa,
And thou art fall'n to give me life in regions of dark death.
On my American plains I feel the struggling afflictions   30
Endured by roots that writhe their arms into the nether deep:
I see a serpent in Canada, who courts me to his love;
In Mexico an eagle, and a lion in Peru;
I see a whale in the South Sea, drinking my soul away.
Oh, what limb-rending pains I feel! Thy fire and my frost
Mingle in howling pains, in furrows by thy lightnings rent.
This is eternal death, and this the torment long foretold.'

A PROPHECY

The Guardian Prince of Albion burns in his nightly tent;
Sullen fires across the Atlantic glow to America's shore,
Piercing the souls of warlike men, who rise in silent night.   40
Washington, Franklin, Paine and Warren, Gates, Hancock
     and Greene
Meet on the coast glowing with blood from Albion's fiery
     prince.

Washington spoke: 'Friends of America, look over the Atlantic
     sea:
A bended bow is lifted in heaven, and a heavy iron chain
Descends link by link from Albion's cliffs across the sea to
     bind
Brothers and sons of America, till our faces pale and yellow,
Heads depressed, voices weak, eyes downcast, hands
     work-bruised,
Feet bleeding on the sultry sands, and the furrows of the whip,
Descend to generations that in future times forget.'

The strong voice ceased; for a terrible blast swept over the
     heaving sea;   50
The eastern cloud rent; on his cliffs stood Albion's wrathful
     prince,
A dragon form clashing his scales. At midnight he arose,
And flamed red meteors round the land of Albion beneath.

His voice, his locks, his awful shoulders, and his glowing eyes
Appear to the Americans upon the cloudy night.

Solemn heave the Atlantic waves between the gloomy nations,
Swelling, belching from its deeps red clouds and raging fires.

Albion is sick; America faints! Enraged the zenith grew.
As human blood shooting its veins all round the orbed heaven
Red rose the clouds from the Atlantic in vast wheels of blood,   60
And in the red clouds rose a wonder o'er the Atlantic sea:
Intense! naked! a human fire fierce glowing, as the wedge
Of iron heated in the furnace. His terrible limbs were fire,
With myriads of cloudy terrors, banners dark and towers
Surrounded. Heat but not light went through the murky
    atmosphere.

The King of England looking westward trembles at the vision.

Albion's Angel stood beside the stone of night, and saw
The terror like a comet, or more like the planet red
That once enclosed the terrible wandering comets in its
    sphere
(Then, Mars, thou wast our centre, and the planets three flew
    round   70
Thy crimson disc; so ere the sun was rent from thy red
    sphere.)
The spectre glowed, his horrid length staining the temple long
With beams of blood, and thus a voice came forth and shook
    the temple:

'The morning comes, the night decays, the watchmen leave
    their stations;
The grave is burst, the spices shed, the linen wrapped up;
The bones of death, the cov'ring clay, the sinews shrunk and
    dried
Reviving shake, inspiring move, breathing, awakening—
Spring like redeemed captives when their bonds and bars are
    burst.
Let the slave grinding at the mill run out into the field;
Let him look up into the heavens and laugh in the bright air;   80
Let the enchained soul shut up in darkness and in sighing,

Whose face has never seen a smile in thirty weary years,
Rise and look out—his chains are loose, his dungeon doors
     are open.
And let his wife and children return from the oppressor's
     scourge;
They look behind at every step and believe it is a dream,
Singing: "The sun has left his blackness, and has found a
     fresher morning.
And the fair moon rejoices in the clear and cloudless night.
For empire is no more, and now the lion and wolf shall
     cease."'

In thunders ends the voice. Then Albion's Angel wrathful
     burnt
Beside the Stone of Night, and, like the eternal lion's howl   90
In famine and war, replied: 'Art thou not Orc, who,
     serpent-formed,
Stands at the gate of Enitharmon to devour her children?
Blasphemous demon, Antichrist, hater of dignities,
Lover of wild rebellion, and transgressor of God's law,
Why dost thou come to angels' eyes in this terrific form?'

The terror answered: 'I am Orc, wreathed round the
     accursed tree.
The times are ended, shadows pass, the morning 'gins to
     break.
The fiery joy, that Urizen perverted to ten commands
What night he led the starry hosts through the wide
     wilderness—
That stony law I stamp to dust, and scatter religion abroad   100
To the four winds as a torn book, and none shall gather the
     leaves.
But they shall rot on desert sands and consume in bottomless
     deeps:
To make the deserts blossom and the deeps shrink to their
     fountains,
And to renew the fiery joy and burst the stony roof—
That pale religious lechery, seeking virginity,
May find it in a harlot, and in coarse-clad honesty
The undefiled, though ravished in her cradle night and morn.
For every thing that lives is holy, life delights in life—

Because the soul of sweet delight can never be defiled.
Fires enwrap the earthly globe, yet Man is not consumed;   110
Amidst the lustful fires he walks; his feet become like brass,
His knees and thighs like silver, and his breast and head like
   gold.'

'Sound! Sound! my loud war-trumpets, and alarm my
   thirteen Angels!
Loud howls the eternal wolf! The eternal lion lashes his tail!
America is darkened, and my punishing demons terrified
Crouch howling before their caverns deep like skins dried in
   the wind.
They cannot smite the wheat, nor quench the fatness of the
   earth.
They cannot smite with sorrows, nor subdue the plough and
   spade.
They cannot wall the city, nor moat round the castle of
   princes.
They cannot bring the stubbed oak to overgrow the hills.   120
For terrible men stand on the shores, and in their robes I see
Children take shelter from the lightnings; there stands
   Washington
And Paine and Warren, with their foreheads reared toward
   the east.
But clouds obscure my aged sight. A vision from afar!
Sound! Sound! my loud war-trumpets, and alarm my
   thirteen Angels.
Ah, vision from afar! Ah, rebel form that rent the ancient
Heavens, eternal viper self-renewed, rolling in clouds!
I see thee in thick clouds and darkness on America's shore,
Writhing in pangs of abhorred birth. Red flames the crest
   rebellious
And eyes of death. The harlot womb oft opened in vain   130
Heaves in enormous circles, now the times are returned
   upon thee,
Devourer of thy parent, now thy unutterable torment renews.
Sound! Sound! my loud war-trumpets, and alarm my
   thirteen Angels.
Ah, terrible birth! A young one bursting! Where is the
   weeping mouth?
And where the mother's milk? Instead those ever-hissing jaws

And parched lips drop with fresh gore. Now roll thou in the
    clouds;
Thy mother lays her length outstretched upon the shore
    beneath.
Sound! Sound! my loud war-trumpets, and alarm my thirteen
    Angels!
Loud howls the eternal wolf! The eternal lion lashes his tail!'

Thus wept the angel voice, and as he wept the terrible blasts   140
Of trumpets blew a loud alarm across the Atlantic deep.
No trumpets answer, no reply of clarion or of fifes;
Silent the Colonies remain and refuse the loud alarm.

On those vast shady hills between America and Albion's
    shore,
Now barred out by the Atlantic sea (called Atlantean hills,
Because from their bright summits you may pass to the
    golden world),
An ancient palace, archetype of mighty emperies,
Rears its immortal pinnacles, built in the forest of God
By Ariston, the king of beauty, for his stolen bride.

Here on their magic seats the thirteen Angels sat perturbed,   150
For clouds from the Atlantic hover o'er the solemn roof.
Fiery the Angels rose, and as they rose deep thunder rolled
Around their shores, indignant burning with the fires of Orc.
And Boston's Angel cried aloud as they flew through the
    dark night.

He cried: 'Why trembles honesty, and like a murderer
Why seeks he refuge from the frowns of his immortal station?
Must the generous tremble and leave his joy to the idle, to
    the pestilence,
That mock him? Who commanded this? What God? What
    Angel?
To keep the gen'rous from experience, till the ungenerous
And unrestrained performers of the energies of nature;   160
Till pity is become a trade, and generosity a science
That men get rich by, and the sandy desert is given to the
    strong.
What God is he, writes laws of peace and clothes him in the
    tempest?

What pitying Angel lusts for tears, and fans himself with sighs?
What crawling villain preaches abstinence and wraps himself
In fat of lambs? No more I follow, no more obedience pay.'

So cried he, rending off his robe and throwing down his
    sceptre
In sight of Albion's Guardian. And all the thirteen Angels
Rent off their robes to the hungry wind and threw their
    golden sceptres
Down on the land of America; indignant they descended   170
Headlong from out their heav'nly heights, descending swift
    as fires
Over the land. Naked and flaming are their lineaments seen
In the deep gloom. By Washington and Paine and Warren
    they stood,
And the flame folded roaring fierce within the pitchy night
Before the demon red, who burnt towards America
In black smoke, thunders and loud winds, rejoicing in its
    terror,
Breaking in smoky wreaths from the wild deep, and gath'ring
    thick
In flames as of a furnace on the land from north to south.
What time the thirteen governors that England sent convene
In Bernard's house, the flames covered the land. They
    arouse, they cry   180
Shaking their mental chains they rush in fury to the sea
To quench their anguish. At the feet of Washington down
    fall'n,
They grovel on the sand and writhing lie, while all
The British soldiers through the thirteen states sent up a
    howl
Of anguish, threw their swords and muskets to the earth and
    ran
From their encampments and dark castles, seeking where to
    hide
From the grim flames and from the visions of Orc, in sight
Of Albion's Angel; who enraged his secret clouds opened
From north to south, and burnt outstretched on wings of
    wrath cov'ring
The eastern sky, spreading his awful wings across the
    heavens.   190

Beneath him rolled his num'rous hosts; all Albion's Angels
    camped
Darkened the Atlantic mountains, and their trumpets shook
    the valleys—
Armed with diseases of the earth to cast upon the abyss,
Their numbers forty millions, must'ring in the eastern sky.

In the flames stood and viewed the armies drawn out in the
    sky
Washington, Franklin, Paine and Warren, Allen, Gates and
    Lee,
And heard the voice of Albion's Angel give the thunderous
    command.
His plagues, obedient to his voice, flew forth out of their
    clouds,
Falling upon America, as a storm to cut them off,
As a blight cuts the tender corn when it begins to appear.   200
Dark is the heaven above, and cold and hard the earth
    beneath,
And as a plague-wind filled with insects cuts off man and
    beast,
And as a sea o'erwhelms a land in the day of an earthquake.

Fury, rage, madness in a wind swept through America,
And the red flames of Orc that folded roaring fierce around
The angry shores, and the fierce rushing of th' inhabitants
    together.
The citizens of New York close their books and lock their
    chests;
The mariners of Boston drop their anchors and unlade;
The scribe of Pennsylvania casts his pen upon the earth;
The builder of Virginia throws his hammer down in fear.   210

Then had America been lost, o'erwhelmed by the Atlantic,
And Earth had lost another portion of the infinite.
But all rush together in the night, in wrath and raging fire;
The red fires raged, the plagues recoiled, then rolled they
    back with fury
On Albion's Angels. Then the pestilence began in streaks of
    red
Across the limbs of Albion's Guardian; the spotted plague
    smote Bristol's

And the leprosy London's spirit, sickening all their bands.
The millions sent up a howl of anguish and threw off their
     hammered mail,
And cast their swords and spears to earth, and stood a naked
     multitude.
Albion's Guardian writhed in torment on the eastern sky,   220
Pale quiv'ring toward the brain his glimmering eyes, teeth
     chattering,
Howling and shuddering, his legs quivering, convulsed each
     muscle and sinew;
Sick'ning lay London's Guardian and the ancient mitred York,
Their heads on snowy hills, their ensigns sick'ning in the sky.
The plagues creep on the burning winds, driven by flames of
     Orc,
And by the fierce Americans rushing together in the night,
Driven o'er the Guardians of Ireland and Scotland and Wales.
They, spotted with plagues, forsook the frontiers, and their
     banners seared
With fires of hell deform their ancient heavens with shame
     and woe.
Hid in his caves the Bard of Albion felt the enormous
     plagues,   230
And a cowl of flesh grew o'er his head, and scales on his back
     and ribs;
And rough with black scales all his Angels fright their
     ancient heavens.
The doors of marriage are open, and the priests in rustling
     scales
Rush into reptile coverts, hiding from the fires of Orc
That play around the golden roofs in wreaths of fierce desire,
Leaving the females naked and glowing with the lusts of
     youth.

For the female spirits of the dead, pining in bonds of
     religion,
Run from their fetters reddening, and in long drawn arches
     sitting;
They feel the nerves of youth renew, and desires of ancient
     times.
Over their pale limbs as a vine when the tender grape
     appears,   240

Over the hills, the vales, the cities, raged the red flames
  fierce;
The heavens melted from north to south, and Urizen, who
  sat
Above all heavens in thunders wrapped, emerged his leprous
  head
From out his holy shrine, his tears in deluge piteous
Falling into the deep sublime. Flagged with grey-browed
  snows
And thunderous visages, his jealous wings waved over the
  deep;
Weeping a dismal howling woe he dark descended, howling
Around the smitten bands, clothed in tears and trembling,
  shudd'ring cold.
His stored snows he poured forth, and his icy magazines
He opened on the deep, and on the Atlantic sea, white
  shiv'ring.   250
Leprous his limbs, all over white, and hoary was his visage,
Weeping in dismal howlings before the stern Americans,
Hiding the demon red with clouds and cold mists from the
  earth:
Till angels and weak men twelve years should govern o'er
  the strong,
And then their end should come, when France received the
  demon's light.

Stiff shudderings shook the heav'nly thrones! France, Spain
  and Italy
In terror viewed the bands of Albion and the ancient
  Guardians
Fainting upon the elements, smitten with their own plagues.
They slow advance to shut the five gates of thir law-built
  heaven,
Filled with blasting fancies and with mildews of despair,   260
With fierce disease and lust, unable to stem the fires of Orc;
But the five gates were consumed, and their bolts and hinges
  melted,
And the fierce flames burnt round the heavens and round
  the abodes of men.

FINIS

MANUSCRIPT LYRICS BETWEEN
INNOCENCE AND *EXPERIENCE*

'I told my love'

I told my love, I told my love,
I told her all my heart,
Trembling, cold, in ghastly fears.
Ah, she doth depart.

Soon as she was gone from me,
A traveller came by
Silently, invisibly.
Oh, was no deny.

'I laid me down'

I laid me down upon a bank
Where love lay sleeping.
I heard among the rushes dank
Weeping, weeping.

Then I went to the heath and the wild,
To the thistles and thorns of the waste,
And they told me how they were beguiled,
Driven out, and compelled to be chaste.

'I saw a chapel'

I saw a chapel all of gold
That none did dare to enter in,
And many weeping stood without,
Weeping, mourning, worshipping.

I saw a serpent rise between
The white pillars of the door,
And he forced and forced and forced;
Down the gold hinges tore.

And along the pavement sweet,
Set with pearls and rubies bright,   10
All his slimy length he drew
Till upon his altar white,

Vomiting his poison out
On the bread and on the wine.
So I turned into a sty
And laid me down among the swine.

'I asked a thief'

I asked a thief to steal me a peach;
He turned up his eyes.
I asked a lithe lady to lie her down;
Holy and meek, she cries.

As soon as I went
An angel came.
He winked at the thief
And smiled at the dame,

And, without one word said,
Had a peach from the tree   10
And, still as a maid,
Enjoyed the lady.

'I heard an angel'

I heard an angel singing,
When the day was springing,
'Mercy, Pity, Peace,
Is the world's release.'

Thus he sung all day
Over the new-mown hay,
Till the sun went down
And haycocks looked brown.

I heard a devil curse
Over the heath and the furze,   10
'Mercy could be no more
If there was nobody poor,

'And pity no more could be
If all were as happy as we.'
At his curse the sun went down,
And the heavens gave a frown.

A Cradle Song

Sleep, sleep, beauty bright,
Dreaming o'er the joys of night.
Sleep, sleep; in thy sleep
Little sorrows sit and weep.

Sweet babe, in thy face
Soft desires I can trace,
Secret joys and secret smiles,
Little pretty infant wiles.

As thy softest limbs I feel,
Smiles as of the morning steal   10
O'er thy cheek and o'er thy breast,
Where thy little heart does rest.

Oh, the cunning wiles that creep
In thy little heart asleep.
When thy little heart does wake,
Then the dreadful lightnings break

From thy cheek and from thy eye,
O'er the youthful harvests nigh,
Infant wiles and infant smiles
Heaven and Earth of peace beguiles.   20

'I feared the fury'

I feared the fury of my wind
Would blight all blossoms fair and true;
And my sun it shined and shined,
And my wind it never blew.

But a blossom fair or true
Was not found on any tree,
For all blossoms grew and grew
Fruitless, false—though fair to see.

'Silent, silent night'

Silent, silent night,
Quench the holy light
Of thy torches bright;

For, possessed of day,
Thousand spirits stray
That sweet joys betray.

Why should joys be sweet
Used with deceit,
Nor with sorrows meet?

But an honest joy   10
Does itself destroy
For a harlot coy.

'Why should I care'

Why should I care for the men of Thames,
Or the cheating waves of chartered streams,
Or shrink at the little blasts of fear
That the hireling blows into my ear?

Though born on the cheating banks of Thames,
Though his waters bathed my infant limbs,
The Ohio shall wash his stains from me.
I was born a slave, but I go to be free.

'O lapwing'

O lapwing, thou flyest around the heath,
Nor seest the net that is spread beneath.
Why dost thou not fly among the cornfields?
They cannot spread nets where a harvest yields.

'Thou hast a lap full of seed'

'Thou hast a lap full of seed
And this is a fine country;
Why dost thou not cast thy seed
And live in it merrily?'

'Shall I cast it on the sand
And turn it into fruitful land?
For on no other ground
Can I sow my seed,
Without tearing up
Some stinking weed.'   10

In a Myrtle Shade

Why should I be bound to thee,
O my lovely myrtle tree?
Love, free love, cannot be bound
To any tree that grows on ground.

Oh how sick and weary I
Underneath my myrtle lie,
Like to dung upon the ground,
Underneath my myrtle bound.

Oft my myrtle signed in vain,
To behold my heavy chain.
Oft my father saw us sigh,
And laughed at our simplicity.

So I smote him, and his gore
Stained the roots my myrtle bore;
But the time of youth is fled,
And grey hairs are on my head.

'As I wandered'

As I wandered the forest,
The green leaves among,
I heard a wild flower
Singing a song:

'I slept in the earth
In the silent night,
I murmured my fears
And I felt delight.

'In the morning I went,
As rosy as morn,
To seek for new joy,
But I met with scorn.'

'Are not the joys'

Are not the joys of morning sweeter
Than the joys of night,
And are the vig'rous joys of youth
Ashamed of the light?

Let age and sickness silent rob
The vineyards in the night,
But those who burn with vig'rous youth
Pluck fruits before the light.

To Nobodaddy

Why art thou silent and invisible,
Father of Jealousy?
Why dost thou hide thyself in clouds
From every searching eye?

Why darkness and obscurity
In all thy words and laws,
That none dare eat the fruit but from
The wily serpent's jaws?

Or is it because secrecy gains females' loud applause?

How to Know Love from Deceit

Love to faults is always blind,
Always is to joy inclined,
Lawless, winged and unconfined,
And breaks all chains from every mind.

Deceit to secrecy confined,
Lawful, cautious and refined,
To everything but interest blind,
And forges fetters for the mind.

Soft Snow

I walked abroad in a snowy day;
I asked the soft snow with me to play.
She played and she melted in all her prime,
And the winter called it a dreadful crime.

An Ancient Proverb

Remove away that black'ning church,
Remove away that marriage hearse,
Remove away that man of blood—
You'll quite remove the ancient curse.

To my Myrtle

To a lovely myrtle bound,
Blossoms show'ring all around,
Oh, how sick and weary I
Underneath my myrtle lie.
Why should I be bound to thee,
O my lovely myrtle tree?

Merlin's Prophecy

The harvest shall flourish in wintry weather,
When two virginities meet together.

The king and the priest must be tied in a tether,
Before two virgins can meet together.

Day

The sun arises in the east,
Clothed in robes of blood and gold;
Swords and spears and wrath increased,
All around his bosom rolled,
Crowned with warlike fires and raging desires.

The Fairy

'Come hither my sparrows,
My little arrows.
If a tear or a smile
Will a man beguile;
If an amorous delay
Clouds a sunshiny day;
If the step of a foot
Smites the heart to its root—
'Tis the marriage ring
Makes each fairy a king.'   10

So a fairy sung—
From the leaves I sprung.
He leaped from the spray
To flee away,
But, in my hat caught,
He soon shall be taught.
Let him laugh, let him cry,
He's my butterfly.
For I've pulled out the sting
Of the marriage ring.   20

'The sword sung on the barren heath'

The sword sung on the barren heath,
The sickle in the fruitful field;
The sword he sung a song of death,
But could not make the sickle yield.

'Abstinence sows sand'

Abstinence sows sand all over
The ruddy limbs and flaming hair;
But desire gratified
Plants fruits of life and beauty there.

'In a wife I would desire'

In a wife I would desire
(What in whores is always found),
The lineaments of gratified desire.

'If you trap the moment'

If you trap the moment before it's ripe,
The tears of repentance you'll certainly wipe;
But if once you let the ripe moment go,
You can never wipe off the tears of woe.

Eternity

He who binds to himself a joy
Does the winged life destroy;
But he who kisses the joy as it flies
Lives in eternity's sunrise.

The Question Answered

What is it men in women do require?
The lineaments of gratified desire.
What is it women do in men require?
The lineaments of gratified desire.

Lacedaemonian Instruction

'Come hither my boy; tell me what thou seest there.'
'A fool tangled in a religious snare'.

Riches

The countless gold of a merry heart,
The rubies and pearls of a loving eye,
The indolent never can bring to the mart,
Nor the secret hoard up in his treasury.

An Answer to the Parson

'Why of the sheep do you not learn peace?'
'Because I don't want you to shear my fleece'.

'The look of love alarms'

The look of love alarms
Because 'tis filled with fire;
But the look of soft deceit
Shall win the lover's hire.

'Her whole life is an epigram'

Her whole life is an epigram, smack-smooth and neatly penned,
Platted quite neat to catch applause—with a sliding noose at the
end.

'An old maid early'

An old maid early, ere I knew
Ought but the love that on me grew;
And now I'm covered o'er and o'er,
And wish that I had been a whore.

Oh, I cannot, cannot find
The undaunted courage of a virgin mind,
For early I in love was crossed,
Before my flower of love was lost.

Motto to the Songs of Innocence and Experience

The good are attracted by men's perceptions,
   And think not for themselves,
Till experience teaches them to catch
   And to cage the fairies and elves.

And then the knave begins to snarl,
   And the hypocrite to howl;
And all his good friends show their private ends,
   And the eagle is known from the owl.

SONGS OF EXPERIENCE (1793)

Introduction

Hear the voice of the bard!
Who present, past, and future sees;
Whose ears have heard
The Holy Word,
That walked among the ancient trees

Calling the lapsed soul,
And weeping in the evening dew;
That might control
The starry pole,
And fallen, fallen light renew!   10

'O Earth, O Earth return!
Arise from out the dewy grass.
Night is worn,
And the morn
Rises from the slumberous mass.

'Turn away no more;
Why wilt thou turn away?
The starry floor,
The wat'ry shore,
Is giv'n thee till the break of day.'   20

Earth's Answer

Earth raised up her head
From the darkness dread and drear.
Her light fled—
Stony dread!—
And her locks covered with grey despair.

'Prisoned on wat'ry shore
Starry jealousy does keep my den.
Cold and hoar,
Weeping o'er,
I hear the father of the ancient men.   10

'Selfish father of men,
Cruel, jealous, selfish fear!
Can delight
Chained in night
The virgins of youth and morning bear?

'Does spring hide its joy
When buds and blossoms grow?
Does the sower
Sow by night?
Or the ploughman in darkness plough?   20

'Break this heavy chain
That does freeze my bones around.
Selfish! Vain!
Eternal bane!
That free love with bondage bound.'

The Clod and the Pebble

'Love seeketh not itself to please,
Nor for itself hath any care,
But for another gives its ease,
And builds a Heaven in Hell's despair.'

So sang a little Clod of Clay,
Trodden with the cattle's feet,
But a Pebble of the brook
Warbled out these metres meet:

'Love seeketh only self to please,
To bind another to its delight,   10
Joys in another's loss of ease,
And builds a Hell in Heaven's despite.'

Holy Thursday

Is this a holy thing to see,
In a rich and fruitful land:
Babes reduced to misery,
Fed with cold and usurous hand?

Is that trembling cry a song?
Can it be a song of joy?
And so many children poor?
It is a land of poverty!

And their sun does never shine,
And their fields are bleak and bare,   10
And their ways are filled with thorns;
It is eternal winter there.

For where'er the sun does shine,
And where'er the rain does fall—
Babe can never hunger there,
Nor poverty the mind appal.

The Chimney-Sweeper

A little black thing among the snow,
Crying 'weep, weep' in notes of woe!
'Where are thy father and mother? Say!'
'They are both gone up to the church to pray.

'Because I was happy upon the heath,
And smiled among the winter's snow,
They clothed me in the clothes of death,
And taught me to sing the notes of woe.

'And because I am happy and dance and sing,
They think they have done me no injury,   10
And are gone to praise God and his priest and king,
Who make up a heaven of our misery.'

Nurse's Song

When the voices of children are heard on the green,
And whisperings are in the dale,
The days of my youth rise fresh in my mind,
My face turns green and pale.

Then come home my children, the sun is gone down,
And the dews of night arise.
Your spring and your day are wasted in play,
And your winter and night in disguise.

The Sick Rose

O rose, thou art sick;
The invisible worm
That flies in the night,
In the howling storm,

Has found out thy bed
Of crimson joy,
And his dark secret love
Does thy life destroy.

The Fly

Little fly,
Thy summer's play
My thoughtless hand
Has brushed away.

Am not I
A fly like thee?
Or art not thou
A man like me?

For I dance
And drink and sing,
Till some blind hand
Shall brush my wing.

If thought is life
And strength and breath,
And the want
Of thought is death,

Then am I
A happy fly,
If I live,
Or if I die.

The Angel

I dreamt a dream!—what can it mean?—
And that I was a maiden queen,
Guarded by an angel mild.
Witless woe was ne'er beguiled!

And I wept both night and day,
And he wiped my tears away,
And I wept both day and night,
And hid from him my heart's delight.

So he took his wings and fled;
Then the morn blushed rosy red.
I dried my tears, and armed my fear
With ten thousand shields and spears.

10

Soon my angel came again.
I was armed; he came in vain,
For the time of youth was fled,
And grey hairs were on my head.

The Tiger

Tiger, tiger, burning bright,
In the forests of the night:
What immortal hand or eye
Could frame thy fearful symmetry?

In what distant deeps or skies,
Burnt the fire of thine eyes?
On what wings dare he aspire?
What the hand dare seize the fire?

And what shoulder, and what art,
Could twist the sinews of thy heart?   10
And when thy heart began to beat,
What dread hand? and what dread feet?

What the hammer? what the chain?
In what furnace was thy brain?
What the anvil? what dread grasp
Dare its deadly terrors clasp?

When the stars threw down their spears,
And watered Heaven with their tears,
Did he smile his work to see?
Did he who made the lamb make thee?   20

Tiger, tiger, burning bright,
In the forests of the night:
What immortal hand or eye
Dare frame thy fearful symmetry?

My Pretty Rose Tree

A flower was offered to me,
Such a flower as May never bore,
But I said, 'I've a pretty rose tree,'
And I passed the sweet flower o'er.

Then I went to my pretty rose tree,
To tend her by day and by night,
But my rose turned away with jealousy,
And her thorns were my only delight.

Ah! Sunflower

Ah! sunflower, weary of time,
Who countest the steps of the sun,
Seeking after that sweet golden clime
Where the traveller's journey is done;

Where the youth pined away with desire,
And the pale virgin shrouded in snow,
Arise from their graves and aspire;
Where my sunflower wishes to go.

The Lily

The modest rose puts forth a thorn,
The humble sheep a threat'ning horn;
While the lily white shall in love delight,
Nor a thorn nor a threat stain her beauty bright.

The Garden of Love

I went to the Garden of Love,
And saw what I never had seen:
A chapel was built in the midst,
Where I used to play on the green.

And the gates of this chapel were shut,
And 'Thou shalt not' writ over the door;
So I turned to the Garden of Love,
That so many sweet flowers bore.

And I saw it was filled with graves,
And tomb-stones where flowers should be,   10
And priests in black gowns were walking their rounds,
And binding with briars my joys and desires.

The Little Vagabond

Dear mother, dear mother, the church is cold,
But the ale-house is healthy and pleasant and warm.
Besides, I can tell where I am used well;
Such usage in Heaven will never do well.

But if at the church they would give us some ale,
And a pleasant fire our souls to regale,
We'd sing and we'd pray all the live-long day,
Nor ever once wish from the church to stray.

Then the parson might preach and drink and sing,
And we'd be as happy as birds in the spring;   10
And modest dame Lurch, who is always at church,
Would not have bandy children, nor fasting, nor birch.

And God, like a father rejoicing to see
His children as pleasant and happy as he,
Would have no more quarrel with the Devil or the barrel,
But kiss him and give him both drink and apparel.

London

I wander through each chartered street,
Near where the chartered Thames does flow,
And mark in every face I meet
Marks of weakness, marks of woe.

In every cry of every man,
In every infant's cry of fear,
In every voice, in every ban,
The mind-forged manacles I hear:

How the chimney-sweeper's cry
Every black'ning church appalls,   10
And the hapless soldier's sigh
Runs in blood down palace walls.

But most through midnight streets I hear
How the youthful harlot's curse
Blasts the new-born infant's tear,
And blights with plagues the marriage hearse.

The Human Abstract

Pity would be no more
If we did not make somebody poor,
And Mercy no more could be
If all were as happy as we.

And mutual fear brings Peace,
Till the selfish loves increase.
Then Cruelty knits a snare,
And spreads his baits with care.

He sits down with holy fears,
And waters the ground with tears;   10
Then Humility takes its root
Underneath his foot.

Soon spreads the dismal shade
Of Mystery over his head,
And the caterpillar and fly
Feed on the Mystery.

And it bears the fruit of Deceit,
Ruddy and sweet to eat,
And the raven his nest has made
In its thickest shade.   20

The gods of the earth and sea
Sought through Nature to find this tree,
But their search was all in vain.
There grows one in the human brain.

Infant Sorrow

My mother groaned, my father wept!
Into the dangerous world I leapt,
Helpless, naked, piping loud,
Like a fiend hid in a cloud.

Struggling in my father's hands,
Striving against my swaddling bands,
Bound and weary, I thought best
To sulk upon my mother's breast.

A Poison Tree

I was angry with my friend;
I told my wrath—my wrath did end.
I was angry with my foe;
I told it not—my wrath did grow.

And I watered it in fears,
Night and morning with my tears,
And I sunned it with smiles,
And with soft deceitful wiles.

And it grew both day and night,
Till it bore an apple bright.   10
And my foe beheld it shine,
And he knew that it was mine,

And into my garden stole
When the night had veiled the pole.
In the morning glad I see
My foe outstretched beneath the tree.

A Little Boy Lost

'Nought loves another as itself,
Nor venerates another so,
Nor is it possible to thought
A greater than itself to know.

'And father, how can I love you,
Or any of my brothers more?
I love you like the little bird
That picks up crumbs around the door.'

The priest sat by and heard the child;
In trembling zeal he seized his hair.   10
He led him by his little coat,
And all admired the priestly care.

And, standing on the altar high,
'Lo, what a fiend is here!' said he,
'One who sets reason up for judge
Of our most holy mystery.'

The weeping child could not be heard;
The weeping parents wept in vain.
They stripped him to his little shirt,
And bound him in an iron chain,   20

And burned him in a holy place,
Where many had been burned before.
The weeping parents wept in vain.
Are such things done on Albion's shore?

A Little Girl Lost

Children of the future age,
Reading this indignant page,
Know that in a former time
Love! sweet love! was thought a crime.

In the age of gold,
Free from winter's cold,
Youth and maiden bright,
To the holy light,
Naked in the sunny beams delight.

Once a youthful pair,   10
Filled with softest care,
Met in garden bright,
Where the holy light
Had just removed the curtains of the night.

There in rising day
On the grass they play.
Parents were afar;
Strangers came not near;
And the maiden soon forgot her fear.

Tired with kisses sweet,   20
They agree to meet
When the silent sleep
Waves o'er heavens deep,
And the weary, tired wanderers weep.

To her father white
Came the maiden bright;
But his loving look,
Like the holy book, .
All her tender limbs with terror shook.

'Ona! pale and weak!   30
To thy father speak.
Oh the trembling fear!
Oh the dismal care,
That shakes the blossoms of my hoary hair!'

To Tirzah

Whate'er is born of mortal birth
Must be consumed with the earth,
To rise from generation free.
Then what have I to do with thee?

The sexes sprung from shame and pride,
Blowed in the morn, in evening died.
But mercy changed death into sleep;
The sexes rose to work and weep.

Thou, mother of my mortal part,
With cruelty didst mould my heart,   10
And with false self-deceiving tears
Didst bind my nostrils, eyes and ears;

Didst close my tongue in senseless clay,
And me to mortal life betray
The death of Jesus set me free.
Then what have I to do with thee?

A Divine Image

Cruelty has a human heart,
And Jealousy a human face;
Terror the human form divine,
And Secrecy the human dress.

The human dress is forged iron;
The human form, a fiery forge;
The human face, a furnace sealed;
The human heart, its hungry gorge.

Europe, a Prophecy (1794)

'Five windows light the caverned man: through one he
  breathes the air;
Through one, hears music of the spheres; through one the
  eternal vine
Flourishes, that he may receive the grapes; through one, can
  look
And see small portions of the eternal world that ever groweth;
Through one, himself pass out what time he please but he will
  not,
For stolen joys are sweet, and bread eaten in secret pleasant.'

So sang a fairy mocking as he sat on a streaked tulip,
Thinking none saw him; when he ceased I started from the
  trees
And caught him in my hat as boys knock down a butterfly.
'How know you this,' said I, 'small sir? Where did you learn
  this song?'   10
Seeing himself in my possession, thus he answered me:
'My master, I am yours; command me, for I must obey.'

'Then tell me what is the material world, and is it dead?'
He laughing answered: 'I will write a book on leaves of flowers,
If you will feed me on love-thoughts, and give me now and then
A cup of sparkling poetic fancies. So when I am tipsy,
I'll sing to you to this soft lute, and show you all alive
The world, when every particle of dust breathes forth its joy.'

I took him home in my warm bosom. As we went along
Wild flowers I gathered, and he showed me each eternal
  flower;   20
He laughed aloud to see them whimper because they were
  plucked.
They hov'red round me like a cloud of incense when I came
Into my parlour and sat down, and took my pen to write;
My fairy sat upon the table, and dictated EUROPE.

PRELUDIUM

The nameless shadowy female rose from out of the breast of
   Orc,
Her snaky hair brandishing in the winds of Enitharmon;
And thus her voice arose:

'O mother Enitharmon, wilt thou bring forth other sons
To cause my name to vanish, that my place may not be found?
For I am faint with travail!—   30
Like the dark cloud disburdened in the day of dismal thunder.

'My roots are brandished in the heavens, my fruits in earth
   beneath
Surge, foam, and labour into life, first born and first consumed,
Consumed and consuming!
Then why shouldst thou, accursed mother, bring me into life?

'I wrap my turban of thick clouds around my lab'ring head,
And fold the sheety waters as a mantle round my limbs—
Yet the red sun and moon
And all the overflowing stars rain down prolific pains.

'Unwilling I look up to heaven! unwilling count the stars!   40
Sitting in fathomless abyss of my immortal shrine,
I seize their burning power
And bring forth howling terrors, all-devouring fiery kings,

'Devouring and devoured, roaming on dark and desolate
   mountains
In forests of eternal death, shrieking in hollow trees.
Ah, mother Enitharmon,
Stamp not with solid form this vig'rous progeny of fires!

'I bring forth from my teeming bosom myriads of flames,
And thou dost stamp them with a signet; then they roam abroad
And leave me void as death.   50
Ah! I am drowned in shady woe, and visionary joy.

'And who shall bind the infinite with an eternal band,
To compass it with swaddling bands? And who shall cherish it
With milk and honey?
I see it smile and I roll inward and my voice is past.'

> She ceased, and rolled her shady clouds
> Into the secret place.

A PROPHECY

> The deep of winter came,
> What time the secret child
Descended through the orient gates of the eternal day.   60
War ceased, and all the troops like shadows fled to their abodes.

Then Enitharmon saw her sons and daughters rise around.
Like pearly clouds they meet together in the crystal house,
And Los, possessor of the moon, joyed in the peaceful night,
Thus speaking while his num'rous sons shook their bright
  fiery wings:

'Again the night is come
That strong Urthona takes his rest,
And Urizen unloosed from chains
Glows like a meteor in the distant north.
Stretch forth your hands and strike the elemental strings!   70
Awake the thunders of the deep,
The shrill winds wake!—
Till all the sons of Urizen look out and envy Los.
Seize all the spirits of life and bind
Their warbling joys to our loud strings;
Bind all the nourishing sweets of earth
To give us bliss, that we may drink the sparkling wine of Los;
And let us laugh at war,
Despising toil and care,
Because the days and nights of joy in lucky hours renew.'   80

'Arise, O Orc, from thy deep den;
First-born of Enitharmon, rise!
And we will crown thy head with garlands of the ruddy vine—
For now thou art bound—
And I may see thee in the hour of bliss, my eldest born.'

The horrent demon rose, surrounded with red stars of fire,
Whirling about in furious circles round the immortal fiend.
Then Enitharmon down descended into his red light,
And thus her voice rose to her children; the distant heavens
 reply.
'Now comes the night of Enitharmon's joy.   90
Who shall I call? Who shall I send?
That Woman, lovely Woman, may have dominion?
Arise, O Rintrah, thee I call! And Palamabron, thee!
Go! Tell the human race that Woman's love is sin,
That an eternal life awaits the worms of sixty winters
In an allegorical abode where existence hath never come.
Forbid all joy, and from her childhood shall the little female
Spread nets in every secret path.

'My weary eyelids draw towards the evening; my bliss is yet
 but new.
Arise, O Rintrah, eldest born, second to none but Orc.   100
O lion Rintrah, raise thy fury from thy forests black;
Bring Palamabron, horned priest, skipping upon the
 mountains,
And silent Elynittria, the silver-bowed queen.
Rintrah, where hast thou hid thy bride?
Weeps she in desert shades?
Alas, my Rintrah, bring the lovely jealous Ocalythron.

'Arise, my son! Bring all thy brethren, O thou king of fire.
Prince of the sun, I see thee with thy innumerable race
Thick as the summer stars,
But each ramping his golden mane shakes;
And thine eyes rejoice because of strength, O Rintrah,
 furious king.'   110

Enitharmon slept
Eighteen hundred years. Man was a dream!—
The night of Nature, and their harps unstrung.
She slept in middle of her nightly song:
Eighteen hundred years, a female dream.

Shadows of men in fleeting bands upon the winds
Divide the heavens of Europe;
Till Albion's Angel, smitten with his own plagues, fled with his
    bands.   120
The cloud bears hard on Albion's shore,
Filled with immortal demons of futurity.
In council gather the smitten Angels of Albion;
The cloud bears hard upon the council house, down rushing
On the heads of Albion's Angels.

One hour they lay buried beneath the ruins of that hall;
But as the stars rise from the salt lake they arise in pain,
In troubled mists o'erclouded by the terrors of struggling
    times.

In thoughts perturbed, they rose from the bright ruins, silent
    following
The fiery king, who sought his ancient temple serpent-formed,
That stretches out its shady length along the island white.   130
Round him rolled his clouds of war; silent the Angel went,
Along the infinite shores of Thames to golden Verulam.
There stand the venerable porches that high-towering rear
Their oak-surrounded pillars, formed of massy stones, uncut
With tool, stones precious. Such eternal in the heavens,
Of colours twelve, few known on earth, give light in the
    opaque,
Placed in the order of the stars when the five senses whelmed
In deluge o'er the earth-born man. Then turned the fluxile
    eyes
Into two stationary orbs, concentrating all things;
The ever-varying spiral ascents to the heavens of heavens   140
Were bended downward, and the nostrils' golden gates shut,
Turned outward, barred and petrified against the infinite.

Thought changed the infinite to a serpent, that which pitieth
To a devouring flame, and Man fled from its face and hid
In forests of night. Then all the eternal forests were divided
Into earths rolling in circles of space, that like an ocean
    rushed
And overwhelmed all except this finite wall of flesh.
Then was the serpent temple formed, image of infinite
Shut up in finite revolutions, and Man became an Angel,
Heaven a mighty circle turning, God a tyrant crowned.   150

Now arrived the ancient Guardian at the southern porch
That, planted thick with trees of blackest leaf, and in a vale
Obscure, enclosed the Stone of Night. Oblique it stood,
   o'erhung
With purple flowers and berries red, image of that sweet
   south
Once open to the heavens and elevated on the human neck,
Now overgrown with hair and covered with a stony roof;
Downward 'tis sunk beneath th' attractive north, that round
   the feet,
A raging whirlpool, draws the dizzy enquirer to his grave.

Albion's Angel rose upon the Stone of Night.
He saw Urizen on the Atlantic,   160
And his brazen book
That kings and priests had copied on earth
Expanded from north to south.

And the clouds and fires pale rolled round in the night of
   Enitharmon,
Round Albion's cliffs and London's walls; still Enitharmon
   slept.
Rolling volumes of grey mist involve churches, palaces,
   towers;
For Urizen unclasped his book, feeding his soul with pity.
The youth of England hid in gloom curse the pained heavens,
   compelled
Into the deadly night to see the form of Albion's Angel.
Their parents brought them forth and aged ignorance
   preaches, canting,   170
On a vast rock, perceived by those senses that are closed
   from thought;
Bleak, dark, abrupt it stands and overshadows London city.
They saw his bony feet on the rock, the flesh consumed in
   flames;
They saw the serpent temple lifted above, shadowing the
   island white;
They heard the voice of Albion's Angel howling in flames of
   Orc,
Seeking the trump of the last doom.

Above the rest the howl was heard from Westminster louder
   and louder.
The guardian of the secret codes forsook his ancient mansion,
Driven out by the flames of Orc; his furred robes and false
   locks
Adhered and grew one with his flesh, and nerves and veins
   shot through them   180
With dismal torment sick, hanging upon the wind. He fled
Grovelling along Great George Street through the Park
   gate; all the soldiers
Fled from his sight; he dragged his torments to the wilderness.

Thus was the howl through Europe!
For Orc rejoiced to hear the howling shadows,
But Palamabron shot his lightnings trenching down his wide
   back,
And Rintrah hung with all his legions in the nether deep.

Enitharmon laughed in her sleep to see (Oh, woman's
   triumph!)
Every house a den, every man bound; the shadows are filled
With spectres, and the windows wove over with curses of iron;   190
Over the doors 'Thou shalt not', and over the chimneys
   'Fear' is written.
With bands of iron round their necks, fastened into the walls,
The citizens; in leaden gyves the inhabitants of suburbs
Walk heavy; soft and bent are the bones of villagers.

Between the cloud of Urizen the flames of Orc roll heavy
Around the limbs of Albion's Guardian, his flesh consuming.
Howlings and hissings, shrieks and groans, and voices of
   despair
Arise around him in the cloudy heavens of Albion. Furious
The red-limbed angel seized, in horror and torment,
The trump of the last doom; but he could not blow the iron
   tube!   200
Thrice he essayed presumptuous to awake the dead to
   judgement.
A mighty spirit leaped from the land of Albion,
Named Newton; he seized the trump and blowed the
   enormous blast!
Yellow as leaves of autumn, the myriads of angelic hosts
Fell through the wintry skies seeking their graves,
Rattling their hollow bones in howling and lamentation.

Then Enitharmon woke, nor knew that she had slept,
And eighteen hundred years were fled
As if they had not been.
She called her sons and daughters   210
To the sports of night
Within her crystal house,
And thus her song proceeds:

'Arise Ethinthus! Though the earth-worm call,
Let him call in vain
Till the night of holy shadows
And human solitude is past!

'Ethinthus, queen of waters, how thou shinest in the sky!
My daughter, how do I rejoice! For thy children flock around
Like the gay fishes on the wave, when the cold moon drinks
    the dew.   220
Ethinthus! thou art sweet as comforts to my fainting soul,
For now thy waters warble round the feet of Enitharmon.

'Manathu-Varcyon! I behold thee flaming in my halls,
Light of thy mother's soul! I see thy lovely eagles round;
Thy golden wings are my delight, and thy flames of soft
    delusion.

'Where is my luring bird of Eden? Leutha, silent love!
Leutha, the many-coloured bow delights upon thy wings:
Soft soul of flowers, Leutha!
Sweet smiling pestilence! I see thy blushing light;
Thy daughters many-changing   230
Revolve like sweet perfumes ascending, O Leutha, silken
    queen!

'Where is the youthful Antamon, prince of the pearly dew?
O Antamon, why wilt thou leave thy mother Enitharmon?
Alone I see thee, crystal form,
Floating upon the bosomed air
With lineaments of gratified desire,
My Antamon, the seven churches of Leutha seek thy love.

'I hear the soft Oothoon in Enitharmon's tents.
Why wilt thou give up woman's secrecy, my melancholy child?
Between two moments bliss is ripe.   240
O Theotormon, robbed of joy, I see thy salt tears flow
Down the steps of my crystal house.

'Sotha and Thiralatha, secret dwellers of dreamful caves,
Arise and please the horrent fiend with your melodious songs.
Still all your thunders golden-hoofed, and bind your horses
    black.
Orc! Smile upon my children!
Smile, son of my afflictions.
Arise, O Orc, and give our mountains joy of thy red light.'

She ceased, for all were forth at sport beneath the solemn moon,
Waking the stars of Urizen with their immortal songs: 250
That Nature felt through all her pores the enormous revelry,
Till morning oped the eastern gate.
Then every one fled to his station, and Enitharmon wept.

But terrible Orc, when he beheld the morning in the east,
Shot from the heights of Enitharmon.
And in the vineyards of red France appeared the light of his
    fury.

The sun glowed fiery red!
The furious terrors flew around!—
On golden chariots raging, with red wheels dropping with
    blood.
The lions lash their wrathful tails;   260
The tigers couch upon the prey and suck the ruddy tide;
And Enitharmon groans and cries in anguish and dismay.

Then Los arose; his head he reared in snaky thunders clad,
And with a cry that shook all Nature to the utmost pole
Called all his sons to the strife of blood.

FINIS

From the annotations to Henry Boyd's
A Translation of the Inferno of Dante Alighieri (*c.*1800)

The grandest poetry is immoral, the grandest characters wicked,
very Satan: Capaneus, Othello (a murderer), Prometheus, Jupiter,
Jehovah, Jesus (a wine-bibber). Cunning and morality are not
poetry, but philosophy. The poet is independent and wicked; the
philosopher is dependent and good.

    Poetry is to excuse vice, and show its reason and necessary
purgation.

'To my friend Butts' (1800)

To my friend Butts I write
My first vision of light.
On the yellow sands sitting
The sun was emitting
His glorious beams
From heaven's high streams.
Over sea, over land,
My eyes did expand
Into regions of air,
Away from all care,   10
Into regions of fire,
Remote from desire.
The light of the morning
Heaven's mountains adorning,
In particles bright
The jewels of light
Distinct shone and clear.
Amazed and in fear
I each particle gazed—
Astonished, amazed,   20
For each was a man
Human-formed. Swift I ran,
For they beckoned to me,
Remote by the sea,
Saying: 'Each grain of sand,
Every stone on the land,
Each rock and each hill,
Each fountain and rill,
Each herb and each tree,
Mountain, hill, earth and sea,   30
Cloud, meteor and star
Are men seen afar'.
I stood in the streams
Of heaven's bright beams
And saw Felpham sweet
Beneath my bright feet,
In soft female charms.
And in her fair arms

My shadow I knew,
And my wife's shadow too,
And my sister and friend.   40
(We like infants descend
In our shadows on earth,
Like a weak mortal birth.)
My eyes more and more
Like a sea without shore
Continue expanding,
The heavens commanding,
Till the jewels of light,
Heavenly men beaming bright,   50
Appeared as one man;
Who complacent began
My limbs to enfold
In his beams of bright gold,
Like dross purged away
All my mire and my clay.
Soft-consumed in delight
In his bosom sun-bright
I remained. Soft he smiled,
And I heard his voice mild,   60
Saying: 'This is my fold,
O thou ram horned with gold,
Who awakest from sleep
On the sides of the deep.
On the mountains around
The roarings resound
Of the lion and wolf,
The loud sea and deep gulf.
These are guards of my fold,
O thou ram horned with gold.'   70
And the voice faded mild.
I remained as a child.
All I ever had known
Before me bright shone.
I saw you and your wife
By the fountains of life.
Such the vision to me
Appeared on the sea.

'With happiness stretched across the hills' (1802)

With happiness stretched across the hills
In a cloud that dewy sweetness distils,
With a blue sky spread over with wings
And a mild sun that mounts and sings,
With trees and fields full of fairy elves
And little devils who fight for themselves
(Rememb'ring the verses that Hayley sung
When my heart knocked against the root of my tongue),
With angels planted in hawthorn bowers
And God himself in the passing hours,   10
With silver angels across my way
And golden demons that none can stay,
With my father hovering upon the wind
And my brother Robert just behind
And my brother John, the evil one,
In a black cloud making his moan
(Though dead, they appear upon my path
Notwithstanding my terrible wrath;
They beg, they entreat, they drop their tears,
Filled full of hopes, filled full of fears),   20

With a thousand angels upon the wind
Pouring disconsolate from behind
To drive them off. And before my way
A frowning thistle implores my stay.
What to others a trifle appears
Fills me full of smiles or tears.
For double the vision my eyes do see,
And a double vision is always with me.
With my inward eye 'tis an old man grey,
With my outward a thistle across my way.   30
'If thou goest back,' the thistle said,
'Thou art to endless woe betrayed.
For here does Theotormon lower,
And here is Enitharmon's bower,
And Los the terrible thus hath sworn,
Because thou backward dost return,
Poverty, envy, old age and fear

Shall bring thy wife upon a bier,
And Butts shall give what Fuseli gave,
A dark black rock and a gloomy cave.'   40

I struck the thistle with my foot
And broke him up from his delving root.
'Must the duties of life each other cross?
Must every joy be dung and dross?
Must my dear Butts feel cold neglect,
Because I give Hayley his due respect?
Must Flaxman look upon me as wild
And all my friends be with doubts beguiled?
Must my wife live in my sister's bane,
Or my sister survive on my love's pain?   50
The curses of Los, the terrible shade,
And his dismal terrors make me afraid.'

So I spoke and struck in my wrath
The old man weltering upon my path.
Then Los appeared in all his power;
In the sun he appeared, descending before
My face in fierce flames. In my double sight
'Twas outward a sun, inward Los in his might.

'My hands are laboured day and night,
And ease comes never in my sight.   60
My wife has no indulgence given,
Except what comes to her from Heaven.
We eat little, we drink less.
This earth breeds not our happiness.
Another sun feeds our life's streams.
We are not warmed with thy beams.
Thou measurest not the time to me
Nor yet the space that I do see.
My mind is not with thy light arrayed.
Thy terrors shall not make me afraid.'   70

When I had my defiance given,
The sun stood trembling in heaven.
The moon that glowed remote below
Became leprous and white as snow,

And every soul of men on the earth
Felt affliction and sorrow and sickness and dearth.
Los flamed in my path and the sun was hot.
With the bows of my mind and the arrows of thought
My bowstring fierce with ardour breathes;
My arrows glow in their golden sheaves.   80
My brothers and father march before.
The heavens drop with human gore.

Now I a fourfold vision see,
And a fourfold vision is given to me.
'Tis fourfold in my supreme delight
And threefold in soft Beulah's night
And twofold always. May God us keep
From single vision and Newton's sleep.

MANUSCRIPT LYRICS OF THE FELPHAM
YEARS (1800–1803)

'When a man has married a wife'

When a man has married a wife he finds out whether
Her knees and elbows are only glued together.

'A woman scaly'

A woman scaly and a man all hairy
Is such a match as he who dares,
Will find the woman's scales scrape off the man's hairs.

'A fairy stepped upon my knee'

A fairy stepped upon my knee,
Singing and dancing merrily.
I said: 'Thou thing of patches, rings,
Pins, necklaces and suchlike things,
Disguiser of the female form,
Thou paltry, gilded pois'nous worm!'
Weeping he fell upon my thigh
And thus in tears did soft reply:
'Knowest thou not, O fairies' lord,
How much by us contemned, abhorred,   10
Whatever hides the female form,
That cannot bear the mental storm?
Therefore in pity still we give
Our lives to make the female live,
And what would turn into disease
We turn to what will joy and please.'

On the Virginity of the Virgin Mary and Joanna Southcott

Whate'er is done to her she cannot know,
And if you'll ask her she will swear it so.
Whether 'tis good or evil none's to blame—
No one can take the pride, no one the shame.

The Golden Net

Three virgins at the break of day:
'Whither young man, whither away?
Alas for woe! alas for woe!'
They cry, and tears for ever flow.
The one was clothed in flames of fire,
The other clothed in iron wire,
The other clothed in tears and sighs,
Dazzling bright before my eyes.
They bore a net of golden twine
To hang upon the branches fine.　　　　10
Pitying I wept to see the woe
That love and beauty undergo.
To be consumed in burning fires
And in ungratified desires,
And in tears clothed night and day,
Melted all my soul away.
When they saw my tears, a smile
That did heaven itself beguile
Bore the golden net aloft,
As on downy pinions soft,　　　　20
Over the morning of my day.
Underneath the net I stray,
Now entreating Burning Fire,
Now entreating Iron Wire,
Now entreating Tears and Sighs:
'Oh, when will the morning rise?'

The Birds

HE:　　Where thou dwellest, in what grove,
　　　　Tell me, fair one, tell me, love;
　　　　Where thou thy charming nest dost build,
　　　　O thou pride of every field.

SHE:　　Yonder stands a lonely tree,
　　　　There I live and mourn for thee;
　　　　Morning drinks my silent tear,
　　　　And evening winds my sorrows bear.

HE: O thou summer's harmony,
       I have lived and mourned for thee;   10
       Each day I mourn along the wood,
       And night hath heard my sorrows loud.

SHE: Dost thou truly long for me,
       And am I thus sweet to thee?
       Sorrow now is at an end,
       O my lover, and my friend

HE: Come, on wings of joy we'll fly
       To where my bower hangs on high;
       Come and make thy calm retreat,
       Among green leaves and blossoms sweet.   20

The Grey Monk

'I die, I die,' the mother said,
'My children die for lack of bread.
What more has the merciless tyrant said?'
The monk sat down on the stony bed.

The blood red ran from the grey monk's side;
His hands and feet were wounded wide,
His body bent, his arms and knees
Like to the roots of ancient trees.

His eye was dry, no tear could flow;
A hollow groan first spoke his woe.   10
He trembled and shuddered upon the bed;
At length with a feeble cry he said:

'When God commanded this hand to write
In the studious hours of deep midnight,
He told me the writing I wrote should prove
The bane of all that on earth I loved.

'My brother starved between two walls;
His children's cry my soul appalls.
I mocked at the rack and griding chain;
My bent body mocks their torturing pain.   20

'Thy father drew his sword in the north;
With his thousands strong he marched forth.
They brother has armed himself in steel,
To avenge the wrongs thy children feel.

'But vain the sword, and vain the bow;
They never can work war's overthrow.
The hermit's prayer, and the widow's tear,
Alone can free the world from fear.

'The hand of vengeance sought the bed
To which the purple tyrant fled;   30
The iron hand crushed the tyrant's head,
And became a tyrant in his stead.

'Until the tyrant himself relent,
The tyrant who first the black bow bent,
Slaughter shall heap the bloody plain;
Resistance and war is the tyrant's gain.

'But the tear of love and forgiveness sweet,
And submission to death beneath his feet—
The tear shall melt the sword of steel,
And every wound it has made shall heal.   40

'A tear is an intellectual thing,
And a sigh is the sword of an angel king,
And the bitter groan of the martyr's woe
Is an arrow from the Almighty's bow.'

Morning

To find the western path,
Right through the gates of Wrath,
I urge my way.
Sweet Mercy leads me on
With soft repentant moan.
I see the break of day.

The war of swords and spears,
Melted by dewy tears,
Exhales on high.
The sun is freed from fears,   10
And with soft grateful tears
Ascends the sky.

'Terror in the house'

Terror in the house does roar,
But Pity stands before the door.

'Mock on'

Mock on, mock on, Voltaire, Rousseau;
Mock on, mock on: 'tis all in vain!
You throw the sand against the wind,
And the wind blows it back again.

And every sand becomes a gem,
Reflected in the beams divine.
Blown back they blind the mocking eye,
But still in Israel's paths they shine.

The atoms of Democritus,
And Newton's particles of light,   10
Are sands upon the Red Sea shore,
Where Israel's tents do shine so bright.

'My Spectre around me'

My Spectre around me night and day
Like a wild beast guards my way;
My Emanation far within
Weeps incessantly for my sin.

A fathomless and boundless deep—
There we wander, there we weep.
On the hungry craving wind
My Spectre follows thee behind.

He scents thy footsteps in the snow,
Wheresoever thou dost go,   10
Through the wintry hail and rain.
'When wilt thou return again?

'Dost thou not in pride and scorn
Fill with tempests all my morn,
And, with jealousies and fears,
Fill my pleasant nights with tears?

'Seven of my sweet loves thy knife
Has bereaved of their life.
Their marble tombs I built with tears,
And with cold and shuddering fears.   20

'Seven more loves weep night and day
Round the tombs where my loves lay;
And seven more loves attend each night
Around my couch with torches bright;

'And seven more loves in my bed
Crown with wine my mournful head,
Pitying and forgiving all
Thy transgressions great and small.

'When wilt thou return and view
My loves, and them to life renew?   30
When wilt thou return and live?
When wilt thou pity as I forgive?'

'Never, never I return.
Still for victory I burn.
Living, thee alone I'll have,
And when dead I'll be thy grave.

'Through the Heaven and Earth and Hell
Thou shalt never, never quell,
I will fly and thou pursue;
Night and morn the flight renew.'   40

'Till I turn from female love,
And root up the infernal grove,
I shall never worthy be
To step into eternity;

'And to end thy cruel mocks
Annihilate thee on the rocks,
And another form create
To be subservient to my fate.

'Let us agree to give up love,
And root up the infernal grove;   50
Then shall we return and see
The worlds of happy eternity,

'And throughout all eternity
I forgive you, you forgive me.
As our dear redeemer said:
"This the wine, and this the bread."'

'O'er my sins'

O'er my sins thou sit and moan;
Hast thou no sins of thy own?
O'er my sins thou sit and weep,
And lull thy own sins fast asleep.

What transgressions I commit,
Are for thy transgressions fit;
They thy harlots, thou their slave,
And my bed becomes their grave.

Poor, pale, pitiable form
That I follow in a storm, 10
Iron tears and groans of lead
Bind around my aching head.

'And let us go to the highest downs
With many pleasing wiles.
The woman that does not love your frowns
Will never embrace your smiles.'

The Smile

There is a smile of love,
And there is a smile of deceit;
And there is a smile of smiles,
In which these two smiles meet.

(And there is a frown of hate,
And there is a frown of disdain;
And there is a frown of frowns
Which you strive to forget in vain,

For it sticks in the heart's deep core,
And it sticks in the deep backbone.) 10
And no smile that ever was smiled,
But only one smile alone—

That betwixt the cradle and grave
It only once smiled can be.
But when it once is smiled
There's an end to all misery.

The Mental Traveller

I travelled through a land of men,
A land of men and women too,
And heard and saw such dreadful things
As cold earth-wanderers never knew.

For there the babe is born in joy
That was begotten in dire woe,
Just as we reap in joy the fruit
Which we in bitter tears did sow.

And if the babe is born a boy   10
He's given to a woman old,
Who nails him down upon a rock,
Catches his shrieks in cups of gold.

She binds iron thorns around his head,
She pierces both his hands and feet,
She cuts his heart out at his side
To make it feel both cold and heat.

Her fingers number every nerve,
Just as a miser counts his gold.
She lives upon his shrieks and cries,
And she grows young as he grows old,   20

Till he becomes a bleeding youth,
And she becomes a virgin bright.
Then he rends up his manacles,
And binds her down for his delight.

He plants himself in all her nerves,
Just as a husbandman his mould,
And she becomes his dwelling-place,
And garden fruitful seventyfold.

An aged shadow soon he fades,
Wand'ring round an earthly cot,   30
Full filled all with gems and gold
Which he by industry had got.

And these are the gems of the human soul,
The rubies and pearls of a lovesick eye,
The countless gold of the aching heart,
The martyr's groan, and the lover's sigh;

They are his meat, they are his drink.
He feeds the beggar and the poor,
And the wayfaring traveller;
For ever open is his door. 40

His grief is their eternal joy;
They make the roofs and walls to ring;
Till from the fire on the hearth
A little female babe does spring.

And she is all of solid fire,
And gems and gold, that none his hand
Dares stretch to touch her baby form,
Or wrap her in his swaddling-band;

But she comes to the man she loves,
If young or old, or rich or poor. 50
They soon drive out the aged host,
A beggar at another's door.

He wanders weeping far away,
Until some other take him in;
Oft blind and age-bent, sore distressed,
Until he can a maiden win.

And to allay his freezing age
The poor man takes her in his arms;
The cottage fades before his sight,
The garden and its lovely charms; 60

The guests are scattered through the land.
For the eye altering, alters all;
The senses roll themselves in fear,
And the flat earth becomes a ball;

The stars, sun, moon, all shrink away,
A desert vast without a bound—
And nothing left to eat or drink,
And a dark desert all around.

The honey of her infant lips,
The bread and wine of her sweet smile,   70
The wild game of her roving eye,
Does him to infancy beguile.

For as he eats and drinks he grows
Younger and younger every day;
And on the desert wild they both
Wander in terror and dismay.

Like the wild stag she flees away;
Her fear plants many a thicket wild.
While he pursues her night and day,
By various arts of love beguiled,   80

By various arts of love and hate;
Till the wide desert planted o'er
With labyrinths of wayward love,
Where roams the lion, wolf and boar;

Till he becomes a wayward babe,
And she a weeping woman old.
Then many a lover wanders here;
The sun and stars are nearer rolled;

The trees bring forth sweet ecstasy
To all who in the desert roam—   90
Till many a city there is built,
And many a pleasant shepherd's home.

But when they find the frowning babe
Terror strikes through the region wide.
They cry: 'The babe, the babe is born,'
And flee away on every side.

For who dare touch the frowning form
His arm is withered to its root;
Lions, boars, wolves, all howling flee,
And every tree does shed its fruit.   100

And none can touch that frowning form,
Except it be a woman old;
She nails him down upon the rock,
And all is done as I have told.

The Land of Dreams

'Awake, awake my little boy,
Thou wast thy mother's only joy.
Why dost thou weep in thy gentle sleep?
Awake, thy father does thee keep.'

'Oh, what land is the Land of Dreams?
What are its mountains and what are its streams?
O father, I saw my mother there,
Among the lilies by waters fair.

'Among the lambs clothed in white,
She walked with her Thomas in sweet delight.   10
I wept for joy; like a dove I mourn.
Oh, when shall I again return?'

'Dear child, I also by pleasant streams
Have wandered all night in the land of dreams;
But though calm and warm the waters wide,
I could not get to the other side.'

'Father, O father, what do we here,
In this land of unbelief and fear?
The Land of Dreams is better far—
Above the light of the morning star.'   20

Mary

Sweet Mary, the first time she ever was there,
Came into the ballroom among the fair.
The young men and maidens around her throng,
And these are the words upon every tongue:

'An angel is here from the heavenly climes,
Or again does return the golden times.
Her eyes outshine every brilliant ray;
She opens her lips—'tis the month of May.'

Mary moves in soft beauty and conscious delight,
To augment with sweet smiles all the joys of the night,   10
Nor once blushes to own to the rest of the fair
That sweet love and beauty are worthy our care.

In the morning the villagers rose with delight,
And repeated with pleasure the joys of the night;
And Mary arose among friends to be free—
But no friend from henceforward thou, Mary, shalt see.

Some said she was proud, some called her a whore,
And some when she passed by shut to the door.
A damp cold came o'er her, her blushes all fled,
Her lilies and roses are blighted and shed.   20

'Oh, why was I born with a different face?
Why was I not born like this envious race?
Why did Heaven adorn me with bountiful hand,
And then set me down in an envious land?

'To be weak as a lamb and smooth as a dove,
And not to raise envy, is called Christian love.
But if you raise envy your merit's to blame
For planting such spite in the weak and the tame.

'I will humble my beauty; I will not dress fine;
I will keep from the ball and my eyes shall not shine.   30
And if any girl's lover forsakes her for me,
I'll refuse him my hand, and from envy be free.'

She went out in morning attired plain and neat;
'Proud Mary's gone mad,' said the child in the street.
She went out in morning in plain neat attire,
And came home in evening bespattered with mire.

She trembled and wept, sitting on the bed-side;
She forgot it was night and she trembled and cried.
She forgot it was night, she forgot it was morn,
Her soft memory imprinted with faces of scorn— 40

With faces of scorn and with eyes of disdain,
Like foul fiends inhabiting Mary's mild brain.
She remembers no face like the human divine;
All faces have envy, sweet Mary, but thine.

And thine is a face of sweet love in despair,
And thine is a face of mild sorrow and care,
And thine is a face of wild terror and fear,
That shall never be quiet till laid on its bier.

The Crystal Cabinet

The maiden caught me in the wild,
Where I was dancing merrily.
She put me into her cabinet,
And locked me up with a golden key.

This cabinet is formed of gold
And pearl, and crystal shining bright,
And within it opens into a world,
And a little, lovely, moony night.

Another England there I saw,
Another London with its Tower, 10
Another Thames and other hills,
And another pleasant Surrey bower,

Another maiden like herself,
Translucent, lovely, shining clear—
Threefold, each in the other closed.
Oh, what a pleasant trembling fear!

Oh, what a smile, a threefold smile,
Filled me, that like a flame I burned!
I bent to kiss the lovely maid,
And found a threefold kiss returned. 20

I strove to seize the inmost form
With ardour fierce and hands of flame,
But burst the crystal cabinet,
And like a weeping babe became:

A weeping babe upon the wild,
And weeping woman, pale, reclined.
And in the outward air again
I filled with woes the passing wind.

Long John Brown and Little Mary Bell

Little Mary Bell had a fairy in a nut;
Long John Brown had the Devil in his gut.
Long John Brown loved little Mary Bell,
And the fairy drew the Devil into the nut-shell.

Her fairy skipped out and her fairy skipped in;
He laughed at the Devil, saying, 'Love is a sin'.
The Devil he raged and the Devil he was wroth,
And the Devil entered into the young man's broth.

He was soon in the gut of the loving young swain,
For John ate and drank to drive away love's pain.   10
But, all he could do, he grew thinner and thinner,
Though he ate and drank as much as ten men for his dinner.

Some said he had a wolf in his stomach day and night;
Some said he had the Devil, and they guessed right.
The fairy skipped about in his glory, joy and pride,
And he laughed at the Devil till poor John Brown died.

Then the fairy skipped out of the old nutshell,
And woe and alack for pretty Mary Bell—
For the Devil crept in when the fairy skipped out,
And there goes Miss Bell with her fusty old nut.   20

William Bond

I wonder whether the girls are mad,
And I wonder whether they mean to kill,
And I wonder if William Bond will die,
For assuredly he is very ill.

He went to church in a May morning
Attended by fairies, one, two and three;
But the angels of providence drove them away,
And he returned home in misery.

He went not out to the field nor fold;
He went not out to the village nor town;   10
But he came home in a black, black cloud,
And took to his bed and there lay down.

And an angel of providence at his feet,
And an angel of providence at his head,
And in the midst a black, black cloud,
And in the midst the sick man on his bed.

And on his right hand was Mary Green,
And on his left hand was his sister Jane,
And their tears fell through the black, black cloud
To drive away the sick man's pain.   20

'O William, if thou dost another love—
Dost another love better than poor Mary—
Go and take that other to be thy wife,
And Mary Green shall her servant be.'

'Yes, Mary, I do another love;
Another I love far better than thee,
And another I will have for my wife.
Then what have I to do with thee?

'For thou art melancholy pale,
And on thy head is the cold moon's shine;   30
But she is ruddy and bright as day,
And the sunbeams dazzle from her eyne.'

Mary trembled and Mary chilled,
And Mary fell down on the right-hand floor—
That William Bond and his sister Jane
Scarce could recover Mary more.

When Mary woke and found her laid
On the right hand of her William dear,
On the right hand of his loved bed,
And saw her William Bond so near,   40

The fairies that fled from William Bond
Danced around her shining head;
They danced over the pillow white,
And the angels of providence left the bed.

'I thought Love lived in the hot sunshine,
But oh, he lives in the moony light;
I thought to find Love in the heat of day,
But sweet Love is the comforter of night.

Seek Love in the pity of other's woe,
In the gentle relief of another's care,   50
In the darkness of night and the winter's snow,
In the naked and outcast, seek Love there.'

MILTON (1804)

From the Preface

And did those feet in ancient time
Walk upon England's mountains green?
And was the holy Lamb of God
On England's pleasant pastures seen?

And did the countenance divine
Shine forth upon our clouded hills?
And was Jerusalem builded here,
Among these dark Satanic mills?

Bring me my bow of burning gold;
Bring me my arrows of desire;   10
Bring me my spear; O clouds, unfold!
Bring me my chariot of fire!

I will not cease from mental fight,
Nor shall my sword sleep in my hand,
Till we have built Jerusalem,
In England's green and pleasant land.

Book Two: Lines 217–end

There is a moment in each day that Satan cannot find,
Nor can his watch-fiends find it. But the industrious find
This moment and it multiply, and when it once is found
It renovates every moment of the day if rightly placed.   220
In this moment Ololon descended to Los and Enitharmon,
Unseen beyond the Mundane Shell, southward in Milton's
   track.

Just in this moment, when the morning odours rise abroad,
And first from the wild thyme, stands a fountain in a rock
Of crystal flowing into two streams. One flows through
   Golgonooza
And through Beulah to Eden, beneath Los's western wall;
The other flows through the aerial void and all the churches,
Meeting again in Golgonooza beyond Satan's seat.

The wild thyme is Los's messenger to Eden, a mighty demon.
Terrible, deadly and poisonous his presence in Ulro dark;   230
Therefore he appears only a small root creeping in grass,
Covering over the rock of odours his bright purple mantle
Beside the fount, above the lark's nest, in Golgonooza.
Luvah slept here in death, and here is Luvah's empty tomb.
Ololon sat beside this fountain on the rock of odours.

Just at the place to where the lark mounts is a crystal gate;
It is the entrance of the first heaven, named Luther. For
The lark is Los's messenger through the twenty-seven
      churches,
That the seven eyes of God, who walk even to Satan's seat
Through all the twenty-seven heavens, may not slumber nor
      sleep.   240
But the lark's nest is at the gate of Los, at the eastern
Gate of wide Golgonooza, and the lark is Los's messenger.
When on the highest lift of his light pinions he arrives
At that bright gate, another lark meets him, and back to back
They touch their pinions, tip tip, and each descend
To their respective earths, and there all night consult with
      angels
Of providence, and with the eyes of God all night in slumbers
Inspired; and at the dawn of day send out another lark
Into another heaven to carry news upon his wings.
Thus are the messengers dispatched till they reach the earth
      again   250
In the east gate of Golgonooza, and the twenty-eighth bright
Lark met the female Ololon descending into my garden.
(Thus it appears to mortal eyes and those of the Ulro
      heavens,
But not thus to Immortals; the lark is a mighty angel.)

For Ololon stepped into the polypus within the Mundane
      Shell.
They could not step into vegetable worlds without becoming
The enemies of humanity, except in a female form,
And as one female; Ololon and all its mighty hosts
Appeared, a virgin of twelve years. Nor time nor space was
To the perception of the virgin Ololon; but as the   260
Flash of lightning, but more quick; the virgin in my garden
Before my cottage stood (for the Satanic space is delusion).

For when Los joined with me he took me in his fiery
   whirlwind;
My vegetated portion was hurried from Lambeth's shades.
He set me down in Felpham's vale and prepared a beautiful
Cottage for me, that in three years I might write all these
   visions
To display Nature's cruel holiness, the deceits of natural
   religion.
Walking in my cottage garden sudden I beheld
The virgin Ololon, and addressed her as a daughter of
   Beulah:

'Virgin of providence, fear not to enter into my cottage.   270
What is thy message to thy friend? What am I now to do?
Is it again to plunge into deeper affliction? Behold me
Ready to obey, but pity thou my shadow of delight.
Enter my cottage, comfort her, for she is sick with fatigue.'

The virgin answered: 'Knowest thou of Milton, who
   descended
Driven from Eternity? Him I seek! Terrified at my act
In great Eternity, which thou knowest, I come him to seek.'

So Ololon uttered in words distinct the anxious thought.
Mild was the voice, but more distinct than any earthly—
That Milton's shadow heard, and, condensing all his fibres   280
Into a strength impregnable of majesty and beauty infinite,
I saw he was the covering cherub, and within him Satan
And Rahab, in an outside which is fallacious (within,
Beyond the outline of identity, in the selfhood deadly).
And he appeared the wicker man of Scandinavia, in whom
Jerusalem's children consume in flames among the stars.

Descending down into my garden, a human wonder of God
Reaching from heaven to earth, a cloud and human form,
I beheld Milton with astonishment, and in him beheld
The monstrous churches of Beulah, the gods of Ulro dark.   290
Twelve monstrous dishumanized terrors, synagogues of
   Satan,
A double twelve and thrice nine: such their divisions.

And these their names and their places within the Mundane Shell.

In Tyre and Sidon I saw Baal and Ashtaroth; in Moab,
    Chemosh;
In Ammon, Molech. (Loud his furnaces rage among the
    wheels
Of Og, and pealing loud the cries of the victims of fire,
And pale his priestesses enfold in veils of pestilence, bordered
With war, woven in looms of Tyre and Sidon by beautiful
    Ashtaroth.)
In Palestine Dagon, sea-monster worshipped o'er the sea;
Thammuz in Lebanon, and Rimmon in Damascus curtained;   300
Osiris, Isis, Orus in Egypt. (Dark their tabernacles on Nile,
Floating with solemn songs, and on the lakes of Egypt nightly
With pomp, even till morning break, and Osiris appear in the
    sky.)
But Belial of Sodom and Gomorrha, obscure demon of
    bribes
And secret assassinations, not worshipped nor adored, but
With the finger on the lips and the back turned to the light;
And Saturn, Jove and Rhea of the isles of the sea remote.
These twelve gods are the twelve spectre sons of the Druid
    Albion.
And these the names of the twenty-seven heavens and their
    churches:
Adam, Seth, Enos, Cainan, Mahalaleel, Jared, Enoch,   310
Methuselah, Lamech (these are giants mighty,
    hermaphroditic),
Noah, Shem, Arphaxad, Cainan the second, Salah, Heber,
Peleg, Reu, Serug, Nahor, Terah (these are the
    female-males,
A male within a female hid as in an ark and curtains),
Abraham, Moses, Solomon, Paul, Constantine,
    Charlemagne,
Luther (these seven are the male-females, the dragon forms,
Religion hid in war, a dragon red and hidden harlot).

All these are seen in Milton's shadow, who is the covering
    cherub,
The spectre of Albion, in which the spectre of Luvah
    inhabits,

In the Newtonian voids between the substances of creation. 320
For the chaotic voids outside of the stars are measured by
The stars, which are the boundaries of kingdoms, provinces
And empires of chaos, invisible to the vegetable man.
The kingdom of Og is in Orion: Sihon is in Ophiuchus;
Og has twenty-seven districts; Sihon's districts twenty-one.
From star to star, mountains and valleys, terrible dimension
Stretched out, compose the Mundane Shell, a mighty
   incrustation
Of forty-eight deformed human wonders of the Almighty,
With caverns whose remotest bottoms meet again beyond
The Mundane Shell in Golgonooza. But the fires of Los rage 330
In the remotest bottoms of the caves, that none can pass
Into Eternity that way, but all descend to Los,
To Bowlahoola and Allamanda, and to Entuthon Benython.

The heavens are the cherub, the twelve gods are Satan.

And the forty-eight starry regions are cities of the Levites,
The heads of the great polypus, fourfold twelve enormity
In mighty and mysterious commingling, enemy with enemy,
Woven by Urizen into sexes from his mantle of years.
And Milton, collecting all his fibres into impregnable
   strength,
Descended down a paved work of all kinds of precious
   stones
   340
Out from the eastern sky, descending down into my cottage
Garden, clothed in black; severe and silent he descended.

The Spectre of Satan stood upon the roaring sea and beheld
Milton within his sleeping humanity. Trembling and
   shudd'ring
He stood upon the waves, a twenty-sevenfold mighty demon.
Gorgeous and beautiful. Loud roll his thunders against
   Milton;
Loud Satan thundered, loud and dark upon mild Felpham
   shore.
Not daring to touch one fibre he howled round upon the sea.

I also stood in Satan's bosom and beheld its desolations,
A ruined man, a ruined building of God not made with   350
    hands:
Its plains of burning sand, its mountains of marble terrible,
Its pits and declivities flowing with molten ore, and fountains
Of pitch and nitre, its ruined palaces and cities and mighty
    works,
Its furnaces of affliction, in which his angels and Emanations
Labour with blackened visages among its stupendous ruins,
Arches and pyramids and porches, colonnades and domes,
In which dwells Mystery, Babylon. Here is her secret place;
From hence she comes forth on the churches in delight;
Here is her cup filled with its poisons, in these horrid vales,
And here her scarlet veil woven in pestilence and war.   360
Here is Jerusalem bound in chains, in the dens of Babylon.

In the eastern porch of Satan's universe Milton stood and
    said:

'Satan, my Spectre, I know my power thee to annihilate
And be a greater in thy place, and be thy tabernacle,
A covering for thee to do thy will: till one greater comes
And smites me as I smote thee, and becomes my covering.
Such are the laws of thy false heavens, but laws of Eternity
Are not such. Know thou, I come to self-annihilation.
Such are the laws of Eternity: that each shall mutually
Annihilate himself for other's good, as I for thee.   370
Thy purpose and the purpose of thy priests and of thy
    churches
Is to impress on men the fear of death; to teach
Trembling and fear, terror, constriction, abject selfishness.
Mine is to teach men to despise death, and to go on
In fearless majesty annihilating self, laughing to scorn
Thy laws and terrors, shaking down thy synagogues as webs.
I come to discover before Heaven and Hell the
    self-righteousness
In all its hypocritic turpitude, opening to every eye
These wonders of Satan's holiness, showing to the earth
The idol-virtues of the natural heart, and Satan's seat   380
Explore, in all its selfish natural virtue, and put off
In self-annihilation all that is not of God alone—
To put off self and all I have, ever and ever. Amen.'

Satan heard, coming in a cloud with trumpets and flaming
  fire,
Saying: 'I am God, the judge of all, the living and the dead.
Fall therefore down and worship me; submit thy supreme
Dictate to my eternal will, and to my dictate bow.
I hold the balances of right and just, and mine the sword.
Seven angels bear my name and in those seven I appear;
But I alone am God, and I alone in Heaven and Earth,   390
Of all that live, dare utter this. Others tremble and bow
Till all things become one great Satan, in holiness
Opposed to mercy, and the divine delusion, Jesus, be no
  more.'

Suddenly around Milton on my path the starry seven
Burned terrible. My path became a solid fire, as bright
As the clear sun, and Milton silent came down on my path.
And there went forth from the starry limbs of the seven
  forms
Human, with trumpets innumerable, sounding articulate
As the seven spake; and they stood in a mighty column of
  fire,
Surrounding Felpham's vale, reaching to the Mundane
  Shell, saying: 400

'Awake, Albion, awake! Reclaim thy reasoning Spectre.
  Subdue
Him to the divine mercy; cast him down into the lake
Of Los, that ever burneth with fire, ever and ever. Amen!
Let the four Zoas awake from slumbers of six thousand
  years.'

Then loud the furnaces of Los were heard, and seen as
  seven heavens
Stretching from south to north over the mountains of Albion.

Satan heard; trembling round his body, he encircled it.
He trembled with exceeding great trembling and
  astonishment,
Howling in his Spectre round his body, hungering to devour,
But fearing for the pain; for if he touches a vital,   410
His torment is unendurable. Therefore he cannot devour,

But howls round it as a lion round his prey continually.
Loud Satan thundered, loud and dark upon mild Felpham's
  shore,
Coming in a cloud with trumpets and with fiery flame,
An awful form eastward, from midst of a bright paved-work
Of precious stones by cherubim surrounded (so permitted—
Lest he should fall apart in his eternal death—to imitate
The eternal great Humanity Divine, surrounded by
His cherubim and seraphim in ever-happy Eternity).
Beneath sat Chaos, Sin on his right hand, Death on his left;   420
And Ancient Night spread over all the heaven his mantle of
  laws.
He trembled with exceeding great trembling and
  astonishment.

Then Albion rose up in the night of Beulah on his couch
Of dread repose, seen by the visionary eye; his face is toward
The east, toward Jerusalem's gates; groaning he sat above
His rocks. London and Bath and Legions and Edinburgh
Are the four pillars of his throne. His left foot near London
Covers the shades of Tyburn; his instep from Windsor
To Primrose Hill, stretching to Highgate and Holloway.
London is between his knees, its basements fourfold.   430
His right foot stretches to the sea on Dover cliffs, his heel
On Canterbury's ruins. His right hand covers lofty Wales,
His left Scotland. His bosom girt with gold involves
York, Edinburgh, Durham and Carlisle, and on the front
Bath, Oxford, Cambridge, Norwich. His right elbow
Leans on the rocks of Erin's land, Ireland, ancient nation.
His head bends over London. He sees his embodied Spectre
Trembling before him, with exceeding great trembling and
  fear.
He views Jerusalem and Babylon; his tears flow down.
He moved his right foot to Cornwall, his left to the rocks of
  Bognor.   440
He strove to rise to walk into the deep, but strength failing
Forbade, and down with dreadful groans he sunk upon his
  couch
In moony Beulah. Los, his strong guard, walks round
  beneath the moon.

Urizen faints in terror striving among the brooks of Arnon
With Milton's spirit. As the ploughman or artificer or
  shepherd,
While in the labours of his calling, sends his thought abroad
To labour in the ocean or in the starry heaven, so Milton
Laboured in chasms of the Mundane Shell—though here
  before
My cottage 'midst the starry seven, where the virgin Ololon
Stood trembling in the porch. Loud Satan thundered on the
  stormy sea,   450
Circling Albion's cliffs in which the fourfold world resides,
Though seen in fallacy outside, a fallacy of Satan's churches.
Before Ololon Milton stood, and perceived the eternal form
Of that mild vision. Wondrous were their acts, by me
  unknown
Except remotely; and I heard Ololon say to Milton:

'I see thee strive upon the brooks of Arnon. There a dread
And awful man I see, o'ercovered with the mantle of years.
I behold Los and Urizen, I behold Orc and Tharmas,
The four Zoas of Albion, and thy spirit with them striving,
In self-annihilation giving thy life to thy enemies.   460
Are those who contemn religion and seek to annihilate it
Become in their feminine portions the causes and promoters
Of these religions? How is that thing, this Newtonian
  phantasm,
This Voltaire and Rousseau, this Hume and Gibbon and
  Bolingbroke,
This natural religion, this impossible absurdity?
Is Ololon the cause of this? Oh, where shall I hide my face?
These tears fall for the little ones, the children of Jerusalem,
Lest they be annihilated in any annihilation.'

No sooner she had spoke but Rehab Babylon appeared
Eastward upon the paved-work across Europe and Asia,   470
Glorious as the midday sun, in Satan's bosom glowing:
A female hidden in a male, religion hidden in war,
Named 'Moral Virtue', cruel twofold monster shining bright,
A dragon red and hidden harlot which John in Patmos saw.

And all beneath the nations innumerable of Ulro
Appeared: the seven kingdoms of Canaan and five Baalim
Of Philistia, into twelve divided, called after the names
Of Israel, as they are in Eden mountain, river and plain,
City and sandy desert intermingled beyond mortal ken.
But turning toward Ololon in terrible majesty, Milton   480
Replied: 'Obey thou the words of the inspired man.
All that can be annihilated must be annihilated,
That the children of Jerusalem may be saved from slavery.
There is a negation, and there is a contrary.
The negation must be destroyed to redeem the contraries.
The negation is the Spectre, the reasoning power in man.
This is a false body, an incrustation over my immortal
Spirit, a selfhood which must be put off and annihilated
    alway.

'To cleanse the face of my spirit by self-examination,
To bathe in the waters of life, to wash off the not-human,   490
I come in self-annihilation and the grandeur of inspiration.
To cast off rational demonstration by faith in the Saviour;
To cast off the rotten rags of memory by inspiration;
To cast off Bacon, Locke and Newton from Albion's
    covering;
To take off his filthy garments, and clothe him with
    imagination;
To cast aside from poetry all that is not inspiration—
That it no longer shall dare to mock with the aspersion of
    madness,
Cast on the inspired by the tame high-finisher of paltry blots,
Indefinite or paltry rhymes, or paltry harmonies,
Who creeps into state government like a caterpillar to
    destroy.   500
To cast off the idiot questioner; who is always questioning
But never capable of answering; who sits with a sly grin
Silent plotting when to question, like a thief in a cave;
Who publishes doubt and calls it knowledge; whose science
    is despair,
Whose pretence to knowledge is envy; whose whole science
    is
To destroy the wisdom of ages to gratify ravenous envy,
That rages round him like a wolf day and night without rest.

He smiles with condescension; he talks of benevolence and
    virtue;
And those who act with benevolence and virtue, they murder
    time on time.
These are the destroyers of Jerusalem; these are the
    murderers   510
Of Jesus, who deny the faith and mock at eternal life,
Who pretend to poetry, that they may destroy imagination
By imitation of Nature's images drawn from remembrance.
These are the sexual garments, the abomination of
    desolation,
Hiding the human lineaments as with an ark and curtains:
Which Jesus rent and now shall wholly purge away with fire,
Till generation is swallowed up in regeneration.'

Then trembled the virgin Ololon and replied in clouds of
    despair:

'Is this our feminine portion, the sixfold Miltonic female?
Terribly this portion trembles before thee, O awful man.   520
Although our human power can sustain the severe
    contentions
Of friendship, our sexual cannot, but flies into the Ulro.
Hence arose all our terrors in Eternity! And now
    remembrance
Returns upon us! Are we contraries, O Milton, thou and I?
O Immortal! how were we led to war the wars of death?
Is this the void outside of existence, which if entered into
Becomes a womb, and is this the death-couch of Albion?
Thou goest to eternal death, and all must go with thee!'

So saying the virgin divided sixfold, and with a shriek
Dolorous that ran through all creation, a double sixfold
    wonder,   530
Away from Ololon she divided and fled into the depths
Of Milton's shadow, as a dove upon the stormy sea.

Then as a moony ark Ololon descended to Felpham's vale
In clouds of blood, in streams of gore, with dreadful
    thunderings,
Into the fires of intellect that rejoiced in Felpham's vale

Around the starry eight. With one accord the starry eight became
One man, Jesus the Saviour, wonderful! Round his limbs
The clouds of Ololon folded as a garment dipped in blood,
Written within and without in woven letters; and the writing
Is the divine revelation in the literal expression,   540
A garment of war. I heard it named the woof of six thousand years.

And I beheld the twenty-four cities of Albion
Arise upon their thrones to judge the nations of the earth;
And the immortal four in whom the twenty-four appear fourfold
Arose around Albion's body. Jesus wept and walked forth
From Felpham's vale, clothed in clouds of blood, to enter into
Albion's bosom, the bosom of death, and the four surrounded him
In the column of fire in Felpham's vale. Then to their mouths the four
Applied their four trumpets, and them sounded to the four winds.

Terror struck in the vale. I stood at that immortal sound;   550
My bones trembled. I fell outstretched upon the path
A moment, and my soul returned into its mortal state,
To resurrection and judgement in the vegetable body.
And my sweet shadow of delight stood trembling by my side.

Immediately the lark mounted with a loud trill from Felpham's vale,
And the wild thyme from Wimbledon's green and empurpled hills;
And Los and Enitharmon rose over the hills of Surrey.
Their clouds roll over London with a south wind; soft Oothoon
Pants in the vales of Lambeth, weeping o'er her human harvest.
Los listens to the cry of the poor man, his cloud   560
Over London in volume terrific, low bended in anger.

Rintrah and Palamabron view the human harvest beneath.
Their winepresses and barns stand open; the ovens are
   prepared,
The waggons ready; terrific, lions and tigers sport and play;
All animals upon the earth are prepared in all their strength
To go forth to the great harvest and vintage of the nations.

Finis

Auguries of Innocence (c. 1804)

To see a world in a grain of sand,
And a heaven in a wild flower—
Hold infinity in the palm of your hand,
And eternity in an hour.
A robin redbreast in a cage
Puts all Heaven in a rage;
A dove-house filled with doves and pigeons
Shudders Hell through all its regions.
A dog starved at his master's gate
Predicts the ruin of the state.   10
A horse misused upon the road
Calls to Heaven for human blood.
Each outcry of the hunted hare
A fibre from the brain does tear.
A skylark wounded in the wing,
A cherubim does cease to sing.
The gamecock clipped and armed for fight
Does the rising sun affright.
Every wolf's and lion's howl
Raises from Hell a human soul.   20
The wild deer wand'ring here and there
Keeps the human soul from care.
The lamb misused breeds public strife,
And yet forgives the butcher's knife.
The bat that flits at close of eve
Has left the brain that won't believe.
The owl that calls upon the night
Speaks the unbeliever's fright.

He who shall hurt the little wren
Shall never be beloved by men.   30
He who the ox to wrath has moved
Shall never be by woman loved.
The wanton boy that kills the fly
Shall feel the spider's enmity.
He who torments the chafer's sprite
Weaves a bower in endless night.
The caterpillar on the leaf
Repeats to thee thy mother's grief.
Kill not the moth nor butterfly,
For the Last Judgement draweth nigh.   40
He who shall train the horse to war
Shall never pass the polar bar.
The beggar's dog and widow's cat:
Feed them and thou wilt grow fat.
The gnat that sings his summer's song
Poison gets from slander's tongue.
The poison of the snake and newt
Is the sweat of envy's foot;
The poison of the honey bee
Is the artist's jealousy.   50
The prince's robes and beggar's rags
Are toadstools on the miser's bags.

A truth that's told with bad intent
Beats all the lies you can invent;
It is right it should be so.
Man was made for joy and woe,
And when this we rightly know
Through the world we safely go.
Joy and woe are woven fine,
A clothing for the soul divine.   60
Under every grief and pine
Runs a joy with silken twine.

The babe is more than swaddling bands.
Throughout all these human lands,
Tools were made and born were hands
(Every farmer understands).
Every tear from every eye

Becomes a babe in eternity;
This is caught by females bright
And returned to its own delight.   70
The bleat, the bark, bellow and roar
Are waves that beat on Heaven's shore.
The babe that weeps the rod beneath
Writes 'Revenge' in realms of death.
The beggar's rags fluttering in air
Does to rags the heavens tear.
The soldier armed with sword and gun
Palsied strikes the summer's sun.
The poor man's farthing is worth more
Than all the gold on Afric's shore.   80
One mite wrung from the lab'rer's hands
Shall buy and sell the miser's lands;
Or, if protected from on high,
Does that whole nation sell and buy.
He who mocks the infant's faith
Shall be mocked in age and death;
He who shall teach the child to doubt
The rotting grave shall ne'er get out;
He who respects the infant's faith
Triumphs over hell and death.   90
The child's toys and the old man's reasons
Are the fruits of the two seasons.
The questioner who sits so sly
Shall never know how to reply.
He who replies to words of doubt
Doth put the light of knowledge out.
The strongest poison ever known
Came from Caesar's laurel crown.
Nought can deform the human race
Like to the armour's iron brace.   100
When gold and gems adorn the plough
To peaceful arts shall envy bow.
A riddle, or the cricket's cry,
Is to doubt a fit reply.
The emmet's inch and eagle's mile
Make lame philosophy to smile.
He who doubts from what he sees

Will ne'er believe, do what you please.
If the sun and moon should doubt
They'd immediately go out.   110

To be in a passion you good may do,
But no good if a passion is in you.
The whore and gambler, by the state
Licenced, build that nation's fate.
The harlot's cry from street to street
Shall weave old England's winding sheet;
The winner's shout, the loser's curse,
Dance before dead England's hearse.
Every night and every morn
Some to misery are born;   120
Every morn and every night
Some are born to sweet delight.
Some are born to sweet delight,
Some are born to endless night.
We are led to believe a lie
When we see not through the eye—
Which was born in a night to perish in a night,
When the soul slept in beams of light.
God appears, and God is light
To those poor souls who dwell in night;   130
But does a human form display
To those who dwell in realms of day.

JERUSALEM (1804–18)

From the preface to Chapter I

Reader, lover of books, lover of Heaven,
And of that God from whom all books are given,
Who in mysterious Sinai's awful cave
To Man the wondrous art of writing gave.
Again he speaks in thunder and in fire:
Thunder of thought, and flames of fierce desire.
Even from the depths of Hell his voice I hear,
Within the unfathomed caverns of my ear.
Therefore I print, nor vain my types shall be;
Heaven, Earth and Hell henceforth shall live in harmony.   10

From the preface to Chapter II

The fields from Islington to Marybone,
To Primrose Hill and Saint John's Wood,
  Were builded over with pillars of gold,
And there Jerusalem's pillars stood.

Her little ones ran on the fields,
The Lamb of God among them seen,
  And fair Jerusalem his bride,
Among the little meadows green.

Pancras and Kentish Town repose
Among her golden pillars high,   10
  Among her golden arches which
Shine upon the starry sky.

The Jews' Harp House and the Green Man,
The ponds where boys to bathe delight,
  The fields of cows by Willan's farm,
Shine in Jerusalem's pleasant sight.

She walks upon our meadows green,
The Lamb of God walks by her side,
  And every English child is seen
Children of Jesus and his bride,   20

Forgiving trespasses and sins,
Lest Babylon with cruel Og,
  With moral and self-righteous law
Should crucify in Satan's synagogue!

What are those golden builders doing
Near mournful ever-weeping Paddington?—
  Standing above that mighty ruin
Where Satan the first victory won,

Where Albion slept beneath the fatal tree,
And the Druid's golden knife   30
  Rioted in human gore,
In offerings of human life.

They groaned aloud on London Stone,
They groaned aloud on Tyburn's brook;
   Albion gave his deadly groan,
And all the Atlantic mountains shook.

   Albion's Spectre from his loins
Tore forth in all the pomp of war.
   Satan his name; in flames of fire
He stretched his Druid pillars far.   40

   Jerusalem fell from Lambeth's vale,
Down through Poplar and Old Bow,
   Through Maldon and across the sea,
In war and howling, death and woe.

   The Rhine was red with human blood,
The Danube rolled a purple tide;
   On the Euphrates Satan stood,
And over Asia stretched his pride.

   He withered up sweet Zion's hill
From every nation of the earth.   50
   He withered up Jeruslem's gates,
And in a dark land gave her birth.

   He withered up the human form
By laws of sacrifice for sin,
   Till it became a mortal worm,
But, oh translucent all within!

   The Divine Vision still was seen,
Still was the human form divine,
   Weeping in weak and mortal clay;
O Jesus, still the form was thine.   60

   And thine the human face, and thine
The human hands and feet and breath,
   Entering through the gates of birth
And passing through the gates of death.

And, O thou Lamb of God, whom I
Slew in my dark self-righteous pride!
    Art thou returned to Albion's land,
And is Jerusalem thy bride?

Come to my arms and never more
Depart, but dwell for ever here.   70
    Create my spirit to thy love;
Subdue my Spectre to thy fear.

Spectre of Albion! Warlike fiend!
In clouds of blood and ruin rolled.
    I here reclaim thee as my own,
My selfhood! Satan! armed in gold.

Is this thy soft family love,
Thy cruel patriarchal pride:
    Planting thy family alone,
Destroying all the world beside?   80

A man's worst enemies are those
Of his own house and family;
    And he who makes his law a curse,
By his own law shall surely die.

In my exchanges every land
Shall walk, and mine in every land;
    Mutual shall build Jerusalem,
Both heart in heart, and hand in hand.

From the preface to Chapter III

I saw a monk of Charlemagne
Arise before my sight.
    I talked with the grey monk as we stood
In beams of infernal light.

Gibbon arose with a lash of steel,
And Voltaire with a racking wheel;
    The schools, in clouds of learning rolled,
Arose with war in iron and gold.

'Thou lazy monk,' they sound afar,
'In vain condemning glorious War,   10
    And in your cell you shall ever dwell.
Rise War, and bind him in his cell.'

    The blood red ran from the grey monk's side;
His hands and feet were wounded wide,
    His body bent, his arms and knees
Like to the roots of ancient trees.

    When Satan first the black bow bent,
And the moral law from the Gospel rent,
    He forged the law into a sword,
And spilled the blood of mercy's lord.   20

    Titus! Constantine! Charlemagne!
O Voltaire! Rousseau! Gibbon! Vain
    Your Grecian mocks and Roman sword
Against this image of his lord.

    For a tear is an intellectual thing!
And a sigh is the sword of an angel king,
    And the bitter groan of a martyr's woe
Is an arrow from the Almighty's bow!

From the preface to Chapter IV

I stood among my valleys of the south
And saw a flame of fire, even as a wheel
Of fire surrounding all the heavens. It went
From west to east against the current of
Creation, and devoured all things in its loud
Fury and thundering course round heaven and earth.
By it the sun was rolled into an orb;
By it the moon faded into a globe
Travelling through the night. For from its dire
And restless fury Man himself shrunk up   10
Into a little root a fathom long.
And I asked a watcher and a holy one

Its name? He answered, 'It is the wheel of religion.'
I wept and said: 'Is this the law of Jesus,
This terrible devouring sword turning every way?'
He answered: 'Jesus died because he strove
Against the current of this wheel. Its name
Is Caiaphas, the dark preacher of death,
Of sin, of sorrow, and of punishment,
Opposing Nature! it is natural religion;   20
But Jesus is the bright preacher of life,
Creating Nature from this fiery law
By self-denial and forgiveness of sin.
Go therefore, cast out devils in Christ's name;
Heal thou the sick of spiritual disease;
Pity the evil, for thou art not sent
To smite with terror and with punishments
Those that are sick, like to the Pharisees
Crucifying and encompassing sea and land
For proselytes to tyranny and wrath.   30
But to the publicans and harlots go!
Teach them true happiness; but let no curse
Go forth out of thy mouth to blight their peace.
For Hell is opened to Heaven: thine eyes beheld
The dungeons burst and the prisoners set free.'

 England! awake! awake! awake!
  Jerusalem thy sister calls!
 Why wilt thou sleep the sleep of death,
  And close her from thy ancient walls?

 Thy hills and valleys felt her feet
  Gently upon their bosoms move;
 Thy gates beheld sweet Zion's ways;
  Then was a time of joy and love.

 And now the time returns again.
  Our souls exult, and London's towers   10
 Receive the Lamb of God, to dwell
  In England's green and pleasant bowers.

Chapter I, lines 925–1011

THE CONFESSION OF ALBION

He felt that love and pity are the same: a soft repose,
Inward complacency of soul, a self-annihilation!

'I have erred! I am ashamed! and will never return more.
I have taught my children sacrifices of cruelty. What shall I
   answer?
I will hide it from Eternals! I will give myself for my children!
Which way soever I turn, I behold humanity and pity!'   930

He recoiled; he rushed outwards; he bore the veil whole
   away.
His fires redound from his dragon altars in errors returning.
He drew the veil of moral virtue, woven for cruel laws,
And cast it into the Atlantic deep, to catch the souls of the
   dead.
He stood between the palm tree and the oak of weeping
Which stand upon the edge of Beulah, and there Albion
   sunk
Down in sick pallid langour. These were his last words,
   relapsing
Hoarse from his rocks, from caverns of Derbyshire and
   Wales
And Scotland, uttered from the circumference into Eternity:

'Blasphemous sons of feminine delusion! God in the dreary
   void   940
Dwells from eternity, wide separated from the human soul.
But thou, deluding image—by whom imbued, the veil I
   rent—
Lo, here is Vala's veil whole, for a law, a terror and a curse!
And therefore God takes vengeance on me; from my
   clay-cold bosom
My children wander, trembling victims of his moral justice.
His snows fall on me and cover me, while in the veil I fold
My dying limbs. Therefore, O manhood, if thou art aught
But a mere fantasy, hear dying Albion's curse!

May God who dwells in this dark Ulro and voidness,
   vengeance take,
And draw thee down into this abyss of sorrow and torture,   950
Like me thy victim. Oh that death and annihilation were the
   same!

'What have I said? What have I done? O all-powerful human
   words!
You recoil back upon me in the blood of the Lamb slain in
   his children.
Two bleeding contraries, equally true, are his witnesses
   against me.
We reared mighty stones; we danced naked around them,
Thinking to bring love into light of day, to Jerusalem's shame
Displaying our giant limbs to all the winds of heaven!
   Sudden
Shame seized us; we could not look on one another for
   abhorrence. The blue
Of our immortal veins and all their hosts fled from our limbs,
And wandered distant in a dismal night clouded and dark.   960
The sun fled from the Briton's forehead, the moon from his
   mighty loins;
Scandinavia fled with all his mountains filled with groans.

'Oh, what is life and what is Man? Oh, what is death?
   Wherefore
Are you, my children, natives in the grave to where I go?
Or are you born to feed the hungry ravenings of destruction,
To be the sport of accident, to waste in wrath and love a
   weary
Life, in brooding cares and anxious labours that prove but
   chaff?
Oh Jerusalem, Jerusalem, I have forsaken thy courts;
Thy pillars of ivory and gold, thy curtains of silk and fine
Linen, thy pavements of precious stones, thy walls of pearl   970
And gold, thy gates of thanksgiving, thy windows of praise,
Thy clouds of blessing, thy cherubims of tender mercy,
Stretching their wings sublime over the little ones of Albion.
O human imagination, O divine body I have crucified!
I have turned my back upon thee into the wastes of moral
   law;

There Babylon is builded in the waste, founded in human
　　desolation.
O Babylon, thy watchman stands over thee in the night;
Thy severe judge all the day long proves thee, O Babylon,
With provings of destruction, with giving thee thy heart's
　　desire.
But Albion is cast forth to the potter, his children to the　　　　980
　　builders
To build Babylon, because they have forsaken Jerusalem.
The walls of Babylon are souls of men, her gates the groans
Of nations, her towers are the miseries of once happy
　　families.
Her streets are paved with destruction, her houses built with
　　death,
Her palaces with Hell and the grave, her synagogues with
　　torments
Of ever-hardening despair, squared and polished with cruel
　　skill.
Yet thou wast lovely as the summer cloud upon my hills,
When Jerusalem was thy heart's desire in times of youth and
　　love.
Thy sons came to Jerusalem with gifts; she sent them away
With blessings on their hands and on their feet, blessings of　　990
　　gold
And pearl and diamond. Thy daughters sang in her courts;
They came up to Jersalem; they walked before Albion.
In the exchanges of London every nation walked,
And London walked in every nation, mutual in love and
　　harmony.
Albion covered the whole earth; England encompassed the
　　nations;
Mutual each within other's bosom in visions of regeneration.
Jerusalem covered the Atlantic mountains and Erythrean,
From bright Japan and China to Hesperia, France and
　　England.
Mount Zion lifted his head in every nation under heaven,
And the Mount of Olives was beheld over the whole earth.　　1000
The footsteps of the Lamb of God were there. But now no
　　more,
No more shall I behold him; he is closed in Luvah's
　　sepulchre.

Yet why these smitings of Luvah, the gentlest, mildest Zoa?
If God was merciful this could not be. O Lamb of God,
Thou art a delusion, and Jerusalem is my sin! O my
    children,
I have educated you in the crucifying cruelties of
    demonstration,
Till you have assumed the providence of God and slain
    your father.
Dost thou appear before me who liest dead in Luvah's
    sepulchre?
Dost thou forgive me, thou who wast dead and art alive?
Look not so merciful upon me, O thou slain Lamb of God,   1010
I die! I die in thy arms, though hope is banished from me.'

Chapter II, lines 800–77

LOS EXPLORES ALBION

Fearing that Albion should turn his back against the Divine
    Vision,   800
Los took his globe of fire to search the interiors of Albion's
Bosom in all the terrors of friendship, entering the caves
Of despair and death to search the tempters out, walking
    among
Albion's rocks and precipices, caves of solitude and dark
    despair,
And saw every minute particular of Albion degraded and
    murdered—
But saw not by whom. They were hidden within in the
    minute particulars
Of which they had possessed themselves, and there they take
    up
The articulations of man's soul, and laughing throw it down
Into the frame, then knock it out upon the plank; and souls
    are baked
In bricks to build the pyramids of Heber and Terah. But Los   810
Searched in vain; closed from the minutia he walked
    difficult.
He came down from Highgate through Hackney and
    Holloway towards London

Till he came to Old Stratford, and thence to Stepney and
    the Isle
of Leutha's Dogs, thence through the narrows of the river's
    side;
And saw every minute particular, the jewels of Albion,
    running down
The kennels of the streets and lanes as if they were abhorred.
Every universal form was become barren mountains of moral
Virtue, and every minute particular hardened into grains of
    sand,
And all the tenderness of the soul cast forth as filth and mire
Among the winding places of deep contemplation intricate.   820
To where the Tower of London frowned dreadful over
    Jerusalem,
A building of Luvah, builded in Jerusalem's eastern gate to
    be
His secluded court; thence to Bethlehem, where was builded
Dens of despair in the house of bread, enquiring in vain
Of stones and rocks he took his way, for human form was
    none.
And thus he spoke, looking on Albion's city with many tears:

'What shall I do? What could I do if I could find these
    criminals?
I could not dare to take vengeance; for all things are so
    constructed
And builded by the divine hand that the sinner shall always
    escape,
And he who takes vengeance alone is the criminal of
    providence.   830
If I should dare to lay my finger on a grain of sand
In way of vengeance, I punish the already punished. Oh,
    whom
Should I pity if I pity not the sinner who is gone astray?
O Albion, if thou takest vengeance, if thou revengest thy
    wrongs,
Thou art for ever lost! What can I do to hinder the sons
Of Albion from taking vengeance, or how shall I them
    persuade?'

So spoke Los, travelling through darkness and horrid
   solitude.
And he beheld Jerusalem in Westminster and Marybone
Among the ruins of the temple, and Vala who is her shadow,
Jerusalem's shadow, bent northward over the island white.   840
At length he sat on London Stone and heard Jerusalem's
   voice:

'Albion, I cannot be thy wife. Thine own minute particulars
Belong to God alone, and all thy little ones are holy.
They are of faith and not of demonstration, wherefore is Vala
Clothed in black mourning upon my river's currents. Vala,
   awake!
I hear thy shuttles sing in the sky, and round my limbs
I feel the iron threads of love and jealousy and despair.'

Vala replied: 'Albion is mine! Luvah gave me to Albion
And now receives reproach and hate. Was it not said of old,
"Set your son before a man and he shall take you and your   850
   sons
For slaves: but set your daughter before a man and she
Shall make him and his sons and daughters your slaves for
   ever"?
And is this faith? Behold, the strife of Albion and Luvah
Is great in the east; their spears of blood rage in the eastern
   heaven.
Urizen is the champion of Albion; they will slay my Luvah.
And thou, O harlot daughter, daughter of despair, art all
This cause of these shakings of my towers on Euphrates.
Here is the house of Albion, and here is thy secluded place,
And here we have found thy sins. And hence we turn thee
   forth
For all to avoid thee, to be astonished at thee for thy sins;   860
Because thou art the impurity and the harlot, and thy children
Children of whoredoms, born for sacrifice, for the meat and
   drink
Offering, to sustain the glorious combat and the battle and
   war,
That Man may be purified by the death of thy delusions.'

So saying, she her dark threads cast over the trembling river
And over the valleys: from the hills of Hertfordshire to the
    hills
Of Surrey, across Middlesex and across Albion's house
Of eternity. Pale stood Albion at his eastern gate,
Leaning against the pillars, and his disease rose from his
    skirts.
Upon the precipice he stood, ready to fall into non-entity.   870

Los was all astonishment and terror; he trembled, sitting on
    the Stone
Of London. But the interiors of Albion's fibres and nerves
    were hidden
From Los; astonished he beheld only the petrified surfaces,
And saw his furnaces in ruins (for Los is the demon of the
    furnaces).
He also saw the four points of Albion reversed inwards.
He seized his hammer and tongs, his iron poker and his
    bellows,
Upon the valleys of Middlesex, shouting loud for aid divine.

Chapter II, lines 927–1058

ERIN MOURNS AT THE TOMB OF ALBION

The Emanations of the grievously afflicted friends of Albion
Concentre in one female form, an aged pensive woman.
Astonished, lovely, embracing the sublime shade, the
    daughters of Beulah
Beheld her with wonder! With awful hands she took   930
A moment of time, drawing it out with many tears and
    afflictions
And many sorrows oblique across the Atlantic vale
(Which is the vale of Rephaim dreadful from east to west,
Where the human harvest waves abundant in the beams of
    Eden),
Into a rainbow of jewels and gold, a mild reflection from
Albion's dread tomb, eight thousand and five hundred years
In its extension; every two hundred years has a door to Eden.

She also took an atom of space, with dire pain opening it, a
    centre
Into Beulah. Trembling the daughters of Beulah dried
Her tears; she ardent embraced her sorrows, occupied in
    labours   940
Of sublime mercy in Rephaim's vale. Perusing Albion's tomb
She sat; she walked among the ornaments solemn mourning.
The daughters attended her shudderings, wiping the
    death-sweat.
Los also saw her in his seventh furnace; he also terrified
Saw the finger of God go forth upon his seventh furnace,
Away from the starry wheels to prepare Jerusalem a place—
When with a dreadful groan the Emanation mild of Albion
Burst from his bosom in the tomb like a pale snowy cloud,
Female and lovely, struggling to put off the human form,
Writhing in pain. The daughters of Beulah in kind arms
    received   950
Jerusalem, weeping over her among the spaces of Erin,
In the ends of Beulah, where the dead wail night and day.

And thus Erin spoke to the daughters of Beulah, in soft tears:

'Albion the vortex of the dead! Albion the generous!
Albion the mildest son of Heaven! The place of holy sacrifice,
Where friends die for each other!—will become the place
Of murder, and unforgiving, near-awaking sacrifice of
    enemies.
The children must be sacrificed (a horror never known
Till now in Beulah!), unless a refuge can be found
To hide them from the wrath of Albion's law, that freezes
    sore   960
Upon his sons and daughters, self-exiled from his bosom.
Draw ye Jerusalem away from Albion's mountains
To give a place for redemption; let Sihon and Og
Remove eastward to Bashan and Gilead, and leave
The secret coverts of Albion and the hidden places of
    America.
Jerusalem, Jerusalem! why wilt thou turn away?
Come ye, O daughters of Beulah, lament for Og and Sihon
Upon the lakes of Ireland from Rathlin to Baltimore;
Stand ye upon the Dargle from Wicklow to Drogheda;

Come and mourn over Albion, the white cliff of the Atlantic,   970
The mountain of giants. All the giants of Albion are become
Weak, withered, darkened! And Jerusalem is cast forth from
    Albion.
They deny that they ever knew Jerusalem, or ever dwelt in
    Shiloh.
The gigantic roots and twigs of the vegetating sons of Albion,
Filled with the little ones, are consumed in the fires of their
    altars.
The vegetating cities are burned and consumed from the
    earth,
And the bodies in which all animals and vegetations, the
    earth and heaven,
Were contained in the all-glorious imagination are withered
    and darkened.
The golden gate of Havilah, and all the garden of God,
Was caught up with the sun in one day of fury and war.   980
The lungs, the heart, the liver shrunk away far distant from
    Man,
And left a little slimy substance floating upon the tides.
In one night the Atlantic continent was caught up with the
    moon,
And became an opaque globe far distant, clad with moony
    beams.
The visions of Eternity, by reason of narrowed perceptions,
Are become weak visions of time and space, fixed into
    furrows of death,
Till deep dissimulation is the only defence an honest man
    has left.
O polypus of death! O Spectre over Europe and Asia,
Withering the human form by laws of sacrifice for sin!
By laws of chastity and abhorrence I am withered up,   990
Striving to create a heaven in which all shall be pure and holy
In their own selfhoods, in natural selfish chastity; to banish
    pity
And dear mutual forgiveness, and to become one great Satan,
Enslaved to the most powerful selfhood; to murder the
    Divine Humanity,
In whose sight all are as the dust, and who chargeth his
    angels with folly.
Ah, weak and wide astray! Ah, shut in narrow doleful form!

Creeping in reptile flesh upon the bosom of the ground!
The eye of Man, a little narrow orb, closed up and dark,
Scarcely beholding the great light, conversing with the void;
The ear, a little shell, in small volutions shutting out   1000
True harmonies, and comprehending great as very small;
The nostrils, bent down to the earth and closed with
    senseless flesh,
That odours cannot them expand, nor joy on them exult;
The tongue, a little moisture fills, a little food it cloys,
A little sound it utters, and its cries are faintly heard.
Therefore they are removed; therefore they have taken root
In Egypt and Philistia, in Moab and Edom and Aram;
In the Erythean Sea their uncircumcision in heart and loins
Be lost for ever and ever. Then they shall arise from self
By self-annihilation, into Jerusalem's courts and into Shiloh,   1010
Shiloh the masculine Emanation among the flowers of
    Beulah.
Lo, Shiloh dwells over France, as Jerusalem dwells over
    Albion.
Build and prepare a wall and curtain for America's shore!
Rush on, rush on, rush on, ye vegetating sons of Albion!
The sun shall go before you in day, the moon shall go
Before you in night. Come on, come on, come on! The Lord
Jehovah is before, behind, above, beneath, around.
He has builded the arches of Albion's tomb, binding the stars
In merciful order, bending the laws of cruelty to peace.
He hath placed Og and Anak, the giants of Albion, for their
    guards;   1020
Building the body of Moses in the valley of Peor, the body
Of divine analogy; and Og and Sihon in the tears of Balaam,
The son of Beor, have given their power to Joshua and Caleb.
Remove from Albion, far remove these terrible surfaces.
They are beginning to form heavens and hells in immense
Circles, the hells for food to the heavens, food of torment,
Food of despair; they drink the condemned soul and rejoice
In cruel holiness in their heavens of chastity and
    uncircumcision.
Yet they are blameless, and iniquity must be imputed only
To the state they are entered into that they may be delivered.   1030
Satan is the state of death and not a human existence;
But Luvah is named Satan, because he has entered that state,

A world where man is by nature the enemy of man,
Because the evil is created into a state, that men
May be delivered time after time evermore. Amen.
Learn therefore, O sisters, to distinguish the eternal human
That walks about among the stones of fire, in bliss and woe
Alternate, from those states or worlds in which the spirit
    travels;
This is the only means to forgiveness of enemies.
Therefore remove from Albion these terrible surfaces,   1040
And let wild seas and rocks close up Jerusalem away from
The Atlantic mountains: where giants dwelt in intellect,
Now given to stony Druids and allegoric generation,
To the twelve gods of Asia, the Spectres of those who sleep,
Swayed by a providence opposed to the divine Lord Jesus,
A murderous providence!—a creation that groans, living on
    death,
Where fish and bird and beast and man and tree and metal
    and stone
Live by devouring, going into eternal death continually.
Albion is now possessed by the war of blood! The sacrifice
Of envy Albion is become, and his Emanation cast out.   1050
Come, Lord Jesus, Lamb of God, descend! For if, O Lord!
If thou hadst been here, our brother Albion had not died.
Arise, sisters! Go ye and meet the Lord, while I remain.
Behold the foggy mornings of the dead on Albion's cliffs,
Ye know that if the Emanation remains in them
She will become an eternal death, an avenger of sin,
A self-righteousness: the proud virgin-harlot! mother of war!
And we also, and all Beulah, consume beneath Albion's
    curse.'

Chapter III, lines 131–899

IN THE WORLD OF THE DEAD ALBION

Then Los heaved his thund'ring bellows on the valley of
    Middlesex,
And thus he chanted his song. The daughters of Albion reply:

'What may Man be? Who can tell? But what may Woman be,
To have power over Man from cradle to corruptible grave?
He who is an infant, and whose cradle is a manger,
Knoweth the infant sorrow, whence it came, and where it
   goeth,
And who weave it a cradle of the grass that withereth away.
This world is all a cradle for the erred wandering phantom,
Rocked by year, month, day and hour, and every two
   moments
Between dwells a daughter of Beulah to feed the human
   vegetable.   140
Entune, daughters of Albion, your hymning chorus mildly!
Cord of affection thrilling ecstatic on the iron reel,
To the golden loom of love, to the moth-laboured woof,
A garment and cradle weaving for the infantine terror,
For fear. At entering the gate into our world of cruel
Lamentation, it flees back and hides in non-entity's dark
   wild,
Where dwells the Spectre of Albion, destroyer of definite
   form.
The sun shall be a scythed chariot of Britain; the moon, a
   ship
In the British ocean created by Los's hammer!—measured
   out
Into days and nights and years and months, to travel with my
   feet   150
Over these desolate rocks of Albion. O daughters of despair!
Rock the cradle, and in mild melodies tell me where found
What you have enwoven with so much tears and care, so
   much
Tender artifice, to laugh, to weep, to learn, to know?
Remember, recollect, what dark befel in wintry days!'

'Oh, it was lost for ever! And we found it not; it came
And wept at our wintry door. Look, look, behold!
   Gwendolen
Is become a clod of clay! Merlin is a worm of the valley!'

Then Los uttered with hammer and anvil: 'Chant! Revoice!
I mind not your laugh, and your frown I not fear! And   160
You must my dictate obey from your gold-beamed looms. Trill

Gentle to Albion's watchman on Albion's mountains; re-echo
And rock the cradle while! Ah me, of that Eternal Man,
And of the cradled infancy in his bowels of compassion!—
Who fell beneath his instruments of husbandry and became
Subservient to the clods of the furrow. The cattle and even
The emmet and earthworms are his superiors and his lords.'

Then the response came warbling from trilling looms in
          Albion:
'We women tremble at the light therefore, hiding fearful
The Divine Vision with curtain and veil and fleshy
          tabernacle.'   170
Los uttered, swift as the rattling thunder upon the mountains,
'Look back into the Church Paul! Look! Three women
          around
The cross! O Albion, why didst thou a female will create?'

And the voices of Bath and Canterbury and York and
          Edinburgh cry
Over the plough of nations in the strong hand of Albion,
          thundering along
Among the fires of the Druid and the deep black thundering
          waters
Of the Atlantic, which poured in impetuous, loud, loud,
          louder and louder.
And the great voice of the Atlantic howled over the Druid
          altars,
Weeping over his children in Stonehenge, in Maldon and
          Colchester,
Round the rocky Peak of Derbyshire, London Stone and
          Rosamond's bower: 180
'What is a wife and what is a harlot? What is a church and
          what
Is a theatre? Are they two and not one? Can they exist
          separate?
Are not religion and politics the same thing? Brotherhood is
          religion;
Oh demonstrations of reason, dividing families in cruelty and
          pride!'

But Albion fled from the Divine Vision, with the plough of
    nations enflaming.
The living creatures maddened, and Albion fell into the
    furrow, and
The plough went over him, and the living was ploughed in
    among the dead.
But his Spectre rose over the starry plough. Albion fled
    beneath the plough
Till he came to the Rock of Ages, and he took his seat upon
    the rock.

Wonder seized all in Eternity to behold the Divine Vision
    open   190
The centre into an expanse! And the centre rolled out into
    an expanse.

In beauty the daughters of Albion divide and unite at will,
Naked and drunk with blood, Gwendolen dancing to the
    timbrel
Of war, reeling up the street of London. She divides in twain,
Among the inhabitants of Albion. The people fall around;
The daughters of Albion divide and unite in jealousy and
    cruelty.
The inhabitants of Albion at the harvest and the vintage
Feel their brain cut round beneath the temples, shrieking,
Bonifying into a skull, the marrow exuding in dismal pain.
They flee over the rocks bonifying; horses, oxen feel the
    knife   200
And while the sons of Albion by severe war and judgement
    bonify,
The hermaphroditic condensations are divided by the knife,
The obdurate forms are cut asunder by jealousy and pity.

Rational philosophy and mathematic demonstration
Is divided in the intoxications of pleasure and affection.
Two contraries war against each other in fury and blood,
And Los fixes them on his anvil; incessant his blows.
He fixes them with strong blows, placing the stones and
    timbers
To create a world of generation from the world of death,
Dividing the masculine and feminine; for the commingling   210
Of Albion's and Luvah's spectres was hermaphroditic.

Urizen wrathful strode above, directing the awful building,
As a mighty temple, delivering form out of confusion.
Jordan sprang beneath its threshold, bubbling from beneath
Its pillars; Euphrates ran under its arches; white sails
And silver oars reflect on its pillars and sound on its echoing
Pavements, where walk the sons of Jerusalem who remain
    ungenerate.
But the revolving sun and moon pass through its porticoes;
Day and night, in sublime majesty and silence, they revolve
And shine glorious within. Hand and Coban arched over the
    sun   220
In the hot noon, as he travelled through his journey; Hyle
    and Skofield
Arched over the moon at midnight, and Los fixed them there
With his thunderous hammer. Terrified the Spectres rage
    and flee.
Canaan is his portico; Jordan is a fountain in his porch,
A fountain of milk and wine to relieve the traveller.
Egypt is the eight steps within; Ethiopia supports his pillars;
Lybia and the lands unknown are the ascent without;
Within is Asia and Greece, ornamented with exquisite art;
Persia and Media are his halls; his inmost hall is great
    Tartary;
China and India and Serbia are his temples for
    entertainment,   230
Poland and Russia and Sweden his soft retired chambers;
France and Spain and Italy and Denmark and Holland and
    Germany
Are the temples among his pillars. Britain is Los's forge;
America, North and South, are his baths of living waters.

Such is the ancient world of Urizen in the Satanic void,
Created from the valley of Middlesex by London's river
From Stonehenge and from London Stone, from Cornwall
    to Caithness.
The four Zoas rush around on all sides in dire ruin;
Furious in pride of selfhood, the terrible Spectres of Albion
Rear their dark rocks among the stars of God, stupendous   240
Works! A world of generation continually creating out of
The hermaphrodite Satanic world of rocky destiny,
And formed into four precious stones, for entrance from
    Beulah.

For the veil of Vala, which Albion cast into the Atlantic deep
To catch the souls of the dead, began to vegetate and petrify
Around the earth of Albion, among the roots of his tree.
This Los formed into the gates and mighty wall, between the
    oak
Of weeping and the palm of suffering beneath Albion's tomb.
Thus in process of time it became the beautiful Mundane
    Shell,
The habitation of the Spectres of the dead, and the place   250
Of redemption and of awaking again into Eternity.

For four universes round the mundane egg remain chaotic.
One to the north, Urthona; one to the south, Urizen;
One to the east, Luvah; one to the west, Tharmas.
They are the four Zoas that stood around the throne divine.
Verulam, London, York and Edinburgh their English names.
But when Luvah assumed the world of Urizen southward,
And Albion was slain upon his mountain and in his tent,
All fell towards the centre, sinking downwards in dire ruin.
In the south remains a burning fire; in the east, a void;   260
In the west, a world of raging waters; in the north, solid
    darkness
Unfathomable, without end. But in the midst of these
Is built eternally the sublime universe of Los and Enitharmon.

And in the north gate, in the west of the north, toward
    Beulah,
Cathedron's looms are builded, and Los's furnaces in the
    south.
A wondrous golden building immense with ornaments sublime
Is bright Cathedron's golden hall, its courts, towers and
    pinnacles.

And one daughter of Los sat at the fiery reel, and another
Sat at the shining loom with her sisters attending round;
Terrible their distress, and their sorrow cannot be uttered.   270
And another daughter of Los sat at the spinning-wheel.
Endless their labour, with bitter food, void of sleep;
Though hungry they labour. They rouse themselves anxious,
Hour after hour labouring at the whirling wheel,
Many wheels—and as many lovely daughters sit weeping.

Yet the intoxicating delight that they take in their work
Obliterates every other evil; none pities their tears,
Yet they regard not pity and they expect no one to pity.
For they labour for life and love, regardless of anyone
But the poor Spectres that they work for, always, incessantly.   280

They are mocked by everyone that passes by. They regard
    not;
They labour. And when their wheels are broken by scorn
    and malice
They mend them sorrowing with many tears and afflictions.

Other daughters weave on the cushion and pillow network
    fine,
That Rahab and Tirzah may exist and live and breathe and
    love.
Ah, that it could be as the daughters of Beulah wish!

Other daughters of Los, labouring at looms less fine,
Create the silk-worm and the spider and the caterpillar
To assist in their most grievous work of pity and compassion.
And others create the woolly lamb and the downy fowl   290
To assist in the work. The lamb bleats; the sea-fowl cries.
Men understand not the distress and the labour and sorrow
That in the interior worlds is carried on in fear and trembling,
Weaving the shudd'ring fears and loves of Albion's families.
Thunderous rage the spindles of iron, and the iron distaff
Maddens in the fury of their hands, weaving in bitter tears
The veil of goats-hair, and purple and scarlet and
    fine-twined linen.

The clouds of Albion's Druid temples rage in the eastern
    heaven,
While Los sat terrified beholding Albion's Spectre, who is
    Luvah,
Spreading in bloody veins in torments over Europe and Asia: 300
Not yet formed, but a wretched torment unformed and
    abyssal
In flaming fire. Within the furnaces the Divine Vision
    appeared
On Albion's hills; often, walking from the furnaces in clouds

And flames among the Druid temples and the starry wheels,
Gathered Jerusalem's children in his arms and bore them like
A shepherd, in the night of Albion which overspread all the
    earth.

'I gave thee liberty and life, O lovely Jerusalem,
And thou hast bound me down upon the stems of vegetation.
I gave thee sheep-walks upon the Spanish mountains,
    Jerusalem;
I gave thee Priam's city and the isles of Grecia lovely.   310
I gave thee Hand and Skofield and the counties of Albion.
They spread forth like a lovely root into the garden of God;
They were as Adam before me, united into one man.
They stood in innocence and their skiey tent reached over
    Asia
To Nimrod's tower, to Ham and Canaan walking with
    Mizraim
Upon the Egyptian Nile, with solemn songs to Grecia
And sweet Hesperia, even to great Chaldea and Tesshina,
Following thee as a shepherd by the four rivers of Eden.
Why wilt thou rend thyself apart, Jerusalem?
And build this Babylon, and sacrifice in secret groves   320
Among the gods of Asia, among the fountains of pitch and
    nitre!
Therefore thy mountains are become barren, Jerusalem!
Thy valleys, plains of burning sand; thy rivers, waters of
    death.
Thy villages die of the famine, and thy cities
Beg bread from house to house, lovely Jerusalem.
Why wilt thou deface thy beauty and the beauty of thy little
    ones
To please thy idols, in the pretended chastities of
    uncircumcision?
Thy sons are lovelier than Egypt or Assyria; wherefore
Dost thou blacken their beauty by a secluded place of rest,
And a peculiar tabernacle, to cut the integuments of beauty   330
Into the veils of tears and sorrows, O lovely Jerusalem?
They have persuaded thee to this; therefore their end shall
    come.
And I will lead thee through the wilderness in shadow of my
    cloud,

And in my love I will lead thee, lovely shadow of sleeping
    Albion.'

This is the song of the Lamb, sung by slaves in evening time.

But Jerusalem faintly saw him, closed in the dungeons of
    Babylon.
Her form was held by Beulah's daughters, but all within
    unseen
She sat at the mills, her hair unbound, her feet naked,
Cut with the flints. Her tears run down; her reason grows like
The wheel of Hand, incessant turning day and night without
    rest.   340
Insane she raves upon the winds, hoarse, inarticulate.
All night Vala hears; she triumphs in pride of holiness
To see Jerusalem deface her lineaments with bitter blows
Of despair, while the Satanic holiness triumphed in Vala,
In a religion of chastity and uncircumcised selfishness,
Both of the head and the heart and loins, closed up in moral
    pride.

But the Divine Lamb stood beside Jerusalem; oft she saw
The lineaments divine and oft the voice heard, and oft she said:

'O Lord and Saviour, have the gods of the heathen pierced
    thee?
Or has thou been pierced in the house of thy friends?   350
Art thou alive, and livest thou for evermore? Or art thou
Not—but a delusive shadow, a thought that liveth not?
Babel mocks, saying there is no God nor Son of God,
That thou, O human imagination, O divine body, art all
A delusion. But I know thee, O Lord, when thou arisest upon
My weary eyes, even in this dungeon and this iron mill.
The stars of Albion cruel rise; thou bindest to sweet
    influences,
For thou also sufferest with me although I behold thee not.
And, although I sin and blaspheme thy holy name, thou
    pitiest me,
Because thou knowest I am deluded by the turning mills,   360
And by these visions of pity and love, because of Albion's
    death.'

Thus spake Jerusalem, and thus the divine voice replied:

'Mild shade of Man, pitiest thou these visions of terror and
  woe!
Give forth thy pity and love; fear not! Lo, I am with thee
  always.
Only believe in me that I have power to raise from death
Thy brother who sleepeth in Albion! Fear not, trembling
  shade.
Behold; in the visions of Elohim Jehovah behold Joseph and
  Mary,
And be comforted, O Jerusalem, in the visions of Jehovah
  Elohim.'

She looked, and saw Joseph the carpenter in Nazareth and
  Mary
His espoused wife. And Mary said: 'If thou put me away   370
  from thee,
Dost thou not murder me?' Joseph spoke in anger and fury:
  'Should I
Marry a harlot and an adulteress?' Mary answered: 'Art thou
  more pure
Than thy maker, who forgiveth sins and calls again her that is
  lost?
Though she hates, he calls her again in love. I love my dear
  Joseph,
But he driveth me away from his presence. Yet I hear the
  voice of God
In the voice of my husband; though he is angry for a moment,
  he will not
Utterly cast me away. If I were pure, never could I taste the
  sweets
Of the forgiveness of sins. If I were holy, I never could
  behold the tears
Of love of him who loves me in the midst of his anger in
  furnace of fire!'

'Ah, my Mary,' said Joseph, weeping over and embracing her
  closely in   380
His arms: 'Doth he forgive Jerusalem, and not exact purity
  from her who is

Polluted? I heard his voice in my sleep, and his angel in my
   dream,

Saying: "Doth Jehovah forgive a debt only on condition that
   it shall

Be paid? Doth he forgive pollution only on conditions of
   purity?

That debt is not forgiven! That pollution is not forgiven!

Such is the forgiveness of the gods, the moral virtues of the

Heathen, whose tender mercies are cruelty. But Jehovah's
   salvation

Is without money and without price, in the continual
   forgiveness of sins,

In the perpetual mutual sacrifice in great Eternity! For
   behold!

There is none that liveth and sinneth not! And this is the
   covenant   390

Of Jehovah: *If you forgive one another, so shall Jehovah forgive*
   you,

That he himself may dwell among you. Fear not then to take

To thee Mary thy wife, for she is with child by the Holy
   Ghost."'

Then Mary burst forth into a song! She flowed like a river of

Many streams in the arms of Joseph and gave forth her tears
   of joy

Like many waters—and emanating into gardens and palaces
   upon

Euphrates, and to forests and floods, and animals wild and
   tame from

Gihon to Hiddekel, and to cornfields and villages and
   inhabitants

Upon Pison and Arnon and Jordan. And I heard the voice
   among

The reapers saying: 'Am I Jerusalem the lost adulteress? Or
   am I   400

Babylon come up to Jerusalem?' And another voice
   answered, saying:

'Does the voice of my Lord call me again? Am I pure through
   his mercy

And pity? Am I become lovely as a virgin in his sight, who am

Indeed a harlot drunken with the sacrifice of idols? Does he

Call her pure as he did in the days of her infancy, when she
Was cast out to the loathing of her person? The Chaldean
   took
Me from my cradle. The Amalekite stole me away upon his
   camels
Before I had ever beheld with love the face of Jehovah, or
   known
That there was a God of mercy. O mercy, O Divine
   Humanity!
O forgiveness and pity and compassion! If I were pure I
   should never   410
Have known thee; if I were unpolluted I should never have
Glorified thy holiness, or rejoiced in thy great salvation.'

Mary leaned her side against Jerusalem; Jerusalem received
The infant into her hands in the visions of Jehovah. Times
   passed on.

Jerusalem fainted over the cross and sepulchre. She heard
   the voice:
'Wilt thou make Rome thy patriarch Druid, and the kings of
   Europe his
Horsemen? Man in the resurrection changes his sexual
   garments at will.
Every harlot was once a virgin, every criminal an infant love.
Repose on me till the morning of the grave. I am thy life.'

Jerusalem replied: 'I am an outcast; Albion is dead.   420
I am left to the trampling foot and the spurning heel.
A harlot I am called; I am sold from street to street.
I am defaced with blows and with the dirt of the prison.
And wilt thou become my husband, O my Lord and Saviour?
Shall Vala bring thee forth? Shall the chaste be ashamed also?
I see the maternal line, I behold the seed of the woman!
Cainah and Ada and Zillah and Naamah wife of Noah,
Shuah's daughter and Tamar, and Rahab the Canaanitess,
Ruth the Moabite, and Bathsheba of the daughters of Heth,
Naamah the Ammonite, Zibeah the Philistine, and Mary.   430
These are the daughters of Vala, mother of the body of death;
But I thy Magdalen behold thy spiritual risen body.
Shall Albion arise? I know I shall arise at the last day!
I know that in my flesh I shall see God; but Emanations
Are weak, they know not whence they are, nor whither tend.'

Jesus replied: 'I am the resurrection and the life.
I die and pass the limits of possibility, as it appears
To individual perception. Luvah must be created
And Vala; for I cannot leave them in the gnawing grave,
But will prepare a way for my banished ones to return.   440
Come now with me into the villages, walk through all the
    cities.
Though thou art taken to prison and judgement, starved in
    the streets,
I will command the cloud to give thee food, and the hard rock
To flow with milk and wine. Though thou seest me not a
    season,
Even a long season and a hard journey and a howling
    wilderness,
Though Vala's cloud hide thee and Luvah's fires follow thee,
Only believe and trust in me. Lo, I am always with thee!'

So spoke the Lamb of God, while Luvah's cloud reddening
    above
Burst forth in streams of blood upon the heavens, and dark
    night
Involved Jerusalem. And the wheels of Albion's sons turned
    hoarse   450
Over the mountains, and the fires blazed on Druid altars,
And the sun set in Tyburn's brook, where victims howl and
    cry.

But Los beheld the Divine Vision among the flames of the
    furnaces.
Therefore he lived and breathed in hope, but his tears fell
    incessant
Because his children were closed from him apart, and
    Enitharmon
Dividing in fierce pain. Also the vision of God was closed in
    clouds
Of Albion's Spectres, that Los in despair oft sat and often
    pondered
On death eternal, in fierce shudders upon the mountains of
    Albion
Walking, and in the vales in howling fierce. Then, to his anvils
Turning, anew began his labours, though in terrible pains.   460

Jehovah stood among the Druids in the valley of Annandale,
When the four Zoas of Albion, the four living creatures, the
  cherubim
Of Albion, tremble before the Spectre in the starry harness
  of the plough
Of nations. And their names are Urizen and Luvah and
  Tharmas and Urthona.

Luvah slew Tharmas, the angel of the tongue, and Albion
  brought him
To justice in his own city of Paris, denying the resurrection.
Then Vala, the wife of Albion, who is the daughter of Luvah,
Took vengeance twelve-fold among the chaotic rocks of the
  Druids,
Where the human victims howl to the moon, and Thor and
  Friga
Dance the dance of death, contending with Jehovah among
  the cherubim.   470
The chariot wheels filled with eyes rage along the howling
  valley
In the dividing of Reuben and Benjamin bleeding from
  Chester's river.

The giants and the witches and the ghosts of Albion dance
  with
Thor and Friga, and the fairies lead the moon along the
  valley of cherubim,
Bleeding in torrents from mountain to mountain, a lovely
  victim.
And Jehovah stood in the gates of the victim, and he appeared
A weeping infant in the gates of birth in the midst of heaven.

The cities and villages of Albion became rock and sand
  unhumanized,
The Druid sons of Albion and the heavens a void around
  unfathomable:
No human form, but sexual, and a little weeping infant pale,
  reflected   480
Multitudinous in the looking-glass of Enitharmon, on all sides
Around in the clouds of the female on Albion's cliffs of the
  dead.

Such the appearance in Cheviot in the divisions of Reuben,
When the cherubim hid their heads under their wings in
   deep slumbers,
When the Druids demanded chastity from Woman and all
   was lost.

'How can the female be chaste, O thou stupid Druid,' cried
   Los,
'Without the forgiveness of sins in the merciful clouds of
   Jehovah,
And without the baptism of repentance to wash away
   calumnies and
The accusations of sin, that each may be pure in their
   neighbour's sight?
O when shall Jehovah give us victims from his flock and
   herds,   490
Instead of human victims by the daughters of Albion and
   Canaan?'

Then laughed Gwendolen, and her laughter shook the
   nations and families of
The dead beneath Beulah, from Tyburn to Golgotha, and
   from
Ireland to Japan. Furious her lions and tigers and wolves
   sport before
Los on the Thames and Medway; London and Canterbury
   groan in pain.

Los knew not yet what was done; he thought it was all in
   vision,
In visions of the dreams of Beulah among the daughters of
   Albion.
Therefore the murder was put apart in the looking-glass of
   Enitharmon.

He saw in Vala's hand the Druid knife of revenge and the
   poison cup
Of jealousy, and thought it a poetic vision of the atmospheres,   500
Till Canaan rolled apart from Albion across the Rhine, along
   the Danube.

And all the land of Canaan suspended over the valley of
Cheviot,
From Bashan to Tyre and from Troy to Gaza of the
Amalekite.
And Reuben fled with his head downwards among the
caverns
Of the Mundane Shell, which froze on all sides round
Canaan on
The vast expanse, where the daughters of Albion weave the
web
Of ages and generations, folding and unfolding it like a veil
of cherubim.
And sometimes it touches the earth's summits, and
sometimes spreads
Abroad into the indefinite Spectre, who is the rational power.

Then all the daughters of Albion became one before Los,
even Vala.   510
And she put forth her hand upon the looms in dreadful
howlings
Till she vegetated into a hungry stomach and a devouring
tongue.
Her hand is a court of justice; her feet, two armies in battle;
Storms and pestilence in her locks; and in her loins
earthquake,
And fire, and the ruin of cities and nations and families and
tongues.
She cries: 'The human is but a worm, and thou, O male,
thou art
Thyself female, a male. A breeder of seed, a son and
husband, and lo,
The human-divine is woman's shadow, a vapour in the
summer's heat.
Go assume papal dignity, thou Spectre, thou male harlot!
Arthur,
Divide into the kings of Europe in times remote, O
woman-born,   520
And woman-nourished, and woman-educated, and
woman-scorned!'

'Wherefore art thou living,' said Los, 'and Man cannot live in
    thy presence?
Art thou Vala, the wife of Albion, O thou lovely daughter of
    Luvah?
All quarrels arise from reasoning, the secret murder and
The violent man-slaughter, these are the Spectre's double
    cave:
The sexual death, living on accusation of sin and judgement,
To freeze love and innocence into the gold and silver of the
    merchant.
Without forgiveness of sin, love is itself eternal death.'

Then the Spectre drew Vala into his bosom, magnificent,
    terrific,
Glittering with precious stones and gold, with garments of
    blood and fire.   530
He wept in deadly wrath of the Spectre, in self-contradicting
    agony,
Crimson with wrath and green with jealousy, dazzling with love
And jealousy immingled; and the purple of the violet
    darkened deep
Over the plough of nations thund'ring in the hand of
    Albion's Spectre.

A dark hermaphrodite they stood, frowning upon London's
    river;
And the distaff and spindle in the hands of Vala, with the
    flax of
Human miseries, turned fierce with the lives of men along
    the valley,
As Reuben fled before the daughters of Albion, taxing the
    nations.

Derby Peak yawned a horrid chasm at the cries of
    Gwendolen and at
The stamping feet of Ragan upon the flaming treadles of her
    loom,   540
That drop with crimson gore, with the loves of Albion and
    Canaan,
Opening along the valley of Rephaim, weaving over the caves
    of Machpelah,

To decide two worlds with a great decision: a world of mercy
  and
A world of justice (the world of mercy for salvation,
To cast Luvah into the wrath, and Albion into the pity,
In the two contraries of humanity, and in the four regions.)

For in the depths of Albion's bosom in the eastern heaven
They sound the clarions strong! They chain the howling
  captives;
They cast the lots into the helmet; they give the oath of blood
  in Lambeth.
They vote the death of Luvah, and they nailed him to   550
They stained him with poisonous blue; they enwove him in
  cruel roots
To die a death of six thousand years bound round with
  vegetation.
The sun was black and the moon rolled a useless globe
  through Britain.

Then left the sons of Urizen the plough and harrow, the
  loom,
The hammer and the chisel, and the rule and compasses,
  from London fleeing
They forged the sword on Cheviot, the chariot of war and
  the battle-axe,
The trumpet fitted to mortal battle, and the flute of summer
  in Annandale.
And all the arts of life they changed into the arts of death in
  Albion:
The hour-glass contemned, because its simple workmanship
Was like the workmanship of the ploughman, and the
  water-wheel   560
That raises water into cisterns broken and burned with fire,
Because its workmanship was like the workmanship of the
  shepherd.
And in their stead intricate wheels invented, wheel without
  wheel,
To perplex youth in their outgoings, and to bind to labours
  in Albion
Of day and night the myriads of Eternity; that they may grind
And polish brass and iron hour after hour, laborious task,

Kept ignorant of its use; that they might spend the days of
  wisdom
In sorrowful drudgery, to obtain a scanty pittance of bread,
In ignorance to view a small portion and think that all,
And call it Demonstration, blind to all the simple rules of life.   570

'Now, now the battle rages round thy tender limbs, O Vala.
Now smile among thy bitter tears: now put on all thy beauty.
Is not the wound of the sword sweet, and the broken bone
  delightful?
Wilt thou now smile among the scythes when the wounded
  groan in the field?
We were carried away in thousands from London, and in tens
Of thousands from Westminster and Marybone: in ships
  closed up,
Chained hand and foot, compelled to fight under the iron
  whips
Of our captains, fearing our officers more than the enemy.
Lift up thy blue eyes, Vala, and put on thy sapphire shoes.
O melancholy Magdalen, behold the morning over Maldon
  break.   580
Gird on thy flaming zone; descend into the sepulchre of
  Canterbury.
Scatter the blood from thy golden brow, the tears from thy
  silver looks;
Shake off the waters from thy wings, and the dust from thy
  white garments.
Remember all thy feigned terrors on the secret couch of
  Lambeth's vale,
When the sun rose in glowing morn, with arms of mighty
  hosts
Marching to battle—who was wont to rise with Urizen's
  harps,
Girt as a sower with his seed to scatter life abroad over
  Albion.
Arise, O Vala! Bring the bow of Urizen; bring the swift
  arrows of light.
How raged the golden horses of Urizen, compelled to the
  chariot of love!
Compelled to leave the plough to the ox, to snuff up the
  winds of desolation,   590

To trample the cornfields in boastful neighings. This is no
    gentle harp;
This is no warbling brook, nor shadow of a myrtle tree,
But blood and wounds and dismal cries, and shadows of the
    oak,
And hearts laid open to the light by the broad grisly sword,
And bowels hid in hammered steel ripped quivering on the
    ground.
Call forth thy smiles of soft deceit; call forth thy cloudy tears.
We hear thy sighs in trumpets shrill when morn shall blood
    renew.'

So sang the Spectre sons of Albion round Luvah's stone of
    trial,
Mocking and deriding at the writhings of their victim on
    Salisbury,
Drinking his Emanation in intoxicating bliss, rejoicing in
    giant dance.   600
For a Spectre has no Emanation but what he imbibes from
    deceiving
A victim; then he becomes her priest and she is his
    tabernacle
And his oak grove, till the victim rend the woven veil,
In the end of his sleep when Jesus calls him from his grave.

Howling the victims on the Druid altars yield their souls
To the stern warriors; lovely sport the daughters round their
    victims,
Drinking their lives in sweet intoxication. Hence arose from
    Bath
Soft deluding odours, in spiral volutions intricately winding
Over Albion's mountains, a feminine indefinite cruel
    delusion.
Astonished, terrified, and in pain and torment, sudden they
    behold   610
Their own parent, the Emanation of their murdered enemy,
Become their Emanation, and their temple and tabernacle.
They knew not this Vala was their beloved mother Vala,
    Albion's wife.

Terrified at the sight of the victim, at his distorted sinews,
The tremblings of Vala vibrate through the limbs of Albion's
  sons,
While they rejoice over Luvah in mockery and bitter scorn.
Sudden they become like what they behold, in howlings and
  deadly pain.
Spasms smite their features, sinews and limbs; pale they look
  on one another.
They turn, contorted; their iron necks bend unwilling
  towards
Luvah; their lips tremble; their muscular fibres are cramped
  and smitten.   620
They become like what they behold! Yet immense in
  strength and power,
In awful pomp and gold, in all the precious unhewn stones of
  Eden,
They build a stupendous building on the Plain of Salisbury:
  with chains
Of rocks round London Stone, of reasonings, of unhewn
  demonstrations
In labyrinthine arches (mighty Urizen the architect), through
  which
The heavens might revolve and Eternity be bound in their
  chain.
Labour unparalleled! A wondrous rocky world of cruel
  destiny,
Rocks piled on rocks reaching the stars, stretching from pole
  to pole.
The building is natural religion and its altars natural morality,
A building of eternal death, whose proportions are eternal
  despair.   630

Here Vala stood turning the iron spindle of destruction
From heaven to earth, howling, invisible! But not invisible
Her two covering cherubs, afterwards named Voltaire and
  Rousseau:
Two frowning rocks on each side of the cove and stone of
  torture,
Frozen sons of the feminine tabernacle of Bacon, Newton
  and Locke.
For Luvah is France, the victim of the Spectres of Albion.

Los beheld in terror; he poured his loud storms on the
    furnaces.
The daughters of Albion, clothed in garments of needlework,
Strip them off from their shoulders and bosoms. They lay
    aside
Their garments; they sit naked upon the stone of trial.   640
The knife of flint passes over the howling victim; his blood
Gushes and stains the fair side of the fair daughters of Albion.
They put aside his curls; they divide his seven locks upon
His forehead; they bind his forehead with thorns of iron.
They put into his hand a reed; they mock, saying: 'Behold
The King of Canaan, whose are seven hundred chariots of
    iron!'
They take off his vesture whole with their knives of flint,
But they cut asunder his inner garments, searching with
Their cruel fingers for his heart. And there they enter in
    pomp,
In many tears; and there they erect a temple and an altar.   650
They pour cold water on his brain in front, to cause
Lids to grow over his eyes in veils of tears, and caverns
To freeze over his nostrils, while they feed his tongue from
    cups
And dishes of painted clay. Glowing with beauty and cruelty
They obscure the sun and the moon; no eye can look upon
    them.

Ah! Alas! At the sight of the victim, and at sight of those who
    are smitten,
All who see become what they behold; their eyes are covered
With veils of tears, and their nostrils and tongues shrunk up,
Their ears bent outwards. As their victim, so are they in the
    pangs
Of unconquerable fear, amidst delights of revenge earth-
    shaking!   660
And as their eye and ear shrunk, the heavens shrunk away;
The Divine Vision became first a burning flame, then a
    column
Of fire, then an awful fiery wheel surrounding earth and
    heaven,
And then a globe of blood wandering distant in an unknown
    night.

Afar into the unknown night the mountains fled away:
Six months of mortality, a summer; and six months of
    mortality, a winter.
The human form began to be altered by the daughters of
    Albion,
And the perceptions to be dissipated into the indefinite,
    becoming
A mighty polypus named Albion's Tree. They tie the veins
And nerves into two knots, and the seed into a double knot.   670
They look forth; the sun is shrunk, the heavens are shrunk
Away in the far remote, and the trees and mountains withered
Into indefinite cloudy shadows in darkness and separation.
By invisible hatreds adjoined, they seem remote and separate
From each other, and yet are a mighty polypus in the deep!
As the mistletoe grows on the oak, so Albion's tree on
    Eternity. Lo,
He who will not commingle in love, must be adjoined by hate!

They look forth from Stonehenge; from the cove round
    London Stone
They look on one another. The mountain calls out to the
    mountain;
Plinlimmon shrunk away; Snowdon trembled. The mountains   680
Of Wales and Scotland beheld the descending war, they
    routed flying.
Red run the streams of Albion; Thames is drunk with
    blood,
As Gwendolen cast the shuttle of war, as Cambel returned
    the beam.
The Humber and the Severn are drunk with the blood of the
    slain.
London feels his brain cut round; Edinburgh's heart is
    circumscribed!
York and Lincoln hide among the flocks because of the
    griding knife;
Worcester and Hereford, Oxford and Cambridge, reel and
    stagger,
Overwearied with howling. Wales and Scotland alone sustain
    the fight!
The inhabitants are sick to death; they labour to divide into
    days

And nights the uncertain periods, and into weeks and
    months. In vain   690
They send the dove and raven, and in vain the serpent over
    the mountains,
And in vain the eagle and lion over the fourfold wilderness.
They return not, but generate in rocky places desolate.
They return not, but build a habitation separate from Man.
The sun forgets his course like a drunken man; he hesitates
Upon the Chisledon hills, thinking to sleep on the Severn.
In vain: he is hurried afar into an unknown night.
He bleeds in torrents of blood as he rolls through heaven
    above;
He chokes up the paths of the sky. The moon is leprous as
    snow,
Trembling and descending down, seeking to rest upon high
    Mona,   700
Scattering her leprous snows in flakes of disease over Albion.
The stars flee remote; the heaven is iron, the earth is sulphur,
And all the mountains and hills shrink up like a withering
    gourd;
As the senses of men shrink together under the knife of flint
In the hands of Albion's daughters, among the Druid temples,
By those who drink their blood and the blood of their
    covenant.

And the twelve daughters of Albion united in Raham and
    Jirzah,
A double female; and they drew out from the rocky stones
Fibres of life to weave. For every female is a golden loom;
The rocks are opaque hardnesses covering all vegetated
    things.   710
And as they wove and cut from the looms, in various divisions
Stretching over Europe and Asia from Ireland to Japan,
They divided into many lovely daughters to be counterparts
To those they wove; for when they wove a male, they divided
Into a female to the woven male. In opaque hardness
They cut the fibres from the rocks; groaning in pain they
    weave,
Calling the rocks Atomic Origins of Existence, denying
    Eternity
By the atheistical Epicurean philosophy of Albion's tree.

Such are the feminine and masculine when separated from
  Man.
They call the rocks Parents of Men and adore the frowning
  chaos,   720
Dancing around in howling pain clothed in the bloody veil,
Hiding Albion's sons within the veil, closing Jerusalem's
Sons without, to feed with their souls the Spectres of Albion:
Ashamed to give love openly to the piteous and merciful man,
Counting him an imbecile mockery. But the warrior
They adore and his revenge cherish with the blood of the
  innocent.
They drink up Dan and Gad to feed with milk Skofield and
  Kotope;
They strip off Joseph's coat and dip it in the blood of battle.

Tirzah sits weeping to hear the shrieks of the dying. Her knife
Of flint is in her hand; she passes it over the howling victim.   730
The daughters weave their work in loud cries over the rock
Of Horeb, still eyeing Albion's cliffs, eagerly seizing and
  twisting
The threads of Vala and Jerusalem running from mountain
  to mountain
Over the whole earth. Loud the warriors rage in Beth Peor
Beneath the iron whips of their captains and consecrated
  banners.
Loud the sun and moon rage in the conflict; loud the stars
Shout in the night of battle, and their spears grow to their
  hands
With blood, weaving the deaths of the mighty into a
  tabernacle
For Rahab and Tirzah, till the great polypus of generation
  covered the earth.

In Verulam the polypus's head, winding around his bulk   740
Through Rochester and Chichester, and Exeter and
  Salisbury,
To Bristol; and his heart beat strong on Salisbury Plain,
Shooting out fibres round the earth, through Gaul and Italy
And Greece, and along the Sea of Rephaim into Judaea
To Sodom and Gomorrha, thence to India, China and
  Japan.

The twelve daughters in Rahab and Tirzah have
   circumscribed the brain
Beneath, and pierced it through the midst with a golden pin.
Blood hath stained her fair side beneath her bosom.

'O thou poor human form!' said she: 'O thou poor child of
   woe!
Why wilt thou wander away from Tirzah; why me compel to
   blind thee?   750
If thou dost go away from me I shall consume upon these
   rocks.
These fibres of thine eyes that used to beam in distant
   heavens
Away from me, I have bound down with a hot iron;
These nostrils, that expanded with delight in morning skies,
I have bent downward with lead melted in my roaring
   furnaces
Of affliction, of love, of sweet despair, of torment
   unendurable.
My soul is seven furnaces; incessant roars the bellows
Upon my terribly flaming heart; the molten metal runs
In channels through my fiery limbs. Oh love, oh pity, oh fear,
Oh pain! Oh the pangs, the bitter pangs of love forsaken.   760
Ephraim was wilderness of joy where all my wild beasts ran;
The River Kanah wandered by my sweet Manasseh's side
To see the boy spring into heavens sounding from my sight!
Go, Noah, fetch the girdle of strong brass; heat it red-hot;
Press it around the loins of this ever-expanding cruelty.
Shriek not so, my only love. I refuse thy joys, I drink
Thy shrieks, because Hand and Hyle are cruel and obdurate
   to me.
Skofield, why art thou cruel? Lo, Joseph is thine! To make
You one, to weave you both in the same mantle of skin.
Bind him down, sisters, bind him down on Ebal, mount of
   cursing.   770
Mahlah, come forth from Lebanon, and Hoglah from Mount
   Sinai;
Come, circumscribe this tongue of sweets, and with a screw
   of iron
Fasten this ear into the rock. Milcah, the task is thine.
Weep not so, sisters; weep not so. Our life depends on this;

Or mercy and truth are fled away from Shechem and Mount
    Gilead,
Unless my beloved is bound upon the stems of vegetation.'

And thus the warriors cry, in the hot day of victory, in songs:

'Look, the beautiful daughter of Albion sits naked upon the
    stone,
Her panting victim beside her; her heart is drunk with blood
Though her brain is not drunk with wine. She goes forth
    from Albion   780
In pride of beauty, in cruelty of holiness, in the brightness
Of her tabernacle, and her ark, and secret place. The
    beautiful daughter
Of Albion delights the eyes of the kings; their hearts and the
Hearts of their warriors glow hot before Thor and Friga. O
    Molech!
O Chemosh! O Bacchus! O Venus! O double god of
    generation.
The heavens are cut like a mantle around from the cliffs of
    Albion
Across Europe, across Africa. In howling and deadly wars
A sheet and veil and curtain of blood is let down from heaven,
Across the hills of Ephraim and down Mount Olivet to
The valley of the Jebusite. Molech rejoices in Heaven;   790
He sees the twelve daughters naked upon the twelve stones,
Themselves condensing to rocks and into the ribs of a man.
Lo, they shoot forth in tender nerves across Europe and Asia;
Lo, they rest upon the tribes, where their panting victims lie.
Molech rushes into the kings, in love to the beautiful
    daughters,
But they frown and delight in cruelty, refusing all other joy.
Bring your offerings, you first-begotten, pampered with milk
    and blood,
Your first-born of seven years old, be they males or females,
To the beautiful daughters of Albion. They sport before the
    kings
Clothed in the skin of the victim! Blood, human blood, is the
    life   800
And delightful food of the warrior! The well-fed warrior's
    flesh

Of him who is slain in war fills the valleys of Ephraim with
Breeding women, walking in pride and bringing forth under
   green trees
With pleasure, without pain, for their food is blood of the
   captive.
Molech rejoices through the land from Havilah to Shur; he
   rejoices
In moral law and its severe penalties. Loud Shaddai and
   Jehovah
Thunder above, when they see the twelve panting victims
On the twelve stones of power, and the beautiful daughters
   of Albion:
"If you dare rend their veil with your spear you are healed of
   love."
From the hills of Camberwell and Wimbledon, from the
   valleys   810
Of Walton and Esher, from Stonehenge and from Maldon's
   cove,
Jerusalem's pillars fall in the rendings of fierce war
Over France and Germany, upon the Rhine and Danube.
Reuben and Benjamin flee; they hide in the valley of
   Rephaim.
Why trembles the warrior's limbs when he beholds thy
   beauty
Spotted with victim's blood, by the fires of thy secret
   tabernacle
And thy ark and holy place? At thy frowns, at thy dire
   revenge,
Smitten as Uzzah of old, his armour is softened; his spear
And sword faint in his hand, from Albion across Great
   Tartary.
O beautiful daughter of Albion, cruelty is thy delight.   820
O virgin of terrible eyes, who dwellest by valleys of springs
Beneath the mountains of Lebanon, in the city of Rehob in
   Hamath,
Taught to touch the harp, to dance in the circle of warriors
Before the kings of Canaan, to cut the flesh from the victim,
To roast the flesh in fire, to examine the infant's limbs
In cruelties of holiness, to refuse the joys of love, to bring
The spies from Egypt, to raise jealousy in the bosoms of the
   twelve

Kings of Canaan, then to let the spies depart to Meribah
  Kadesh
To the place of the Amalekite. I am drunk with unsatiated
  love;
I must rush again to war, for the virgin has frowned and
  refused.   830
Sometimes I curse, and sometimes bless thy fascinating
  beauty.
Once Man was occupied in intellectual pleasures and
  energies,
But now my soul is harrowed with grief and fear and love
  and desire.
And now I hate and now I love, and intellect is no more;
There is no time for anything but the torments of love and
  desire.
The feminine and masculine shadows soft, mild and
  ever-varying
In beauty, are shadows now no more, but rocks in Horeb.'

Then all the males combined into one male, and every one
Became a ravening eating cancer growing in the female,
A polypus of roots of reasoning, doubt, despair and death,   840
Going forth and returning from Albion's rocks to Canaan,
Devouring Jerusalem from every nation of the earth.

Envying stood the enormous form, at variance with itself
In all its members, in eternal torment of love and jealousy,
Driven forth by Los time after time from Albion's cliffy
  shore,
Drawing the free loves of Jerusalem into infernal bondage;
That they might be born in contentions of chastity, and in
Deadly hate between Leah and Rachel, daughters of deceit
  and fraud,
Bearing the images of various species of contention,
And jealousy, and abhorrence, and revenge, and deadly
  murder,   850
Till they refuse liberty to the male. And not like Beulah,
Where every female delights to give her maiden to her
  husband;
The female searches sea and land for gratifications to the
Male genius, who in return clothes her in gems and gold,

And feeds her with the food of Eden. Hence all her beauty
   beams.
She creates at her will a little moony night and silence,
With spaces of sweet gardens and a tent of elegant beauty,
Closed in by a sandy desert and a night of stars shining,
And a little tender moon and hovering angels on the wing.
And the male gives a time and revolution to her space   860
Till the time of love is passed in every-varying delights.
For all things exist in the human imagination,
And thence in Beulah they are stolen by secret amorous
   theft,
Till they have had punishment enough to make them
   commit crimes.
Hence rose the tabernacle in the wilderness and all its
   offerings—
From male and female loves in Beulah and their jealousies.
But no one can consummate female bliss in Los's world
   without
Becoming a generated mortal, a vegetating death.

And now the Spectres of the dead awake in Beulah. All
The jealousies become murderous, uniting together in
   Rahab.   870
A religion of chastity, forming a commerce to sell loves,
With moral law, an equal balance, not going down with
   decision.
Therefore the male, severe and cruel, filled with stern
   revenge;
Mutual hate returns, and mutual deceit and mutual fear.

Hence the infernal veil grows in the disobedient female,
Which Jesus rends and the whole Druid law removes away
From the inner sanctuary: a false holiness hid within the
   centre.
For the sanctuary of Eden is in the camp, in the outline,
In the circumference, and every minute particular is holy.
Embraces are comminglings from the head even to the feet,   880
And not a pompous High Priest entering by a secret place.

Jerusalem pined in her inmost soul over wandering Reuben,
As she slept in Beulah's night hid by the daughters of Beulah.

And this the form of mighty Hand sitting on Albion's cliffs
Before the face of Albion, a mighty threat'ning form.

His bosom wide and shoulders huge, overspreading,
    wondrous,
Bear three strong sinewy necks and three awful and terrible
    heads,
Three brains in contradictory council brooding incessantly,
Neither daring to put in act its councils, fearing each other:
Therefore rejecting ideas as nothing, and holding all wisdom   890
To consist in the agreements and disagreements of ideas,
Plotting to devour Albion's body of humanity and love.

Such form the aggregate of the twelve sons of Albion took,
    and such
Their appearance when combined; but often by birth-pangs
    and loud groans
They divide to twelve. The key-bones and the chest dividing
    in pain,
Disclose a hideous orifice, thence issuing, the giant-brood
Arise as the smoke of the furnace, shaking the rocks from
    sea to sea,
And there they combine into three forms, named Bacon and
    Newton and Locke,
In the oak groves of Albion which overspread all the earth.

Chapter IV, lines 21–291

JERUSALEM, VALA, AND THE DAUGHTERS OF ALBION

Naked Jerusalem lay before the gates upon Mount Zion,
The hill of giants, all her foundations levelled with the dust.

Her twelve gates thrown down, her children carried into
    captivity,
Herself in chains: this from within was seen in a dismal night
Outside, unknown before in Beulah, and the twelve gates
    were filled
With blood, from Japan eastward to the Giants' Causeway,
    west

Into Erin's continent. And Jerusalem wept upon Euphrates'
banks

Disorganised—an evanescent shade, scarce seen or heard
among

Her children's Druid temples, dropping with blood wandered
weeping;

And thus her voice went forth in the darkness of Philistia: 30

'My brother and my father are no more! God hath forsaken
me.

The arrows of the Almighty pour upon me and my children.

I have sinned and am an outcast from the divine presence!

My tents are fall'n! My pillars are ruins! My children dashed

Upon Egypt's iron floors and the marble pavements of Assyria.

I melt my soul in reasonings among the towers of Heshbon;

Mount Zion is become a cruel rock; and no more dew

Nor rain, no more the spring of the rock appears, but cold,

Hard and obdurate are the furrows of the mountain of wine
and oil.

The mountain of blessing is itself a curse and an
astonishment;   40

The hills of Judaea are fallen with me into the deepest hell,

Away from the nations of the earth, and from the cities of the
nations.

I walk to Ephraim; I seek for Shiloh; I walk like a lost sheep

Among the precipices of despair. In Goshen I seek for light

In vain, and in Gilead for a physician and a comforter.

Goshen hath followed Philistia, Gilead hath joined with Og!

They are become narrow places in a little and dark land;

How distant far from Albion! His hills and his valleys no more

Receive the feet of Jerusalem; they have cast me quite away,

And Albion is himself shrunk to a narrow rock in the midst of
the sea!   50

The plains of Sussex and Surrey, their hills of flocks and
herds,

No more seek to Jerusalem nor to the sound of my holy ones.

The fifty-two counties of England are hardened against me

As if I was not their mother; they despise me and cast me out.

London covered the whole earth; England encompassed the
nations;

And all the nations of the earth were seen in the cities of
Albion.

My pillars reached from sea to sea; London beheld me come
From my east and from my west. He blessed me and gave
His children to my breasts, his sons and daughters to my
  knees.
His aged parents sought me out in every city and village.   60
They discerned my countenance with joy; they showed me to
  their sons,
Saying: "Lo Jerusalem is here! She sitteth in our secret
  chambers.
Levi and Judah and Issachar, Ephraim, Manasseh, Gad and
  Dan
Are seen in our hills and valleys. They keep our flocks and
  herds;
They watch them in the night, and the Lamb of God appears
  among us."
The river Severn stayed his course at my command;
Thames poured his waters into my basins and baths;
Medway mingled with Kishon; Thames received the heavenly
  Jordan.
Albion gave me the whole earth to walk up and down, to pour
Joy upon every mountain, to teach songs to the shepherd and
  ploughman.   70
I taught the ships of the sea to sing the songs of Zion.
Italy saw me, in sublime astonishment. France was wholly
  mine,
As my garden and as my secret bath. Spain was my heavenly
  couch;
I slept in his golden hills; the Lamb of God met me there;
There we walked as in our secret chamber among our little
  ones.
They looked upon our loves with joy; they beheld our secret
  joys,
With holy raptures of adoration rapt sublime in the visions of
  God.
Germany, Poland and the north wooed my footsteps; they
  found
My gates in all their mountains and my curtains in all their
  vales;
The furniture of their houses was the furniture of my
  chamber.   80
Turkey and Grecia saw my instruments of music; they arose,

They seized the harp, the flute, the mellow horn of
  Jerusalem's joy;
They sounded thanksgivings in my courts. Egypt and Lybia
  heard.
The swarthy sons of Ethiopia stood round the Lamb of God
Enquiring for Jerusalem; he led them up my steps to my altar.
And thou, America! I once beheld thee, but now behold no
  more
Thy golden mountains, where my cherubim and seraphim
  rejoiced
Together among my little ones. But now my altars run with
  blood!
My fires are corrupt! My incense is a cloudy pestilence
Of seven diseases! Once a continual cloud of salvation rose   90
From all my myriads; once the fourfold world rejoiced among
The pillars of Jerusalem, between my winged cherubim.
But now I am closed out from them in the narrow passages
Of the valleys of destruction, into a dark land of pitch and
  bitumen,
From Albion's tomb afar and from the fourfold wonders of
  God
Shrunk to a narrow doleful form in the dark land of Cabul.
There is Reuben and Gad and Joseph and Judah and Levi,
  closed up
In narrow vales. I walk and count the bones of my beloveds
Along the valley of destruction, among these Druid temples
Which overspread all the earth in patriarchal pomp and cruel
  pride.   100
Tell me, O Vala, thy purposes. Tell me wherefore thy
  shuttles
Drop with the gore of the slain; why Euphrates is red with
  blood;
Wherefore in dreadful majesty and beauty outside appears
Thy masculine from thy feminine, hardening against the
  heavens
To devour the human! Why dost thou weep upon the wind
  among
These cruel Druid temples? O Vala! Humanity is far above
Sexual organisation and the visions of the night of Beulah,
Where sexes wander in dreams of bliss among the
  Emanations,

Where the masculine and feminine are nursed into youth
    and maiden
By the tears and smiles of Beulah's daughters, till the time
    of sleep is past.   110
Wherefore then do you realize these nets of beauty and
    delusion,
In open day to draw the souls of the dead into the light,
Till Albion is shut out from every nation under heaven?
Encompassed by the frozen net and by the rooted tree,
I walk weeping in pangs of a mother's torment for her
    children.
I walk in affliction; I am a worm, and no living soul!
A worm going to eternal torment, raised up in a night
To an eternal night of pain, lost, lost, lost, for ever!'

Beside her Vala howled upon the winds in pride and beauty,
Lamenting among the timbrels of the warriors, among the
    captives   120
In cruel holiness; and her lamenting songs were from Arnon
And Jordan to Euphrates. Jerusalem followed, trembling,
Her children in captivity, listening to Vala's lamentation
In the thick cloud and darkness. And the voice went forth from
The cloud: 'Oh rent in sunder from Jerusalem the harlot
    daughter,
In an eternal condemnation, in fierce burning flames
Of torment unendurable! And if once a delusion be found
Woman must perish, and the heavens of heavens remain no
    more.

'My father gave to me command to murder Albion
In unreviving death; my love, my Luvah, ordered me in night   130
To murder Albion, the king of men. He fought in battles
    fierce;
He conquered Luvah my beloved. He took me and my
    father;
He slew them. I revived them to life in my warm bosom.
He saw them issue from my bosom; dark in jealousy
He burned before me. Luvah framed the knife, and Luvah
    gave
The knife into his daughter's hand. Such thing was never
    known

Before in Albion's land: that one should die a death never to
    be revived.
For in our battles we the slain men view with pity and love;
We soon revive them in the secret of our tabernacles.
But I, Vala, Luvah's daughter, keep his body embalmed in
    moral laws   140
With spices of sweet odours of lovely jealous stupefaction
Within my bosom, lest he arise to life and slay my Luvah.
Pity me then, O Lamb of God! O Jesus, pity me!
Come into Luvah's tents, and seek not to revive the dead!'

So sang she, and the spindle turned furious as she sang.
The children of Jerusalem, the souls of those who sleep,
Were caught into the flax of her distaff and in her cloud,
To weave Jerusalem a body according to her will,
A dragon form on Zion hill's most ancient promontory.

The spindle turned in blood and fire. Loud sound the
    trumpets   150
Of war; the cymbals play loud before the captains,
With Cambel and Gwendolen in dance and solemn song,
The cloud of Rahab vibrating with the daughters of Albion.
Los saw terrified; melted with pity and divided in wrath
He sent them over the narrow seas in pity and love,
Among the four forests of Albion which overspread all the
    earth.
They go forth and return, swift as a flash of lightning.
Among the tribes of warriors, among the stones of power,
Against Jerusalem they rage through all the nations of
    Europe,
Through Italy and Grecia, to Lebanon and Persia and India.   160

The serpent temples through the earth, from the wide plain
    of Salisbury,
Resound with cries of victims, shouts and songs and dying
    groans
And flames of dusky fire, to Amalek, Canaan and Moab.
And Rahab like a dismal and indefinite hovering cloud
Refused to take a definite form. She hovered over all the
    earth,
Calling the definite 'sin', defacing every definite form,

Invisible or visible, stretched out in length or spread in
   breadth:
Over the temples drinking groans of victims, weeping in pity,
And joying in the pity, howling over Jerusalem's walls.

Hand slept on Skiddaw's top, drawn by the love of beautiful   170
Cambel; his bright-beaming counterpart divided from him,
And her delusive light beamed fierce above the mountain,
Soft, invisible, drinking his sighs in sweet intoxication,
Drawing out fibre by fibre. Returning to Albion's tree
At night and in the morning to Skiddaw, she sent him over
Mountainous Wales into the loom of Cathedron, fibre by
   fibre.
He ran in tender nerves across Europe to Jerusalem's shade
To weave Jerusalem a body repugnant to the Lamb.

Hyle on East Moor in rocky Derbyshire raved to the moon
For Gwendolen; she took up in bitter tears his anguished
   heart   180
That, apparent to all in Eternity, glows like the sun in the
   breast.
She hid it in his ribs and back; she hid his tongue with teeth,
In terrible convulsions pitying and gratified, drunk with pity,
Glowing with loveliness before him, becoming apparent
According to his changes. She rolled his kidneys round
Into two irregular forms, and looking on Albion's dread tree
She wove two vessels of seed, beautiful as Skiddaw's snow,
Giving them bends of self-interest and selfish natural virtue.
She hid them in his loins; raving he ran among the rocks,
Compelled into a shape of moral virtue against the Lamb,   190
The invisible lovely one giving him a form according to
His law: a form against the Lamb of God, opposed to mercy
And playing in the thunderous loom in sweet intoxication,
Filling cups of silver and crystal with shrieks and cries, with
   groans
And dolorous sobs, the wine of lovers in the winepress of
   Luvah.

'O sister Cambel,' said Gwendolen, as their long beaming
   light
Mingled above the mountain, 'What shall we do to keep

These awful forms in our soft bands? Distracted with
    trembling,
I have mocked those who refused cruelty and I have admired
The cruel warrior. I have refused to give love to Merlin the
    piteous;   200
He brings to me the images of his love, and I reject in
    chastity
And turn them out into the streets for harlots, to be food
To the stern warrior. I am become perfect in beauty over my
    warrior.
For men are caught by love, woman is caught by pride:
That love may only be obtained in the passages of death.
Let us look, let us examine. Is the cruel become an infant,
Or is he still a cruel warrior? Look sisters, look! Oh, piteous!
I have destroyed wand'ring Reuben who strove to bind my
    will;
I have stripped off Joseph's beautiful integument for my
    beloved,
The cruel one of Albion, to clothe him in gems of my zone.   210
I have named him Jehovah of Hosts. Humanity is become
A weeping infant in ruined lovely Jerusalem's folding cloud.

'In Heaven love begets love, but fear is the parent of earthly
    love!
And he who will not bend to love must be subdued by fear.
I have heard Jerusalem's groans; from Vala's cries and
    lamentations
I gather our eternal fate! Outcasts from life and love!
Unless we find a way to bind these awful forms to our
Embrace, we shall perish annihilate, discovered our
    delusions.
Look, I have wrought without delusion. Look! I have wept!
And given soft milk mingled together with the spirits of
    flocks,   220
Of lambs and doves, mingled together in cups and dishes
Of painted clay. The mighty Hyle is become a weeping
    infant;
Soon shall the Spectres of the dead follow my weaving
    threads.'

The twelve daughters of Albion attentive listen in secret
  shades,
On Cambridge and Oxford beaming, soft uniting with
  Rahab's cloud,
While Gwendolen spoke to Cambel, turning soft the
  spinning reel,
Or throwing the winged shuttle, or drawing the cords with
  softest songs.
The golden cords of the looms animate beneath their
  touches soft
Along the island white, among the Druid temples, while
  Gwendolen
Spoke to the daughters of Albion standing on Skiddaw's top.   230

So saying, she took a falsehood and hid it in her left hand,
To entice her sisters away to Babylon on Euphrates.
And thus she closed her left hand and uttered her falsehood;
Forgetting that falsehood is prophetic, she hid her hand
  behind her,
Upon her back behind her loins, and thus uttered her deceit.

'I heard Enitharmon say to Los: "Let the daughters of
  Albion
Be scattered abroad and let the name of Albion be forgotten.
Divide them into three! Name them Amalek, Canaan and
  Moab.
Let Albion remain a desolation without an inhabitant,
And let the looms of Enitharmon and the furnaces of Los   240
Create Jerusalem and Babylon and Egypt and Moab and
  Amalek,
And Helle and Hesperia and Hindustan and China and
  Japan.
But hide America, for a curse, an altar of victims and a holy
  place."
See, sisters: Canaan is pleasant; Egypt is as the Garden of
  Eden;
Babylon is our chief desire, Moab our bath in summer.
Let us lead the stems of this tree; let us plant it before
  Jerusalem
To judge the friend of sinners to death without the veil,
To cut her off from America, to close up her secret ark,

And the fury of Man exhaust in war. Woman permanent
  remain.

See how the fires of our loins point eastward to Babylon.   250

Look, Hyle is become an infant love. Look! Behold! See him
  lie

Upon my bosom! Look! Here is the lovely wayward form

That gave me sweet delight by his torments beneath my veil.

By the fruit of Albion's tree I have fed him with sweet milk,

By contentions of the mighty for sacrifice of captives.

Humanity, the great delusion, is changed to war and
  sacrifice;

I have nailed his hands on Bath Rabbim and his feet on
  Heshbon's wall.

Oh, that I could live in his sight. Oh, that I could bind him to
  my arm.'

So saying, she drew aside her veil from Mam-Tor to
  Dovedale,

Discovering her own perfect beauty to the daughters of
  Albion   260

And Hyle a winding worm beneath, and not a weeping
  infant.

Trembling and pitying she screamed and fled upon the
  wind;

Hyle was a winding worm and herself perfect in beauty.

The deserts tremble at his wrath; they shrink themselves in
  fear.

Cambel trembled with jealousy. She trembled! She envied!

The envy ran through Cathedron's looms into the heart

Of mild Jerusalem, to destroy the Lamb of God, Jerusalem

Languished upon Mount Olivet, east of mild Zion's hill.

Los saw the envious blight above his seventh furnace

On London's tower on the Thames. He drew Cambel in
  wrath   270

Into his thundering bellows, heaving it for a loud blast,

And with the blast of his furnace upon fishy Billingsgate,

Beneath Albion's fatal tree, before the gate of Los,

Showed her the fibres of her beloved to ameliorate

The envy. Loud she laboured in the furnace of fire

To form the mighty form of Hand according to her will,
In the furnaces of Los and in the winepress treading day and
   night.
Naked among the human clusters, bringing wine of anguish
To feed the afflicted in the furnaces, she minded not
The raging flames, though she returned instead of beauty   280
Deformity. She gave her beauty to another, bearing abroad
Her struggling torment in her iron arms, and like a chain
Binding his wrists and ankles with the iron arms of love.

Gwendolen saw the infant in her sister's arms. She howled
Over the forests with bitter tears, and over the winding worm
Repentant, and she also in the eddying wind of Los's bellows
Began her dolorous task of love, in the winepress of Luvah
To form the worm into a form of love by tears and pain.
The sisters saw; trembling ran through their looms,
   softening mild
Towards London. Then they saw the furnaces opened, and
   in tears   290
Began to give their souls away in the furnaces of affliction.

Chapter IV, lines 426–end

RECONCILIATION AND JOY

And thus Los replies upon his watch. The valleys listen
   silent;
The stars stand still to hear. Jerusalem and Vala cease to
   mourn;
His voice is heard from Albion. The Alps and Apennines
Listen; Hermon and Lebanon bow their crowned heads.
Babel and Shinar look toward the western gate; they sit down   430
Silent at his voice; they view the red globe of fire in Los's
   hand
As he walks from furnace to furnace, directing the labourers.
And this is the song of Los, the song that he sings on his
   watch:

'O lovely mild Jerusalem! O Shiloh of Mount Ephraim!
I see thy gates of precious stones, thy walls of gold and silver.
Thou art the soft reflected image of the sleeping man
Who, stretched on Albion's rocks, reposes amidst his
    twenty-eight
Cities, where Beulah lovely terminates in the hills and
    valleys of Albion:
Cities not yet embodied in time and space. Plant ye
The seeds, O sisters, in the bosom of time and space's
    womb,   440
To spring up for Jerusalem. Lovely shadow of sleeping
    Albion,
Why wilt thou rend thyself apart and build an earthly
    kingdom,
To reign in pride, and to oppress, and to mix the cup of
    delusion?
O thou that dwellest with Babylon, come forth, O lovely one!

'I see thy form, O lovely mild Jerusalem, winged with six
    wings
In the opacous bosom of the sleeper, lovely threefold
In head and heart and reins, three universes of love and
    beauty.
Thy forehead bright, 'Holiness to the Lord' with gates of
    pearl,
Reflects Eternity beneath thy azure wings of feathery down,
Ribbed delicate and clothed with feathered gold and azure
    and purple   450
From thy white shoulders shadowing, purity in holiness!
Thence feathered with soft crimson of the ruby bright as fire,
Spreading into the azure wings, which like a canopy
Bends over thy immortal head, in which Eternity dwells.
Albion, beloved land, I see thy mountains, and thy hills,
And valleys, and thy pleasant cities: 'Holiness to the Lord'.
I see the Spectres of thy dead, O Emanation of Albion.

'Thy bosom white, translucent, covered with immortal gems,
A sublime ornament not obscuring the outlines of beauty,
Terrible to behold for thy extreme beauty and perfection: 460
Twelvefold here all the tribes of Israel I behold
Upon the holy land. I see the River of Life and Tree of Life.

I see the new Jerusalem descending out of Heaven
Between thy wings of gold and silver, feathered immortal,
Clear as the rainbow, as the cloud of the sun's tabernacle.

'Thy reins covered with wings translucent, sometimes
  covering
And sometimes spread abroad, reveal the flames of holiness
Which like a robe covers, and like a veil of seraphim
In flaming fire unceasing burns from eternity to eternity.
Twelvefold I there behold Israel in her tents;   470
A pillar of cloud by day, a pillar of fire by night
Guides them. There I behold Moab and Ammon and
  Amalek.
There bells of silver round thy knees, living, articulate
Comforting sounds of love and harmony; and on thy feet
Sandals of gold and pearl; and Egypt and Assyria before me,
The isles of Javan, Philistia, Tyre and Lebanon.'

Thus Los sings upon his watch, walking from furnace to
  furnace.
He seizes his hammer every hour; flames surround him as
He beats. Seas roll beneath his feet; tempests muster
Around his head; the thick hailstones stand ready to obey   480
His voice in the black cloud. His sons labour in thunders
At his furnaces; his daughters at their looms sing woes.
His Emanation separates in milky fibres, agonising
Among the golden looms of Cathedron, sending fibres of
  love
From Golgonooza with sweet visions for Jerusalem,
  wanderer.

Nor can any consummate bliss without being generated
On earth, of those whose Emanations weave the loves
Of Beulah for Jerusalem and Shiloh in immortal
  Golgonooza:
Concentering in the majestic form of Erin in eternal tears,
Viewing the winding worm on the deserts of Great Tartary,   490
Viewing Los in his shudderings, pouring balm on his
  sorrows.
So dread is Los's fury, that none dare him to approach
Without becoming his children in the furnaces of affliction.

And Enitharmon like a faint rainbow waved before him,
Filling with fibres from his loins, which reddened with
    desire,
Into a globe of blood beneath his bosom, trembling in
    darkness
Of Albion's clouds. He fed it with his tears and bitter groans,
Hiding his Spectre in invisibility from the timorous shade;
Till it became a separated cloud of beauty, grace and love
Among the darkness of his furnaces dividing asunder; till   500
She separated stood before him, a lovely female, weeping.
Even Enitharmon separated outside, and his loins closed
And healed after the separation; his pains he soon forgot,
Lured by her beauty outside of himself in shadowy grief.
Two wills they had, two intellects, and not as in times of old.

Silent they wandered hand in hand, like two infants
    wand'ring,
From Enion in the deserts, terrified at each other's beauty,
Envying each other yet desiring, in all-devouring love,
Repelling weeping Enion, blind and age-bent, into the
    fourfold
Deserts. Los first broke silence and began to utter his love: 510

'O lovely Enitharmon, I behold thy graceful forms
Moving beside me, till intoxicated with the woven labyrinth
Of beauty and perfection my wild fibres shoot in veins
Of blood through all my nervous limbs. Soon overgrown in
    roots
I shall be closed from thy sight. Seize therefore in thy hand
The small fibres as they shoot around me, draw out in pity,
And let them run on the winds of thy bosom. I will fix them
With pulsations; we will divide them into sons and
    daughters,
To live in thy bosom's translucence as in an eternal morning.'

Enitharmon answered: 'No! I will seize thy fibres and weave   520
Them: not as thou wilt but as I will. For I will create
A round womb beneath my bosom, lest I also be overwoven
With love. Be thou assured I never will be thy slave.
Let Man's delight be love, but Woman's delight be pride.
In Eden our loves were the same; here they are opposite.

I have loves of my own; I will weave them in Albion's
    Spectre.
Cast thou in Jerusalem's shadows thy loves: silk of liquid
Rubies, jacinths, crysolites, issuing from thy furnaces. While
Jerusalem divides thy care, whilst thou carest for Jerusalem,
Know that I never will be thine. Also thou hidest Vala;   530
From her these fibres shoot to shut me in a grave.
You are Albion's victim; he has set his daughter in your
    path.'

Los answered, sighing like the bellows of his furnaces:

'I care not! The swing of my hammer shall measure the
    starry round.
When in Eternity man converses with man they enter
Into each other's bosom (which are universes of delight)
In mutual interchange, and first their Emanations meet,
Surrounded by their children. If they embrace and
    commingle
The human fourfold forms mingle also in thunders of
    intellect,
But, if the Emanations mingle not, with storms and agitations   540
Of earthquakes and consuming fires they roll apart in fear.
For man cannot unite with man but by their emanations,
Which stand, both male and female, at the gates of each
    humanity.
How then can I ever again be united as man with man
While thou, my Emanation, refusest my fibres of dominion?
When souls mingle and join through all the fibres of
    brotherhood,
Can there be any secret joy on earth greater than this?'

Enitharmon answered: 'This is Woman's world, nor need
    she any
Spectre to defend her from Man. I will create secret places,
And the masculine names of the places Merlin and Arthur.   550
A triple female tabernacle for moral law I weave,
That he who loves Jesus may loathe, terrified, female love,
Till God himself become a male subservient to the female.'

She spoke in scorn and jealousy, alternate torments, and
So speaking she sat down on Sussex shore, singing lulling
Cadences and playing in sweet intoxication among the
   glistening
Fibres of Los, sending them over the ocean eastward into
The realms of dark death. O perverse to thyself; contrarious
To thy own purposes. For when she began to weave,
Shooting out in sweet pleasure, her bosom in milky love   560
Flowed into the aching fibres of Los—yet contending
   against him
In pride, sending his fibres over to her objects of jealousy
In the little lovely allegoric night of Albion's daughters,
Which stretched abroad, expanding east and west and north
   and south
Through all the world of Erin and of Los and all their
   children.

A sullen smile broke from the Spectre in mockery and scorn,
Knowing himself the author of their divisions and
   shrinkings. Gratified
At their contentions, he wiped his tears, he washed his
   visage.

'The man who respects woman shall be despised by Woman,
And deadly cunning and mean abjectness only shall enjoy
   them.   570
For I will make their places of joy and love excrementitious,
Continually building, continually destroying in family feuds.
While you are under the dominion of a jealous female,
Unpermanent for ever because of love and jealousy,
You shall want all the minute particulars of life.'

Thus joyed the Spectre in the dusky fires of Los's forge,
   eyeing
Enitharmon, who at her shining looms sings lulling
   cadences;
While Los stood at his anvil in wrath, the victim of their love
And hate, dividing the space of love with brazen compasses
In Golgonooza, and in Udan-Adan, and in Entuthon of
   Urizen.   580

The blow of his hammer is justice, the swing of his hammer
    mercy;
The force of Los's hammer is eternal forgiveness. But
His rage or his mildness were vain; she scattered his love on
    the wind
Eastward into her own centre, creating the female womb
In mild Jerusalem around the Lamb of God. Loud howl
The furnaces of Los! Loud roll the wheels of Enitharmon.
The four Zoas in all their faded majesty burst out in fury
And fire. Jerusalem took the cup which foamed in Vala's hand
Like the red sun upon the mountains in the bloody day,
Upon the hermaphroditic winepresses of love and wrath.   590

Though divided by the cross and nails and thorns and spear
In cruelties of Rahab and Tirzah, permanent endure
A terrible indefinite hermaphroditic form,
A winepress of love and wrath, double, hermaphroditic,
Twelvefold in allegoric pomp, in selfish holiness:
The Pharisaion, the Grammateis, the Presbyterion,
The Archiereus, the Iereus, the Saddusaion, double
Each withoutside of the other, covering eastern heaven.

Thus was the covering cherub revealed, majestic image
Of selfhood, body put off, the Antichrist accursed,   600
Covered with precious stones. A human dragon terrible
And bright stretched over Europe and Asia gorgeous,
In three nights he devoured the rejected corse of death.

His head dark, deadly, in its brain encloses a reflection
Of Eden all-perverted, Egypt on the Gihon many-tongued
And many-mouthed, Ethiopia, Lybia, the Sea of Rephaim.
Minute particulars in slavery I behold among the brick-kilns
Disorganized, and there is Pharaoh in his iron court,
And the dragon of the river, and the furnaces of iron.

Outwoven from Thames and Tweed and Severn, awful
    streams,   610
Twelve ridges of stone frown over all the earth in tyrant pride,
Frown over each river, stupendous works of Albion's Druid
    sons.
And Albion's forests of oaks covered the earth from pole to
    pole.

His bosom wide reflects Moab and Ammon, on the River
Pison, since called Arnon. There is Heshbon beautiful,
The rocks of Rabbath on the Arnon, and the fish-pools of
    Heshbon
Whose currents flow into the Dead Sea by Sodom and
    Gomorrah.
Above his head high-arching wings, black, filled with eyes,
Spring upon iron sinews from the *scapulae* and *os humeri*;
There Israel in bondage to his generalizing gods,   620
Molech and Chemosh. And in his left breast in Philistia,
In Druid temples over the whole earth with victim's sacrifice,
From Gaza to Damascus, Tyre and Sidon, and the gods
Of Javan, through the isles of Grecia and all Europe's kings.
Where Hiddekel pursues his course among the rocks
Two wings spring from his ribs of brass, starry, black as night,
But translucent their blackness as the dazzling of gems.

His loins enclose Babylon on Euphrates beautiful,
And Rome in sweet Hesperia; there Israel scattered abroad
In martyrdoms and slavery I behold. Ah, vision of sorrow!   630
Enclosed by eyeless wings, glowing with fire as the iron
Heated in the smith's forge, but cold the wind of their dread
    fury.

But in the midst of a devouring stomach, Jerusalem
Hidden within the covering cherub as in a tabernacle
Of threefold workmanship, in allegoric delusion and woe.
There the seven Kings of Canaan and five Baalim of
    Philistia,
Sihon and Og, the Anakim and Emim, Nephilim and
    Gibborim,
From Babylon to Rome. And the wings spread from Japan,
Where the Red Sea terminates the world of generation and
    death,
To Ireland's farthest rocks where giants builded their
    causeway   640
Into the Sea of Rephaim; but the sea o'erwhelmed them all.

A double female now appeared within the tabernacle:
Religion hid in war, a dragon red and hidden harlot—
Each within other, but, without, a warlike mighty one

Of dreadful power, sitting upon Horeb pondering dire
And mighty preparations, mustering multitudes innumerable
Of warlike sons among the sands of Midian and Aram.
For multitudes of those who sleep in Alla descend,
Lured by his warlike symphonies of tabret, pipe and harp,
Burst the bottoms of the graves and funeral arks of Beulah.   650
Wandering in that unknown night beyond the silent grave,
They become one with the Antichrist and are absorbed in
   him.
The feminine separates from the masculine and both from
   Man,
Ceasing to be his Emanations, life to themselves assuming.
And while they circumscribe his brain, and while they
   circumscribe
His heart, and while they circumscribe his loins, a veil and net
Of veins of red blood grows around them like a scarlet robe,
Covering them from the sight of Man like the woven veil of
   sleep;
Such as the flowers of Beulah weave to be their funeral
   mantles,
But dark, opaque, tender to touch, and painful, and agonizing   660
To the embrace of love and to the mingling of soft fibres
Of tender affection—that no more the masculine mingles
With the feminine, but the sublime is shut out from the
   pathos
In howling torment, to build stone walls of separation,
   compelling
The pathos to weave curtains of hiding secrecy from the
   torment.

Bowen and Conwenna stood on Skiddaw, cutting the fibres
Of Benjamin from Chester's river. Loud the river, loud the
   Mersey
And the Ribble thunder into the Irish sea, as the twelve sons
Of Albion drank and imbibed the life and eternal form of
   Luvah.
Cheshire and Lancashire and Westmorland groan in anguish;   670
As they cut the fibres from the rivers he sears them with hot
Iron of his forge, and fixes them into bones of chalk and rock.
Conwenna sat above; with solemn cadences she drew
Fibres of life out from the bones into her golden loom.

Hand had his furnace on Highgate's heights, and it reached
To Brockley Hills across the Thames; he with double
   Boadicea
In cruel pride cut Reuben apart from the hills of Surrey,
Commingling with Luvah and with the sepulchre of Luvah.
For the male is a furnace of beryl; the female is a golden
   loom.

Los cries: 'No individual ought to appropriate to himself,   680
Or to his Emanation, any of the universal characteristics
Of David or of Eve, of the woman or of the Lord,
Of Reuben or of Benjamin, of Joseph or Judah or Levi.
Those who dare appropriate to themselves universal
   attributes
Are the blasphemous selfhoods, and must be broken asunder.
A vegetated Christ and a virgin Eve are the hermaphroditic
Blasphemy; by his maternal birth he is that evil one,
And his maternal humanity must be put off eternally,
Lest the sexual generation swallow up regeneration.
Come, Lord Jesus; take on thee the Satanic body of holiness.'   690

So Los cried in the valleys of Middlesex in the spirit of
   prophecy,
While in selfhood Hand and Hyle and Bowen and Skofield
   appropriate
The divine names, seeking to vegetate the Divine Vision
In a corporeal and ever-dying vegetation and corruption.
Mingling with Luvah in one, they become one great Satan.

Loud scream the daughters of Albion beneath the tongs and
   hammer;
Dolorous are their lamentations in the burning forge.
They drink Reuben and Benjamin as the iron drinks the fire;
They are red hot with cruelty, raving along the banks of
   Thames
And on Tyburn's brook among the howling victims, in
   loveliness.   700
While Hand and Hyle condense the little ones and erect them
   into
A mighty temple even to the stars; but they vegetate
Beneath Los's hammer, that life may not be blotted out.

For Los said: 'When the individual appropriates universality
He divides into male and female; and when the male and
    female
Appropriate individuality, they become an eternal death.
Hermaphroditic worshippers of a god of cruelty and law!
Your slaves and captives you compel to worship a god of
    mercy.
These are the demonstrations of Los, and the blows of my
    mighty hammer.'

So Los spoke. And the giants of Albion, terrified and
    ashamed   710
With Los's thunderous words, began to build trembling
    rocking-stones,
For his words roll in thunders and lightnings among the
    temples;
Terrified, rocking to and fro upon the earth, and sometimes
Resting in a circle in Maldon or in Strathness or Jura,
Plotting to devour Albion and Los the friend of Albion,
Denying in private, mocking God and eternal life, and in
    public
Collusion calling themselves Deists, worshipping the
    maternal
Humanity, calling it Nature, and Natural Religion.

But still the thunder of Los peals loud, and thus the
    thunder's cry:
'These beautiful witchcrafts of Albion are gratified by cruelty.   720
It is easier to forgive an enemy than to forgive a friend.
The man who permits you to injure him deserves your
    vengeance;
He also will receive it. Go, Spectre, obey my most secret
    desire,
Which thou knowest without my speaking. Go to these
    fiends of righteousness,
Tell them to obey their humanities, and not pretend holiness
When they are murderers. As far as my hammer and anvil
    permit
Go, tell them that the worship of God is honouring his gifts
In other men, and loving the greatest men best, each
    according

To his genius, which is the Holy Ghost in Man. There is no
  other
God than that God who is the intellectual fountain of
  humanity.   730
He who envies or calumniates, which is murder and cruelty,
Murders the Holy One. Go, tell them this and overthrow
  their cup,
Their bread, their altar table, their incense and their oath,
Their marriage and their baptism, their burial and
  consecration.
I have tried to make friends by corporeal gifts but have only
Made enemies; I never made friends but by spiritual gifts,
By severe contentions of friendship and the burning fire of
  thought.
He who would see the Divinity must see him in his children:
One first, in friendship and love; then a divine family; and in
  the midst
Jesus will appear. So he who wishes to see a vision, a perfect
  whole,   740
Must see it in its minute particulars, organized: and not as
  thou,
O fiend of righteousness, pretendest. Thine is a disorganized
And snowy cloud, brooder of tempest and destructive war.
You smile with pomp and rigour; you talk of benevolence
  and virtue.
I act with benevolence and virtue and get murdered time
  after time.
You accumulate particulars, and murder by analysing, that
  you
May take the aggregate. And you call the aggregate Moral
  Law;
And you call that swelled and bloated form, a Minute
  Particular.
But general forms have their vitality in particulars; and every
Particular is a man, a divine member of the divine Jesus.'   750

So Los cried at his anvil, in the horrible darkness weeping.

The Spectre builded stupendous works, taking the starry
  heavens
Like to a curtain and folding them according to his will,

Repeating the Smaragdine Table of Hermes to draw Los down
Into the indefinite, refusing to believe without demonstration.
Los reads the stars of Albion; the Spectre reads the voids
Between the stars, among the arches of Albion's tomb
   sublime:
Rolling the sea in rocky paths, forming Leviathan
And Behemoth, the war by sea enormous and the war
By land astounding, erecting pillars in the deepest hell   760
To reach the heavenly arches. Los beheld undaunted; furious
His heaved hammer. He swung it round and at one blow,
In unpitying ruin driving down the pyramids of pride,
Smiting the Spectre on his anvil, and the integuments of his
   eye
And ear unbinding in dire pain, with many blows
Of strict severity self-subduing, and with many tears
   labouring.

Then he sent forth the Spectre; all his pyramids were grains
Of sand, and his pillars dust on the fly's wing, and his starry
Heavens a moth of gold and silver mocking his anxious grasp.
Thus Los altered his Spectre, and every ratio of his reason   770
He altered time after time, with dire pain and many tears,
Till he had completely divided him into a separate space.

Terrified Los sat to behold, trembling and weeping and
   howling.
'I care not whether a man is good or evil; all that I care
Is whether he is a wise man or a fool. Go! Put off holiness
And put on intellect, or my thundrous hammer shall drive thee
To wrath which thou condemnest, till thou obey my voice.'

So Los terrified cries, trembling and weeping and howling!
   'Beholding,
What do I see? The Briton, Saxon, Roman, Norman
   amalgamating
In my furnaces into one nation, the English, and taking refuge   780
In the loins of Albion; the Canaanite united with the fugitive
Hebrew, whom she divided into twelve and sold into Egypt,
Then scattered the Egyptian and Hebrew to the four winds.
This sinful nation created in our furnaces and looms is
   Albion.'

So Los spoke. Enitharmon answered in great terror in
    Lambeth's vale:
'The poet's song draws to its period, and Enitharmon is no
    more.
For if he be that Albion I can never weave him in my looms;
But when he touches the first fibrous thread, like filmy dew
My looms will be no more and I, annihilate, vanish for ever.
Then thou wilt create another female according to thy will.'   790

Los answered swift as the shuttle of gold: 'Sexes must vanish
    and cease
To be, when Albion arises from his dread repose, O lovely
    Enitharmon.
When all their crimes, their punishments, their accusations
    of sin,
All their jealousies, revenges, murders, hidings of cruelty in
    deceit
Appear only in the outward spheres of visionary space and
    time,
In the shadows of possibility by mutual forgiveness for
    evermore,
And in the vision and in the prophecy. That we may foresee
    and avoid
The terrors of creation and redemption and judgement,
    beholding them
Displayed in the emanative visions of Canaan in Jerusalem
    and in Shiloh,
And in the shadows of remembrance, and in the chaos of the
    spectre,   800
Amalek, Edom, Egypt, Moab, Ammon, Asshur, Philistia,
    around Jerusalem:
Where the Druids reared their rocky circles to make
    permanent remembrance
Of sin, and the Tree of Good and Evil sprang from the rocky
    circle and snake
Of the Druid, along the Valley of Rephaim from Camberwell
    to Golgotha,
And framed the Mundane Shell, cavernous in length,
    breadth and height.'

Enitharmon heard. She raised her head like the mild moon:

'O Rintrah! O Palamabron! What are your dire and awful
purposes?

Enitharmon's name is nothing before you; you forget all my
love!

The mother's love of obedience is forgotten, and you seek a
love

Of the pride of dominion that will divorce Ocalythron and
Elynittria   810

Upon East Moor in Derbyshire and along the valleys of
Cheviot.

Could you love me, Rintrah, if you pride not in my love,

As Reuben found mandrakes in the field and gave them to
his mother?

Pride meets with pride upon the mountains in the stormy day,

In that terrible day of Rintrah's plough and of Satan's
driving the team.

Ah! then I heard my little ones weeping along the valley.

Ah! then I saw my beloved ones fleeing from my tent.

Merlin was like thee, Rintrah, among the giants of Albion;

Judah was like Palamabron. O Simeon! O Levi! ye fled away.

How can I hear my little ones weeping along the valley,   820

Or how upon the distant hills see my beloved's tents?'

Then Los again took up his speech as Enitharmon ceased:

'Fear not, my sons, this waking death; he is become one with
me.

Behold him here! We shall not die! We shall be united in
Jesus.

Will you suffer this Satan, this body of doubt that seems but
is not,

To occupy the very threshold of eternal life? If Bacon,
Newton, Locke

Deny a conscience in Man, and the communion of saints
and angels,

Contemning the Divine Vision and fruition, worshipping the
Deus

Of the heathen, the god of this world, and the goddess Nature,

Mystery, Babylon the Great, the Druid dragon and hidden
harlot,   830

Is it not that signal of the morning which was told us in the
beginning?'

Thus they converse upon Mam-Tor; the graves thunder
under their feet.

Albion cold lays on his rock; storms and snows beat round him,
Beneath the furnaces and the starry wheels and the immortal
tomb.
Howling winds cover him; roaring seas dash furious against him.
In the deep darkness broad lightnings glare, long thunders roll.

The weeds of death enwrap his hands and feet, blown
incessant
And washed incessant by the for-ever restless sea-waves
foaming abroad
Upon the white rock. England, a female shadow, as deadly
damps
Of the mines of Cornwall and Derbyshire, lays upon his
bosom heavy,   840
Moved by the wind in volumes of thick cloud, returning,
folding round
His loins and bosom, unremovable by swelling storms and
loud rending
Of enraged thunders. Around them the starry wheels of
their giant sons
Revolve; and over them the furnaces of Los, and the
immortal tomb around,
Erin sitting in the tomb to watch them unceasing night and
day.
And the body of Albion was closed apart from all nations.

Over them the famished eagle screams on bony wings, and
around
Them howls the wolf of famine; deep heaves the ocean
black, thundering
Around the wormy garments of Albion, then pausing in
deathlike silence.

Time was finished! The breath divine breathed over Albion   850
Beneath the furnaces and starry wheels and in the immortal
tomb;
And England, who is Britannia, awoke from death on
Albion's bosom.
She awoke pale and cold; she fainted seven times on the
body of Albion.

'Oh piteous sleep, oh piteous dream! O God, O God, awake. I have slain

In dreams of chastity and moral law; I have murdered Albion! Ah!

In Stonehenge and on London Stone and in the oak groves of Maldon

I have slain him in my sleep with the knife of the Druid. Oh England,

O all ye nations of the earth, behold ye the jealous wife.

The eagle and the wolf and monkey and owl and the king and priest were there.'

Her voice pierced Albion's clay-cold ear; he moved upon the rock. 860

The breath divine went forth upon the morning hills. Albion moved

Upon the rock; he opened his eyelids in pain. In pain he moved

His stony members; he saw England. Ah! shall the dead live again?

The breath divine went forth over the morning hills. Albion rose

In anger, the wrath of God breaking bright flaming on all sides around

His awful limbs. Into the heavens he walked, clothed in flames,

Loud thund'ring, with broad flashes of flaming lightning and pillars

Of fire, speaking the words of Eternity in human forms, in direful

Revolutions of action and passion, through the four elements on all sides

Surrounding his awful members. Thou seest the sun in heavy clouds 870

Struggling to rise above the mountains. In his burning hand

He takes his bow, then chooses out his arrows of flaming gold;

Murmuring the bowstring breathes with ardour! Clouds roll round the

Horns of the wide bow; loud sounding winds sport on the mountain brows

Compelling Urizen to his furrow, and Tharmas to his
    sheepfold,
And Luvah to his loom. Urthona he beheld mighty labouring
    at
His anvil, in the great Spectre Los unwearied labouring and
    weeping.
Therefore the sons of Eden praise Urthona's Spectre in songs:
Because he kept the Divine Vision in time of trouble.

As the sun and moon lead forward the visions of Heaven and
    Earth,   880
England, who is Britannia, entered Albion's bosom rejoicing,
Rejoicing in his indignation, adoring his wrathful rebuke.
She who adores not your frowns will only loathe your smiles.

Then Jesus appeared standing by Albion, as the good
    shepherd
By the lost sheep that he hath found; and Albion knew that it
Was the Lord, the universal humanity. And Albion saw his
    form,
A man, and they conversed as man with man, in ages of
    eternity.
And the divine appearance was the likeness and similitude of
    Los.

Albion said: 'O Lord, what can I do? My selfhood cruel
Marches against thee deceitful from Sinai and from Edom   890
Into the wilderness of Judah to meet thee in his pride.
I behold the visions of my deadly sleep of six thousand years
Dazzling around thy skirts like a serpent of precious stones
    and gold.
I know it is my self, O my divine creator and redeemer.'

Jesus replied: 'Fear not, Albion; unless I die thou canst not
    live.
But if I die I shall arise again and thou with me.
This is friendship and brotherhood; without it Man is not.'

So Jesus spoke. The covering cherub coming on in darkness
Overshadowed them and Jesus said: 'Thus do men in
    Eternity,
One for another to put off by forgiveness every sin.'   900

Albion replied: 'Cannot Man exist without mysterious
Offering of self for another? Is this friendship and
   brotherhood?
I see thee in the likeness and similitude of Los my friend.'

Jesus said: 'Wouldest thou love one who never died
For thee, or ever die for one who had not died for thee?
And if God dieth not for Man and giveth not himself
Eternally for Man, Man could not exist. For Man is love,
As God is love. Every kindness to another is a little death
In the divine image, nor can Man exist but by brotherhood.'

So saying the cloud overshadowing divided them asunder.   910
Albion stood in terror, not for himself but for his friend
Divine; and self was lost in the contemplation of faith,
And wonder at the divince mercy and at Los's sublime
   honour.

'Do I sleep amidst danger to friends? O my cities and
   counties!
Do you sleep? Rouse up, rouse up! Eternal death is abroad.'

So Albion spoke and threw himself into the furnaces of
   affliction.
All was a vision, all a dream. The furnaces became
Fountains of living waters flowing from the Humanity
   Divine.
And all the cities of Albion rose from their slumbers, and all
The sons and daughters of Albion on soft clouds waking
   from sleep.   920
Soon all around remote the heavens burnt with flaming fires,
And Urizen and Luvah and Tharmas and Urthona arose
   into
Albion's bosom. Then Albion stood before Jesus in the
   clouds
Of Heaven, fourfold among the visions of God in Eternity.

'Awake! Awake, Jerusalem! O lovely Emanation of Albion,
Awake and overspread all nations as in ancient time.
For lo! the night of death is past and the eternal day
Appears upon our hills. Awake Jerusalem, and come away.'

So spake the vision of Albion, and in him so spake in my
   hearing
The universal father. Then Albion stretched his hand into
   infinitude   930
And took his bow. Fourfold the vision: for bright beaming
   Urizen
Laid his hand on the south and took a breathing bow of
   carved gold;
Luvah his hand stretched to the east and bore a silver bow
   bright shining;
Tharmas westward a bow of brass pure flaming, richly
   wrought;
Urthona northward in thick storms a bow of iron terrible
   thundering.

And the bow is a male and female, and the quiver of the
   arrows of love
Are the children of this bow, a bow of mercy and
   loving-kindness, laying
Open the hidden heart in wars of mutual benevolence, wars
   of love;
And the hand of Man grasps firm between the male and
   female loves.
And he clothed himself in bow and arrows in awful state,
   fourfold   940
In the midst of his twenty-eight cities, each with his bow
   breathing.

Then each an arrow flaming from his quiver fitted carefully.
They drew fourfold the unreprovable string, bending
   through the wide heavens
The horned bow fourfold. Loud sounding flew the flaming
   arrow fourfold.

Murmuring the bow-string breathes with ardour. Clouds roll
   round the horns
Of the wide bow; loud sounding winds sport on the
   mountain's brows.
The Druid Spectre was annihilate, loud thund'ring,
   rejoicing, terrific vanishing,
Fourfold annihilation. And at the clangour of the arrows of
   intellect

The innumerable chariots of the Almighty appeared in
    Heaven,
And Bacon and Newton and Locke, and Milton and
    Shakespeare and Chaucer,   950
A sun of blood-red wrath surrounding Heaven on all sides
    around,
Glorious, incomprehensible by mortal man; and each chariot
    was sexual threefold.

And every man stood fourfold. Each four faces had: one to
    the west,
One toward the east, one to the south, one to the north. The
    horses fourfold.
And the dim chaos brightened beneath, above, around! Eyed
    as the peacock,
According to the human nerves of sensation, the four rivers
    of the water of life.

South stood the nerves of the eye. East in rivers of bliss the
    nerves of the
Expansive nostrils. West flowed the parent sense, the tongue.
    North stood
The labyrinthine ear. Circumscribing and circumcising, the
    excrementitious
Husk and covering into vacuum evaporating, revealing the
    lineaments of Man,   960
Driving outward the body of death in an eternal death and
    resurrection,
Awaking it to life among the flowers of Beulah, rejoicing in
    unity
In the four senses, in the outline, the circumference and
    form, for ever
In forgiveness of sins which is self-annihilation. It is the
    covenant of Jehovah.

The four living creatures, chariots of Humanity Divine
    incomprehensible,
In beautiful paradises expand. These are the four rivers of
    paradise
And the four faces of humanity fronting the four cardinal
    points
Of Heaven, going forward, forward, irresistible from eternity
    to eternity.

And they conversed together in visionary forms dramatic,
    which bright
Redounded from their tongues in thunderous majesty, in
    visions,   970
In new expanses, creating exemplars of memory and of
    intellect,
Creating space, creating time according to the wonders divine
Of human imagination, throughout all the three regions
    immense
Of childhood, manhood and old age; and the all-tremendous
    unfathomable non-ens
Of death was seen in regenerations terrific or complacent,
    varying
According to the subject of discourse. And every word and
    every character
Was human, according to the expansion or contraction, the
    translucence or
Opaquenes of nervous fibres. Such was the variation of time
    and space,
Which vary according as the organs of perception vary, and
    they walked
To and fro in Eternity as one man, reflecting each in each
    and clearly seen   980
And seeing, according to fitness and order. And I heard
    Jehovah speak
Terrific from his holy place and saw the words of the mutual
    covenant divine
On chariots of gold and jewels, with living creatures starry
    and flaming
With every colour: lion, tiger, horse, elephant, eagle, dove,
    fly, worm,
And the all-wondrous serpent clothed in gems and rich
    array, humanize
In the forgiveness of sins according to the covenant of
    Jehovah. They cry:

'Where is the covenant of Priam, the moral virtues of the
    heathen?
Where is the Tree of Good and Evil that rooted beneath the
    cruel heel
Of Albion's Spectre, the patriarch Druid? Where are all his
    human sacrifices

For sin, in war and in the Druid temples of the accuser of
   sin, beneath   990
The oak groves of Albion that covered the whole earth
   beneath his Spectre?
Where are the kingdoms of the world and all their glory that
   grew on desolation,
The fruit of Albion's poverty-tree, when the triple-headed
   Gog-Magog giant
Of Albion taxed the nations into desolation, and then gave
   the spectrous oath?'

Such is the cry from all the Earth, from the living creatures
   of the Earth
And from the great city of Golgonooza in the shadowy
   generation,
And from the thirty-two nations of the Earth among the
   living creatures,

All human forms identified, even tree, metal, earth and
   stone. All
Human forms identified, living, going forth, and returning
   wearied
Into the planetary lives of years, months, days and hours,
   reposing   1000
And then awaking into his bosom in the life of immortality.

And I heard the name of their Emanations; they are named
   Jerusalem.
The End of the Song of Jerusalem

The Everlasting Gospel (c.1818)

If moral virtue was Christianity
Christ's pretensions were all vanity,
And Caiaphas and Pilate men
Praiseworthy, and the lion's den,
And not the sheepfold, allegories
Of God and Heaven and their glories.
The moral Christian is the cause

Of the unbeliever and his laws.
The Roman virtues, warlike fame,
Take Jesus' and Jehovah's name.   10
For what is Antichrist, but those
Who against sinners Heaven close
With iron bars in virtuous state,
And Rhadamanthus at the gate?

What can this Gospel of Jesus be?
What life and immortality?
What was it that he brought to light
That Plato and Cicero did not write?
The heathen deities wrote them all,
These moral virtues, great and small.   20
What is the accusation of sin
But moral virtues' deadly gin?
The moral virtues in their pride
Did o'er the world triumphant ride
In wars and sacrifice for sin,
And souls to Hell ran trooping in—
The accuser, holy God of all
This pharisaic worldly ball,
Amidst them in his glory beams
Upon the rivers and the streams.   30
Then Jesus rose and said to me,
'Thy sins are all forgiven thee.'
Loud Pilate howled, loud Caiaphas yelled
When they the Gospel light beheld.
It was when Jesus said to me,
'Thy sins are all forgiven thee'.
The Christian trumpets loud proclaim
Through all the world in Jesus' name
Mutual forgiveness of each vice,
And oped the gates of Paradise.   40
The moral virtues in great fear
Formed the cross and nails and spear,
And the accuser standing by
Cried out 'Crucify, crucify.
Our moral virtues ne'er can be,
Nor warlike pomp and majesty,
For moral virtues all begin

In the accusations of sin,
And all the heroic virtues end
In destroying the sinners' friend.   50
Am I not Lucifer the Great,
And you my daughters in great state,
The fruit of my mysterious Tree
Of Good and Evil, and misery,
And death, and Hell, which now begin
On everyone who forgives sin?'

Was Jesus born of a virgin pure
With narrow soul and looks demure?
If he intended to take on sin
The mother should an harlot been,   60
Just such a one as Magdalen
With seven devils in her pen.
Or were Jew virgins still more cursed,
And more sucking devils nursed?
Or what was it which he took on
That he might bring salvation?
A body subject to be tempted,
From neither pain nor grief exempted,
Or such a body as might not feel
The passions that with sinners deal?   70
Yes, but they say he never fell;
Ask Caiaphas, for he can tell:
'He mocked the Sabbath, and he mocked
The Sabbath's God, and he unlocked
The evil spirits from their shrines,
And turned fishermen to divines:
O'erturned the tent of secret sins,
And its golden cords and pins.
'Tis the bloody shrine of war
Pinned around from star to star,   80
Halls of justice, hating vice,
Where the devil combs his lice.
He turned the devils into swine
That he might tempt the Jews to dine
(Since which a pig has got a look
That for a Jew may be mistook).
"Obey your parents." What says he?

"Woman, what have I to do with thee?"
He scorned earth's parents, scorned earth's God,
And mocked the one and the other's rod;   90
His seventy disciples sent
Against religion and government.
They by the sword of justice fell,
And him their cruel murderer tell.
He left his father's trade to roam,
A wand'ring vagrant without home,
And thus he others' labour stole,
That he might live above control.
The publicans and harlots he
Selected for his company,   100
And from the adulteress turned away
God's righteous law, that lost its prey.'

Was Jesus gentle, or did he
Give any marks of gentility?
When twelve years old he ran away,
And left his parents in dismay.
When after three days' sorrow found,
Loud at Sinai's trumpet sound:
'No earthly parents I confess—
My heavenly Father's business.   110
Ye understand not what I say,
And angry, force me to obey.
Obedience is a duty then,
And favour gains with God and men.'
John from the wilderness loud cried;
Satan gloried in his pride.
'Come,' said Satan, 'come away;
I'll soon see if you'll obey.
John for disobedience bled,
But you can turn the stones to bread.   120
God's high king and God's high priest
Shall plant their glories in your breast,
If Caiaphas you will obey,
If Herod you, with bloody prey
Feed with the sacrifice, and be
Obedient, fall down, worship me.'
Thunders and lightnings broke around,

And Jesus' voice in thunder's sound:
'Thus I seize the spiritual prey.
Ye smiters with disease, make way.   130
I come your king and god to seize;
Is God a smiter with disease?'
The god of this world raged in vain.
He bound old Satan in his chain,
And, bursting forth, his furious ire
Became a chariot of fire.
Throughout the land he took his course,
And traced diseases to their source.
He cursed the scribe and Pharisee,
Trampling down hypocrisy.   140
Where'er his chariot took its way
There gates of death let in the day,
Broke down from every chain and bar,
And Satan in his spiritual war
Dragged at his chariot wheels. Loud howled
The god of this world; louder rolled
The chariot wheels, and louder still
His voice was heard from Zion's hill,
And in his hand the scourge shone bright.
He scourged the merchant Canaanite   150
From out the temple of his mind,
And in his body tight does bind
Satan and all his hellish crew.
And thus with wrath he did subdue
The serpent bulk of Nature's dross,
Till he had nailed it to the cross.
He took on sin in the virgin's womb
And put it off on the cross and tomb,
To be worshipped by the Church of Rome.

Did Jesus teach doubt, or did he   160
Give any lessons of philosophy,
Charge visionaries with deceiving
Or call men wise for not believing?

Was Jesus humble, or did he
Give any proofs of humility,
Boast of high things with humble tone

And give with charity a stone?
When the rich learned Pharisee
Came to consult him secretly,
Upon his heart with iron pen   170
He wrote: 'Ye must be born again.'
He was too proud to take a bribe.
He spoke with authority, not like a scribe.
He says with most consummate art:
'Follow me; I am meek and lowly of heart'—
As that is the only way to escape
The miser's net and the glutton's trap.
What can be done with such desperate fools
Who follow after the heathen schools
(I was standing by when Jesus died;   180
What I called 'humility' they called 'pride')?
He who loves his enemies betrays his friends;
This surely is not what Jesus intends,
But the sneaking pride of heroic schools
And the scribes' and Pharisees' virtuous rules.
For he acts with honest triumphant pride,
And this is the cause that Jesus died.
He did not die with Christian ease,
Asking pardon of his enemies.
If he had, Caiaphas would forgive;   190
Sneaking submission can always live.
He had only to say that God was the Devil,
And the Devil was God, like a Christian civil,
Mild Christian regrets to the Devil confess
For affronting him thrice in the wilderness—
He had soon been bloody Caesar's elf,
And at the last he would have been Ceasar himself—
Like Dr Priestley and Bacon and Newton.
Poor spiritual knowledge is not worth a button,
For thus the Gospel Sir Isaac confutes: 200
'God can only be known by his attributes,
And as for the indwelling of the Holy Ghost
Or of Christ and his Father—it's all a boast,
And pride and vanity of the imagination,
That disdains to follow this world's fashion.'
To teach doubt and experiment
Certainly was not what Christ meant.

What was he doing all that time
From twelve years old to manly prime?
Was he then idle, or the less   210
About his father's business?
Or was his wisdom held in scorn
Before his wrath began to burn
In miracles throughout the land
That quite unnerved Caiaphas' hand?
If he had been Antichrist, creeping Jesus,
He'd have done any thing to please us—
Gone sneaking into synagogues,
And not used the elders and priests like dogs,
But humble as a lamb or ass   220
Obeyed himself to Caiaphas.
God wants not Man to humble himself;
This is the trick of the ancient elf.
This is the race that Jesus ran:
Humble to God, haughty to Man,
Cursing the rulers before the people
Even to the Temple's highest steeple.
And when he humbled himself to God,
Then descended the cruel rod:
'If thou humblest thyself thou humblest me;   230
Thou also dwell'st in eternity.
Thou art a man. God is no more.
Thy own humanity learn to adore,
For that is my spirit of life.
Awake! Arise to spiritual strife,
And thy revenge abroad display
In terrors at the Last Judgement day.
God's mercy and long-suffering
Is but the sinner to judgement to bring.
Thou on the cross for them shalt pray,   240
And take revenge at the last day.'
Jesus replied, and thunders hurled:
'I never will pray for the world.
Once I did so when I prayed in the garden;
I wished to take with me a bodily pardon.'
Can that?—which was of woman born
In the absence of the morn,
When the soul fell into sleep

And archangels round it weep,
Shooting out against the light   250
Fibres of a deadly night,
Reasoning upon its own dark fiction
In doubt, which is self-contradiction.
Humility is only doubt,
And does the sun and moon blot out,
Rooting over with thorns and stems
The buried soul and all its gems
(This life's dim windows of the soul),
Distorts the heavens from pole to pole,
And leads you to believe a lie   260
When you see with, not through, the eye—
That was born in a night, to perish in a night,
When the soul slept in the beams of light.
Was Jesus chaste, or did he
Give any lessons of chastity?
The morning blushed fiery red;
Mary was found in adulterous bed.
Earth groaned beneath, and Heaven above
Trembled at discovery of love.
Jesus was sitting in Moses' chair;   270
They brought the trembling woman there.
'Moses commands she be stoned to death';
What was the sound of Jesus breath?
He laid his hand on Moses' law;
The ancient heavens in silent awe,
Writ with curses from pole to pole,
All away begans to roll.
The earth trembling and naked lay
In secret bed of mortal clay,
On Sinai felt the hand divine   280
Putting back the bloody shrine.
And she heard the breath of God
As she heard by Eden's flood.
'Good and evil are no more.
Sinai's trumpets, cease to roar!
Cease, finger of God, to write!
The heavens are not clean in thy sight;
Thou art good and thou alone,
Nor may the sinner cast one stone.

To be good only is to be   290
A devil, or else a Pharisee.
Thou angel of the presence divine,
That didst create this body of mine,
Wherefore hast thou writ these laws
And created Hell's dark jaws?
My presence I will take from thee:
A cold leper thou shalt be.
Though thou wast so pure and bright
That Heaven was impure in thy sight;
Though thy oath turned Heaven pale;   300
Though thy covenant built Hell's jail;
Though thou didst all to chaos roll
With the serpent for its soul—
Still the breath divine does move,
And the breath divine is love.
Mary, fear not; let me see
The seven devils that torment thee.
Hide not from my sight thy sin,
That forgiveness thou may'st win.
Has no man condemned thee?'   310
'No man, Lord!' 'Then what is he
Who shall accuse thee? Come ye forth,
Fallen fiends of heav'nly birth,
That have forgot your ancient love,
And driven away my trembling dove.
You shall bow before her feet,
You shall lick the dust for meat,
And though you cannot love, but hate,
Shall be beggars at love's gate.
What was thy love? Let me see it.   320
Was it love, or dark deceit?'
'Love too long from me has fled.
'Twas dark deceit to earn my bread.
'Twas covet, or 'twas custom, or
Some trifle not worth caring for:
That they may call a shame and sin
Love's temple that God dwelleth in,
And hide in secret hidden shrine
The naked human form divine,
And render that a lawless thing   330

On which the soul expands its wing.
But this, O Lord, this was my sin,
When first I let these devils in
In dark pretence to chastity:
Blaspheming love, blaspheming thee.
Thence rose secret adulteries,
And thence did covet also rise.
My sin thou hast forgiven me;
Canst thou forgive my blasphemy?
Canst thou return to this dark hell,   340
And in my burning bosom dwell,
And canst thou die, that I may live,
And canst thou pity, and forgive?'
Then rolled the shadowy man away
From the limbs of Jesus to make them his prey,
An ever-devouring appetite
Glittering with festering venoms bright,
Crying: 'Crucify this cause of distress,
Who don't keep the secrets of holiness!
All mental powers by diseases we bind,   350
But he heals the deaf and the dumb and the blind.
Whom God has afflicted for secret ends
He comforts and heals, and calls them friends.'
But when Jesus was crucified,
Then was perfected his glitt'ring pride;
In three nights he devoured his prey,
And still he devours the body of clay.
For dust and clay is the serpent's meat,
Which never was made for Man to eat.

I am sure this Jesus will not do,   360
Either for Englishman or Jew.
The vision of Christ that thou dost see
Is my vision's greatest enemy.
Thine has a great hook nose like thine;
Mine has a snub nose like to mine.
Thine is the friend of all mankind;
Mine speaks in parables to the blind.
Thine loves the same world that mine hates.
Thy Heaven-doors are my Hell-gates.
Socrates taught what Melitus   370

Loathed as a nation's bitterest curse,
And Caiaphas was, in his own mind,
A benefactor to mankind.
Both read the Bible day and night,
But thou read'st black where I read white.

From the annotations to Bishop Berkeley's Siris (c.1820)

Jesus considered imagination to be the real man and says, I will not leave you orphans and I will manifest to you. He says also the spiritual body, or angel, as little children always behold the face of the heavenly Father.

Harmony and proportion are qualities, and not things. The harmony and proportion of a horse are not the same with those of a bull. Everything has its own harmony and proportion, two inferior qualities in it. For its reality is its imaginative form.

Knowledge is not by deduction, but immediate by perception or sense at once. Christ addresses himself to the man, not to his reason. Plato did not bring life and immortality to light; Jesus only did this.

Jesus supposes everything to be evident to the child and to the poor and unlearned. Such is the Gospel.

The whole Bible is filled with imagination and visions from end to end, and not with moral virtues. That is the baseness of Plato, and the Greek and all warriors. The moral virtues are continual accusers of sin, and promote eternal wars and dominancy over others.

God is not a mathematical diagram.

The natural body is an obstruction to the soul or spiritual body.

Man is all imagination. God is Man and exists in us and we in him.

What Jesus came to remove was the heathen or platonic philosophy which blinds the eye of imagination, the real man.

LATE LYRICS

'Grown old in love'

Grown old in love from seven till seven times seven,
I oft have wished for Hell, for ease from Heaven.

'Madman I have been called'

Madman I have been called; fool they call thee.
I wonder which they envy, thee or me?

'He's a blockhead'

He's a blockhead who wants a proof of what he can't perceive,
And he's a fool who tries to make such a blockhead believe.

'I am no Homer's hero'

I am no Homer's hero you all know;
I profess not generosity to a foe.
My generosity is to my friends,
That for their friendship I may make amends.
The generous to enemies promotes their ends,
And becomes the enemy and betrayer of his friends.

'The angel that presided o'er my birth'

The angel that presided o'er my birth
Said: 'Little creature formed of joy and mirth,
Go love without the help of any king on earth.'

'Some men created for destruction'

Some men created for destruction come
Into the world, and make the world their home.
Be they as vile and base as e'er they can,
They'll still be called 'The World's' honest man.

Imitation of Pope: A Compliment to the Ladies

Wondrous the gods; more wondrous are the men;
More wondrous, wondrous still the cock and hen;
More wondrous still the table, stool, and chair—
But ah! more wondrous still the Charming Fair!

'If I e'er grow'

If I e'er grow to man's estate
Oh, give to me a woman's fate:
May I govern all, both great and small,
Have the last word, and take the wall.

'You don't believe'

You don't believe—I won't attempt to make ye.
You are asleep—I won't attempt to wake ye.
Sleep on, sleep on, while in your pleasant dreams
Of reason you may drink of life's clear streams
Reason and Newton, they are quite two things,
For so the swallow and the sparrow sings.
Reason says 'Miracle', Newton says 'Doubt'.
Aye, that's the way to make all Nature out:
Doubt, doubt, and don't believe without experiment.
That is the very thing that Jesus meant   10
When he said: 'Only believe.' Believe and try,
Try, try, and never mind the reason why.

'Great things are done'

Great things are done when men and mountains meet;
This is not done by jostling in the street.

'If you play a game of chance'

If you play a game of chance, know before you begin;
If you are benevolent you will never win.

'I rose up'

I rose up at the dawn of day:
'Get thee away, get thee away!
Pray'st thou for riches? Away, away!
This is the throne of Mammon grey.'

Said I: 'This sure is very odd;
I took it to be the throne of God.
For everything besides I have;
It is only for riches that I can crave.

'I have mental joy and mental health,
And mental friends and mental wealth;   10
I've a wife I love and that loves me;
I've all but riches bodily.

'I am in God's presence night and day,
And he never turns his face away.
The accuser of sins by my side does stand,
And he holds my money-bag in his hand.

'For my worldly things God makes him pay,
And he'd pay for more if to him I would pray.
And so you may do the worst you can do;
Be assured, Mr Devil, I won't pray to you.   20

'Then if for riches I must not pray,
God knows I little of prayers need say.
So as a church is known by its steeple,
If I pray it must be for other people.

'He says if I do not worship him for a God
I shall eat coarser food and go worse shod;
So as I don't value such things as these,
You must do, Mr Devil, just as God please.'

'Why was Cupid a boy'

Why was Cupid a boy,
And why a boy was he?
He should have been a girl,
For aught that I can see.

For he shoots with his bow
And the girl shoots with her eye,
And they both are merry and glad
And laugh when we do cry.

And to make Cupid a boy
Was the Cupid-girl's mocking plan;   10
For a boy can't interpret the thing
Till he is become a man.

And then he's so pierced with care,
And wounded with arrowy smarts,
That the whole business of his life
Is to pick out the heads of the darts.

'Twas the Greeks' love of war
Turned Love into a boy,
And woman into a statue of stone;
And away fled every joy.   20

'Great men and fools'

Great men and fools do often me inspire;
But the greater fool the greater liar.

To God

If you have formed a circle to go into,
Go into it yourself, and see how you would do.

'Since all the riches'

Since all the riches of this world
May be gifts from the Devil and earthly kings,
I should suspect that I worshipped the Devil
If I thanked my God for worldly things.

'To Chloe's breast'

To Chloe's breast young Cupid slyly stole,
But he crept in at Myra's pocket-hole.

'Anger and wrath'

Anger and wrath my bosom rends;
I thought them the errors of friends.
But all my limbs with warmth glow;
I find them the errors of the foe.

Notes

1 *To Spring.* The extremely free blank verse of this sonnet (and of parts of its companion poems) tends to fall into septenaries, or seven-stress lines, such as Blake used extensively in the prophetic writings.
ll. 2–3. *turn . . . western isle*: Dan. II: 18.

2 *To Autumn.* The ending imitates that of Milton's *Lycidas*, and both poems run through the annual cycle of vegetation.

To Winter

3 l. 16. *Mount Hecla*: either Hekla in Iceland or Hecla in the Western Isles.

To Morning

4 l. 8. *buskined.* Buskins (or half-boots) were sometimes associated with the goddess Diana, who is perhaps also alluded to in the motifs of virginity and hunting.

Song ('*I love the jocund dance*').

6 l. 11. *White or brown*: varieties of bread.

7 *Mad Song.* George Saintsbury (*A History of English Prosody* (London, 1910), iii. 11) judged that for 'pure verse-effect' there were 'few pieces in English to beat' this lyric. Analysing his texts in terms of traditional feet (and coping with irregularities under the rubric of 'substituted feet') Saintsbury believed that Blake in the lyrics and shorter prophetic books was the greatest English prosodist since Shakespeare.

9 *Song* ('*When early morn*'). To be read (unlike its preceding companion poem) as a satire on the kind of love that is happier with sexual deprivation than with sexual fulfilment.

10 *King Edward the Third.* This impressive short play, or commencement of a longer play, concerns the build-up to an ambiguous event in 14th-c. history, the Battle of Crécy (1346), which may be thought of as a great national triumph, or an appalling slaughter by a marauding invader. Blake has modelled his drama on the Tudor, particularly Shakespearian, chronicle play, and his source is the French chronicler Froissart.

Scene I

11 ll. 43–5. *revenge . . . Paris*: alludes to the execution of Olivier de Clisson and others by the French king in 1343.

l. 46. *here in Brittany.* Blake has confused Brittany (scene of Edward's 1343 campaign) with Normandy, which Edward chose for his 1346 excursion on Harcourt's advice, and which his armies thoroughly looted and terrorized.

ll. 47–9. In the context (of taking 'a just revenge') Edward means that Brittany too will now be devastated, but Blake is too sophisticated to allow an explicit reference to this to disturb the stately high-flown rhetoric of the king.

Scene III

14 l. 8. *Philip*: Philip of Valois, the French king.

15 ll. 56–7. *distemper . . . running away*. Edward was making his withdrawal eastwards across northern France when obliged to confront the French at Crécy.

16 l. 99. *gilt . . . blood: King John* II. i. 316.

17 l. 106. *not . . . parted with*: reminiscent of *Hamlet* II. ii. 216.

18 ll. 158–9. *a candle half burned out: 2 Henry IV* I. ii. 156.

ll. 159–60. *pig . . . pattle*: supposedly Welsh pronunciations of 'big' and 'battle'; a consonantal device employed also by Shakespeare for Fluellen in *Henry V*.

l. 175. *ribs of death: Comus* 562.

l. 176. *mortal dart*: as possessed by Milton's Death (*Paradise Lost* ii. 729).

ll. 184–5. *more . . . servants*: from the French epigram to the effect that no man is a hero to his valet.

Scene IV

22 *natural philosopher: As You Like It* III. ii. 33.

Scene V

23 l. 6. *wons*: dwells.

24 l. 43. The allegedly glorious occasion of Crécy left some 6,000 French dead; and England was soon to be ravaged by the Black Death. An anonymous account of Blake towards the end of his life has him enjoying a conversation with the spirit of Edward III, in which Blake challenged the latter on his 'butcheries'; the king is supposed to have replied 'what you and I call carnage is a trifle unworthy of notice . . . destroying five thousand men is doing them no real injury . . . their important parts being immortal, it is merely removing them from one state of existence to another' (G. E. Bentley, Jr., *Blake Records* (Oxford 1969), 299).

25 *Scene VI*. Blake's short play or dramatic fragment ends with a song on British liberty, anticipating the equally unusual conclusion to *Marriage of Heaven and Hell*.

l. 1. *Trojan Brutus*: draws on the legend that Britain was founded by survivors from Troy, under the leadership of Brutus.

25 l. 12. *navies black*: just as the Greek ships in the *Iliad* are consistently black.

ll. 15–16. Though here Albion is addressed as female it need not follow that Blake's later male figure, the giant Albion, undergoes a sex-change. It is orthodox to use feminine pronouns for countries, which is all Albion is seen as at this date (and the female pronouns in the last stanza of the song mainly refer to Liberty).

26 l. 51. *prevented*: anticipated.

28 *Song First by a Shepherd*. The second shepherd's song which was a companion is a close variant of 'Laughing Song' in *Innocence*.

[*The Cynic's First Song*]. Sung by 'Quid the Cynic' in Blake's prose satire 'An Island in the Moon'; the character represents Blake himself. Quid also sings a version of 'The Little Boy Lost' from *Songs of Innocence*.

l. 2. *yellow vest*. Vest, as in modern American English, means waistcoat. A yellow one was probably dandified.

29 l. 18. Presumably a reference to morbid dissection in medical research and teaching, a practice much distrusted in Blake's day.

l. 22. Vitamin-C deficiency and typhus. The ravages of these diseases in the navy were finally arrested in the 1780s by naval medical administrators.

30 [*Miss Gittipin's First Song*]. Miss Gittipin is also a character in 'An Island in the Moon', and has not been definitely identified. Her main trait is her hankering after fashionable London pleasures, though here she celebrates rustic festivities.

[*The Cynic's Second Song*].

31 l. 7. *fingerfooted*: with feet of finger-like slimness.

l. 23. *the pip*: a common disease of birds.

[*Obtuse Angle's Song*]. Uttered by another unidentified character in 'An Island in the Moon'. He also sings a version of 'Holy Thursday' from *Songs of Innocence*.

ll. 4–5. *South . . . Sherlock*. Richard South and William Sherlock, two Anglican divines of the latter 17th century, who engaged in a pamphlet controversy. South was celebrated as a preacher, and Sherlock for his *Practical Discourse Concerning Death* (1689).

l. 6. *Sutton*. Thomas Sutton, founder of the Charterhouse, a boys' school and home for the aged.

32 [*The Lawgiver's Song*]. Steelyard the Lawyer in 'An Island in the Moon' is Blake's friend Flaxman (see note to 'With happiness stretched across the hills' 47).

34 *All Religions are One*. Each of the paragraphs here and in *There is No Natural Religion* was printed by Blake on a separate sheet and decorated

with ornament and illustration, making this venture almost certainly the prototype for the publication of most of Blake's verse. Blake never bound up these sheets and, while the order followed here is that favoured by modern scholarship, many alternative orders are possible, limited chiefly by Blake's numbering of the majority of his propositions.

The voice . . . wilderness. The phrase is applied in all the gospels to John the Baptist, and derives from Isa. 40: 3.

Spirit of Prophecy: Rev. 19: 10.

35 *There is No Natural Religion* (1 and 2). 'Natural religion' is the standard 18th-c. term for any religious belief which relies on reason and our knowledge of the physical world, and not on revelation. Always allowing for the problem of ordering Blake's plates, in these two sequences he seems, characteristically, to be attacking such a position both from within and from without. The duality of this approach, in such a context, perhaps owes something to Hume's recently published *Dialogues Concerning Natural Religion* (1779). See also note to 'The Tiger'.

ratio. Blake's complicated use of this term includes a play on Latin *ratio* (reason) and here perhaps also the sense, current in the 18th century, of 'ration'.

37 *Tiriel*. Almost certainly Blake's first long mythological poem, *Tiriel* fulfils more obviously than any other of his works his ideal of dealing with universal, permanent psychological types and states. Tiriel has elements of Lear (dying king evicted by children whom he curses, and dependent on daughter), of Oedipus (blind, deposed king, also laying a curse on his offspring, and, led by daughter, finding a haven where he dies), of Odin (half-blind father of many sons who wanders disguised among men), and of other analogues (Moses, Theseus, etc.) mentioned in the notes. Blake's procedure is more or less to reverse the moral standing of his archetypes, and he depicts Tiriel in the last forty lines as recognizing the wickedness of all his past actions and beliefs. In the manner of several of the sources the narrative concerns a family: all the characters appear to be related to one another.

l. 1. *And*. As with several Blake texts, the effect of a fragment is deliberately sought by the device of incomplete syntax.   *Tiriel*. The name seems to have been invented by the alchemical writer Cornelius Agrippa, and denotes the spiritual agency common to earthly elements (sulphur and mercury) and a heavenly body (Mercury). The name would also have appealed to Blake for its Hebrew/Old Testament feel, and Tiriel is a patriarch in a pastoral society who has inherited a legacy of cruel laws.

l. 2. *Myratana*: perhaps derived from Jacob Bryant's alleged Amazonian queen of Mauretania, Myrina.

37 l. 21. *Serpents, not sons*: cf. *King Lear* IV. ii. 40, 'Tigers, not daughters'.

l. 24. *Heuxos, Yuva*: both probably Blake's coinages. The first is evidently Greek in inspiration. Yuva, given Blake's conventions for naming in this poem, may be a daughter.

38 l. 32. The dispute about burial outside gates and Myratana's Amazonian connection in a general way recall Theseus (burier of the seven against Thebes, husband of Hippolyta, and a major figure in *Oedipus at Colonus*).

l. 34. *Zazel*. Tiriel's brother also bears a Hebrew-sounding name (cf. Azazel: scapegoat) which is found in Cornelius Agrippa.

l. 55. *Har*: probably attractive to Blake as a Hebrew word rather than for its specific meaning (which is 'mountain').

l. 56. *Heva*: Blake's coinage, but evoking 'Eve'.

39 l. 57. *Mentha*. The name has a Greek form, and may be thought to combine 'Mnemosyne' (Memory) and 'Athena' (Wisdom). True to the convention that *Tiriel* is part of a larger body of narrative, Mnetha is introduced as if already known to the reader.

40 l. 88. *Bless thy poor eyes*: cf. *Lear* IV. i. 54.

41 l. 119. *did . . . thee*: reminiscent of Lear's delusion about Edgar in *Lear* III. iv.

42 l. 142. *Ijim*: a Hebrew name, found at Isa. 13: 22: but a plural, denoting something like 'jackals'.

44 l. 183. *Lotho*: Blake's Germanic-sounding coinage.

l. 197. Cf. *Paradise Lost* iv. 800 (of Satan).

l. 200. *so I'll keep him*. The second link between Ijim and a veteran of Troy. Like Aeneas carrying Anchises he bears his father on his shoulders; and he subdues a multiform enemy, as Menelaus subdues Proteus while returning to Sparta.

45 l. 215. *Matha*: presumably a mythological region or aspect of the world, rather than a person (in 'Ossian' the name is borne by a man).   *Orcus*: a Latin term for the underworld and its god.

l. 225. *centre*: of the earth.

l. 226. *pestilence . . . lakes*: cf. Lear's cursing of Regan (*Lear* II. iv. 167–9).

46 l. 242. *Hela*: a Norse name for the goddess of Hell.

l. 250. This climax to the tribulations brought down by Tiriel echoes the last of the punishments of Egypt wrought on behalf of Moses: the slaying of the first-born.

l. 253. *silent of the night*: 2 *Henry VI* I. iv. 19.

50 l. 339. *lack of mother's nourishment*. There was widespread antagonism in England in the late 18th century to the use of wet-nurses.

l. 346. *repugnant*: unwilling, resistant.

l. 350. *Returns my thirsty hissings*: cf. *Paradise Lost* x. 518.

From the annotations to Swedenborg's Divine Love and Wisdom. Allusions to Emanuel Swedenborg (1688–1772), the Swedish Christian mystic and founder of a millenarian sect, are scattered throughout Blake's work. He seems to have known at least five of Swedenborg's books, of which he annotated two, and he attended the first conference of the Swedenborgian Church in London in 1789, though he seems not to have become a member.

51 *The Book of Thel*. The poem is, most immediately, a text about death and the purpose of human life (and in this regard it is indebted to Job, even to the number of Thel's interlocutors). It also incorporates, more allusively, four ancient themes: a world that is parallel to ours and contains the elements of the latter in pre-existent forms; a fall from Paradise; sexual initiation; a descent to the underworld. Each has been emphasized at the expense of others by various critics, who disagree particularly over the meaning of the poem's closing events. Any single reading is simplistic.

Thel. In Greek this is the root element in the vocabulary of wishing and willing.

ll. 3–4. *wisdom ... bowl*: Eccles. 12: 6, Job 28: 12–15 are the most important of several biblical echoes, and golden bowls are part of the traditional altar-furniture of the tabernacle in the Bible.

l. 5. *Mne Seraphim*. Blake has taken a name from Cornelius Agrippa, 'Bne Seraphim', and made the first element look more Greek.

l. 8. *river of Adona*. Milton has a river Adonis (*Paradise Lost* i. 450). This is one of *Thel*'s links with Spenser's Garden of Adonis, but Blake has not wanted it to be emphatic. There is a very broad resemblance between Thel's lament and that of Spenser's Venus over the transience of the garden (*Faerie Queene* III. vi. 40).

52 l. 12. This imagery may derive from a passage in Swedenborg's *Wisdom of the Angels* which Blake ringed in his copy.

l. 13. *shadows in the water*: cf. Job 14: 2.

l. 16. *lay me down*: *Paradise Lost* x. 777. There are several parallels between Adam's state of mind just after the fall and Thel's. And Blake may be recalling James Hervey's *Meditations among the Tombs* (1746) i. 83, a work that influences *Thel* at several points.

l. 19. *walketh ... evening time*: cf. Gen. 3: 8.

l. 22. *gilded butterfly*: *Lear* V. iii. 13.

ll. 25–9. *Rejoice ... vales*. The whole encounter with the lily is indebted to Matt. 7: 28–33.

52 l. 36. *meekin*: probably Blake's dialect-like coinage, combining the senses of timid and weak.

53 l. 55. *Luvah*: Blake's equivalent of the Greek sun-god Helios, who is normally envisaged as a charioteer.

ll. 57–63. Blake's ingenious personification has water-vapour turning to dew and re-evaporating in the morning to descend as refreshing rain.

54 ll. 79–80. The worm, as the associate of death, should be stronger than a little infant (and, perhaps, more repellent).

l. 94. *crown . . . away*: Rev. 3: 11.

55 ll. 106–7. *given . . . return*. The Clod's role is broadly comparable to that of the Sybil in Book 6 of the *Aeneid*, enabling Aeneas' descent to the underworld.

l. 108. *northern*: probably because the north entrance to the cave of the nymphs (as described in Book 13 of the *Odyssey*) is for mortals, and the southern for gods. There was some tradition of interpreting this cave as an image of mortal life. Twin gates, and the 'porter' or gatekeeper, are further tenuous links with Spenser's Garden of Adonis.

l. 113. *list'ning*. The verb could still take a direct object in Blake's day.

56 *Songs of Innocence*. (For the significance of the title see the general note to *Songs of Experience* below.) The various orders in which Blake bound up different copies of the *Songs* offer his editor many choices in the matter, though not an unlimited number: there are some groupings that remain very constant. The order adopted here tries to be faithful to as many of these groupings as possible. It is slightly unusual in the three songs placed after 'Introduction' (two of which, moreover, were later transferred to *Experience*); but they are so arranged in the copy which Geoffrey Keynes regarded as personally preferred by Blake, and Keynes used this arrangement in his own editions. This way of starting the collection also makes good literary sense, establishing its predominant motif of the threatened/guarded child in night ('innocent' in the sense of unharmed) versus the free, joyful child in day.

Introduction

l. 18. Refers to the manufacture of ink or watercolour.

57 *The Little Girl Lost*. In all but one of the known copies of the twin volume, *Songs of Innocence and Experience*, this and its sequel 'Little Girl Found' are inserted among the Experience lyrics, and they are omitted from several of the known copies of the Innocence lyrics published separately. Blake's motif is essentially the traditional one of the child nurtured by animals. His affirmative treatment of the

child's experience is in keeping with the ancient belief that such children can have superior powers. There was a revived, rationalistic interest in the subject in the 18th century. The 16th-c. 'Babes in the Wood' and 'Children in the Wood' ballads had made the topic an occasion for sentimental fear; Blake would have been aware of the ballads through their appearance in Percy's *Reliques* and in chapbooks.

The Little Girl Found

59 ll. 18–19. *pressed With feet*. 'Pressed' probably has the sense 'hastened', but the whole phrase is just possibly a Latinism (see *Aeneid* vi. 197), and hence means 'halted'.

l. 30. *allay*. The intransitive sense would have been almost obsolete in Blake's day.

The Shepherd

61 l. 4. The phrase recalls many in the Psalms (e.g. 71: 8).

On Another's Sorrow

62 l. 22. cf. Rev. 7: 17, 21: 4.

l. 27. *man of woe*: cf. Isa. 53: 3.

64 *The Schoolboy*. In a few copies of the combined lyrics this poem is included among the Experience songs.

The Little Black Boy

65 l. 28. *be like him*: 1 John 3: 2.

66 *The Voice of the Ancient Bard*. In a few copies of the combined lyrics this poem is included among the Experience songs.

67 *Nurse's Song*. A version also appeared in 'An Island in the Moon' sung by Mrs Nannicantipot (a coarsely irreligious character) as her mother's (but the modern sense of 'nanny' existed in Blake's day, so she is perhaps herself a nurse).

68 *Holy Thursday*. Blake describes the combined service for all the charity schools in London which was held in St Paul's, generally on the first Thursday in May, from 1782 onwards.

l. 5. *multitude*. There may have been 6,000 children present at these services.

l. 6. *in companies they sit*: perhaps in groups according to their schools. But there is also an important echo of the feeding of the five thousand (Mark 6: 39).

l. 9. *mighty wind*. The Pentecostal wind is called a 'rushing mighty wind' (Acts 2: 2). Pentecost is celebrated at Whitsun, seven weeks after Easter.

The Divine Image

68 ll. 10–11: *Paradise Lost* 3: 44.

The Little Boy Lost

71 l. 8. The will o' the wisp traditionally lured men into swampy places, but Milton's adaptation of the idea to describe Satan (*Paradise Lost* ix. 634–42) is surely echoed here.

Night

72 ll. 42–3. Cf. Isa. 11: 6.

l. 45. *life's river*. Rev. 22: 1.

74 *The Marriage of Heaven and Hell*. Blake's title enshrines an impossible and absurd notion, which is nevertheless the kind of event which becomes possible in apocalypses. This tension informs the whole work. *The Marriage* attacks errors about Man's moral and spiritual life (especially those which interchange and confound the heavenly and hellish in him), but at another level does not admit the possibility of error, celebrating as it does the whole of existence in all its plurality and diversity (and in particular the diverse inner worlds of all living things). This is matched in the unusual tone of the work, at once vehement and affable (indeed comic), expressing both 'opposition' and 'friendship'. Much of it consists of 'Memorable Fancies', which are parodies of Swedenborg, yet also tributes to his visionary writings. For all its plainness of utterance, *The Marriage* is full of obliqueness and ambiguity.

The Argument. According to Alicia Oistriker, the leading modern authority on Blake's prosody, the first example of free verse in English.

l. 2. *swag*: droop down heavily.

l. 5. *vale of death*. The valley and its dangerous path are a reminiscence of Bunyan's Valley of the Shadow of Death, which in turn derives from Ps. 23: 4 and Jer. 2: 6.

l. 12. *bleached bones*. For this image see Ezek. 37.

l. 17. *serpent walks*. Many biblical commentators held that before the Fall the serpent had an upright posture.

thirty-three years. The time elapsed since 1757 (Blake's birth-year and Swedenborg's date for a Last Judgement), and also Christ's age at his crucifixion and resurrection.

folded up. John 20: 5–7 emphasizes the disposition of Christ's empty grave-clothes.

Edom: alludes to the eventual triumph of the dispossessed Esau over Jacob (see Gen. 27).

Isaiah xxxiv and xxxv. The imagery of the work's 'Argument' draws on the latter chapter.

Attraction . . . existence. There may be an echo here of a remark by the French free thinker Baron d'Holbach.

75 *called Satan*. In Job Satan is one of the 'sons of God' (1: 6) and the tormentor of Job on God's instructions.

the comforter: John 14: 16.

76 *cuts . . . way. Faerie Queene* II. viii. 5.

77 *Excess of joy*. For Milton's Satan (*Paradise Lost* i. 123) God the tyrant reigns 'in the excess of joy'.

78 *Sublime*: a noun, and an important aesthetic positive for Blake.

79 *all gods . . . ours*: a thought more in the spirit of enlightenment religious historiography than of the Old Testament.

King David: traditionally the composer of the Psalms.

three years: Isa. 20: 3.

Diogenes the Grecian: the Greek philosopher (*c.*400–*c.*325 BC) whose main tenet, as expressed in his own practice, was that humans should live in as simple and unartificial a manner as possible.

80 *perception of the infinite*: Ezek. 4. Despite the allusion to North America Blake may also see Ezekiel's fakir-like action (he lay 390 days on his left side, and 40 on his right) as an example of how 'the philosophy of the east taught the first principles of perception'.

six thousand years: an interval often mentioned by Blake and, according to a long-standing tradition in Christian theology, the age of the world. There is also an even older tradition to the effect that this is the life-span of the world. Blake's remark amounts to a declaration that the apocalypse is imminent.

Tree of Life: Gen. 3: 24, Rev. 22: 2.

by corrosives: with etched plates rather than with conventional letter-press.

81 *The giants*. Blake, like some ancient authors, seems to conflate the Giants and the Titans, both of whom rebelled against the Gods and were defeated and imprisoned. A second-generation Titan, Prometheus, made mankind out of clay (cf. 'The Argument' above) and was chained to a rock.

a sword: Matt. 10: 34, 25: 31–3.

Tempter: the Satan of Job.

he took me. The five stages of this trip mirror the sequence in the 'printing-house in Hell'.

83 *fixed stars*. Swedenborg held that spirits and angels populated all the bodies in the solar system, becoming progressively less spiritual beyond the orbit of Mars. Moreover, with the discovery of Uranus in 1781 there was no longer a 'void' beyond Saturn.

83 *Analytics*. The two treatises of the *Analytics* are concerned with the science of logic.

84 *Paracelsus or Jacob Behmen*. Paracelsus was an extremely influential exponent of occult and alchemical thought in the early 16th century. Behmen, or Boehme, born in 1575, was a German mystic whose vision, in its own fashion, centred on progression through contraries.

blue ... pink. The sequence is accurate for the light emitted by a cooling body as its wavelength increases.

Bray a fool ... out of him: Prov. 27: 22.

ten commandments. Blake's references to Christ's violations of the sixth and eighth commandments (forbidding murder and theft) are obscure, but may be clarified by reference to *Everlasting Gospel* 93–8. The other transgressions are mentioned at Mark 2: 27–8, John 8: 2–11, Matt. 27: 13–14, 10: 14.

85 *Elijah*: 2 Kgs. 2: 11.

A Song of Liberty. While this section may have been composed later than the rest of *The Marriage*, and evidently emphasizes social and political questions not previously mentioned in the work, it was consistently employed by Blake as its conclusion (and as a structural device is anticipated in his *Edward III*). Such a blending of the moral/epistemological/religious and the social/political is indeed the whole tendency of Blake's writing in the years of the French Revolution. All these strands are present in the closing sentence.

Female groaned. Another point of close connection with the rest of *The Marriage*, since this is the revival of 'eternal Hell' announced at the outset. The event continues to be paired with the story of Christ, and here starts with a momentous birth. This whole section has connections with Milton's 'Ode on the Morning of Christ's Nativity'. For the 'Eternal Female' see also a passage in Blake's 'Vision of the last Judgement', Geoffrey Keynes, *The Complete Writings of William Blake* (1966), 609.

The Eternal ... the earth. This verse should be compared with Rev. 12: 1–2.

thy dungeon. The Bastille was sacked in 1789.

keys, O Rome: emblem of the Pope's spiritual power.

Flagged: covered.

86 *stony law*. The ten commandments were written on stone tablets.

loosing ... dens of night. In Blake's story of the 'son of fire' there is generally a reminiscence of Phaeton, who disobediently drove the chariot of the sun and scorched the earth.

Empire. Probably combines the idea of monarchy and England's recently lost American colonies.

Visions of the Daughters of Albion. The predominantly dramatic procedure of the work, evidently understood by Blake to be the form taken by the 'visions' of English women (one of many references to visual perception in the poem), is a highly original experiment on his part. Each speaker displays responses to three levels of our existence; philosophical, moral (especially sexual), and political. The sexual theme is the leading one, and is astonishingly emancipated in its treatment. The effect is typically Blakian, in that each of the conflicting ideologies is explored and expressed, rather than judged, though there is clearly an implicit verdict in favour of Oothoon. There is nothing to choose between the other two figures, however, in unsatisfactoriness: they amount to a dismaying, disabling predicament for Oothoon.

l. 1. *Theotormon*: Blake's coinage, but perhaps indebted to 'The Huron', as the name of Voltaire's hero in *L'Ingénu* is Anglicized (the first translation of Voltaire's tale was published in 1768). *L'Ingénu*'s situation of triangular love, involving a young American native and a corrupt *ancien régime* aristocrat who forces himself upon the heroine, seems to be generally an influence in *Visions*. Blake has given all the main names in the poem a phonetic similarity, as if they belonged to the same lost language (in which 'Albion' could also be a name). 'Oothoon' is also an adaptation, being a reminiscence of 'Oithona' in the 'Ossian' tales (she is a hero's wife who is ravished by an enemy).

87 l. 27. *jealous dolphins*. Dolphins have an association with the sea-nymph Galatea, who was wooed by the Cyclops Polyphemus and, in the most famous version of her story, hated his uncouth courtship; she was discovered by him with her lover Acis, whom Polyphemus killed. This version has evident, though not straightforwardly treated, connections with Blake's Oothoon (moreover it is told, in Ovid, *Metamorphoses* xiii, as a lamentation by the female victim to a female audience: Galatea to Scylla).

l. 29. *signet*: the mark or stamp of a name (here as branded on a slave).

89 ll. 71–82. In this important section the falsity of Locke's denial of innate ideas in Man is deduced from the diverse and highly specialized instinctual drives and capacities which animals possess (which evidently cannot be explained by anything they have learned through their sensory apparatus). And if Locke is wrong Man must have 'thoughts . . . hid of old' analogous to those of animals.

91 l. 122. *Urizen*: probably the earliest surviving allusion by Blake to a figure that he was to write about a great deal. Characteristically, he is mentioned as if he needed no introduction, and in fact several of his

later traits have evidently already been determined by Blake. The form of his name fits the conventions of the poem, though it must have been a formation from 'horizon', and perhaps Greek *horizein* 'to limit'. The name is stressed on the first syllable.

91 ll. 133-44. Blake associates the expenditure of natural wealth and manpower on war with enclosure and the decline of agriculture. Hostilities between Britain and revolutionary France commenced in February 1793.   *fat-fed . . . drum*: the recruited soldier.

l. 136. *the parson claim the labour of the farmer*: in tithes.

l. 146. *wake her womb*. In the sexual physiology of Blake's day the whole reproductive apparatus of a woman was thought to participate in arousal and orgasm, with the female equivalent of male ejaculation occurring at the ovary.

95 *America, a Prophecy*. In so far as *America* has a naturalistic content it is like that of Blake's earlier *The French Revolution* (1791): the first, triggering phase of a revolution. But the transactions of humans and human institutions are no longer the main subject; there is a brief episode of conflict which stands for the whole War of Independence, and even the more extensive account of preliminaries has little to do with historical fact. *America* and its successor *Europe* are the only works which Blake subtitled 'prophecies' (although it has become conventional to call all his blank-verse narratives 'prophetic'). 'Prophecy' in this context has nothing to do with prediction; Blake is a 'prophet' in relation to the events of his time (and this explains much about the mode of *America* and *Europe*) in the same fashion as the Old Testament prophets—as a man of vision or imagination who can discern the purposes and agencies behind the history his readers are witnessing.

l. 1. *shadowy daughter of Urthona*: not a named element in Blake's mythology, and an example of its plasticity. She reappears in the Preludium to *Europe* (which seems to be a post-coital continuation of that to *America*) invoking Enitharmon as her mother, who is not a consort of Urthona.   *Orc*. Orc here commences his memorable if fairly brief activity in Blake's myths (he is only mentioned once in *Jerusalem*). His name clearly derives from the Latin word *Orcus* for the underworld and its god.

l. 6. *pestilence . . . heaven*. Comets and meteors were sometimes supposed to carry pestilence.

97 ll. 68-71. In this astronomical myth of Blake's own invention Mars stood at the centre of the solar system, with Mercury, Venus, and the Earth as satellites, and contained the comets and the sun.

l. 75. All the gospels except Matthew mention the spices used for Christ's burial; John 20: 7 refers to the wrapping up of Christ's discarded grave-clothes.

ll. 76–7. A vision that derives from, but modifies, Ezek. 37: 1–10.

l. 77. *inspiring*: breathing in.

l. 79. *grinding at the mill*: Matt. 24: 41.

ll. 93–4. 1 John 2: 22.

98 l. 103. *deserts blossom*: Isa. 35: 1.

l. 111. *Amidst . . . he walks*: Dan. 3: 25.

ll. 111–12. *feet . . . like gold*: Dan. 2: 32–3.

100 l. 145. *Atlantean*: as mighty as Atlas.

l. 149. *Ariston*. No Ariston is traditionally associated with Atlantis or with beauty. Ariston king of Sparta did steal a friend's wife, but Blake may be thinking of Plato's story that Poseidon lord of Atlantis captured a mortal bride.

101 l. 166. *fat of lambs*: Deut. 32: 14.

l. 180. *Bernard's*: Sir Francis Bernard, governor of Massachusetts.

102 ll. 198–206. This passage has the closest resemblances to one that influences *America* at several points: Christ's final overwhelming of the rebel angels in *Paradise Lost* viii. 824–65.

103 l. 223. *mitred York*: alludes to York, one of England's two archdioceses, or to its archbishop.

l. 230. *Bard of Albion*: perhaps the poet laureate William Whitehead.

l. 233. *doors of marriage are open*. Blake married Catherine Boucher in 1782.

104 ll. 254–5. Evidently, until the French Revolution. There are a number of events in the two revolutions that are separated by twelve years, and it is not clear which Blake would have thought decisive.

l. 262. *five gates*: the five physical senses.

105 *Manuscript Lyrics between* Innocence *and* Experience. In Blake's notebook entries of this period there are many drafts for Experience lyrics, which have not been reproduced. Several of the poems that have been included were lightly deleted in the notebook, but had been brought to a sufficiently final form to justify printing here. These are: 'I saw a chapel', 'I asked a thief', 'I heard an angel', 'Why should I care', 'O lapwing', 'Are not the joys', 'Soft Snow', 'In a Myrtle Shade', and 'Day'. One group of poems was recopied by Blake elsewhere in his notebook and put under the heading 'Several Questions Answered': they are 'Eternity', 'The look of love', and 'The Question Answered'. He added to them the couplet, 'Soft deceit and idleness, | These are beauty's sweetest dress'.

107 *A Cradle Song*. Presumably devised as an *Experience* parallel to 'A Cradle Song', but rejected in favour of 'Infant Sorrow'.

108 *'Why should I care'*
  l. 2. *chartered*. See note to 'London' 1.

109 *'Thou hast a lap full of seed'*
  l. 2. *country*: possibly, by a device for which there are precedents, a bawdy equivocation for 'cunt'.

  In a Myrtle Shade. The myrtle, a motif peculiar to the lyrics of this period, has strong connotations of licit and illicit love. The shrub is sacred to Venus, and Pliny refers to its use in conjugal rites, which continued (in Germany, for example) into the modern period. In Greek legend Myrrha, the incestuous mother of Adonis, was turned into a myrtle, and at her festivals married women wore myrtle crowns. There is a folk tradition that dreaming of myrtle prognosticates lovers or second marriages. For an important Virgilian association see note to 'My Spectre around me' 42.

  l. 3. *free love*. See note to 'Earth's Answer' 25.

111 *How to Know Love from Deceit.* This poem-title is deleted in the notebook.

112 *Merlin's Prophecy.* The tradition of Merlin the prophet and of the 'Prophecies of Merlin' are both due to the medieval historian Geoffrey of Monmouth. Part 5 of *The History of the Kings of Britain* consists of the prophecies, which are enigmatic predictions of calamity and unnatural phenomena in Britain. But Geoffrey's *History* was a rare book, especially in English, and Blake's unnatural events are anyway more in the spirit of the latter part of the group of sayings which Lear's Fool calls a prophecy by Merlin (*Lear* III. ii. 85–90).

114 *Lacedaemonian Instruction.* 'Lacedaemonian' means 'Spartan'. Blake characteristically associates Sparta's celebrated military culture with religion.

  'Her whole life is an epigram'

115 l. 1. *smack-smooth*: perfectly smooth.

117 *Songs of Experience.* Some four years after he first issued the Innocence collection Blake started to put out copies in which these poems were combined with a second group entitled *Songs of Experience*, the two being headed with a joint title and the subtitle 'Showing the Contrary States of the Human Soul': for a joint 'motto' to the enlarged volume, never used, see the preceding item. He continued to issue *Innocence* on its own, but it is virtually certain that *Experience* was only published as a companion to *Innocence*, never independently. This harmonizes with Blake's use elsewhere, at this period, of the terms 'innocence' and 'experience': the former was used rather frequently and deliberately (and affirmatively: see for example *Visions of the Daughters of Albion* 165) whereas 'experience' is not a common or a weighted term. When

Blake used the latter in the title of his new collection of lyrics it was as an antonym to 'innocence' that carried no special significance (except that it may have had a pejorative force due to another writer's deployment of it: Milton uses 'experience' on several occasions with reference to the Fall).

Introduction

ll. 6–7. At Gen. 3: 8 the God walks in the garden 'in the cool of the day' and calls Adam and Eve, but note that Milton has Eve dream of Satan doing almost the same (*Paradise Lost* v. 35–9).

l. 9. Milton's term for the night sky as seen by Adam and Eve (*Paradise Lost* iv. 724).

Earth's Answer

118 l. 25. *free love*. It is uncertain when in the 19th century this phrase entered English in the sense of an ideal of unconstrained choice of sexual partner, but Blake's use of it here almost amounts to that meaning.

Holy Thursday

l. 4. *usurous*: because of the extent to which the lending of money with interest would lie behind the wealth with which the charity schools are endowed. Less specifically, a gift that is usurous is not a gift at all.

121 *The Tiger*. The rhyme-scheme and metre, and some elements of the expression, in this song may be indebted to Crashaw's 'Hymn of the Church in Meditation of the Day of Judgement', a paraphrase of the famous liturgical poem *Dies Irae*. The tenor of the poem may be conceived as an enquiry as to whether God-the-creator exists given the character of creation: this traditional Epicurean line of thought had been reopened by Hume in *Dialogues concerning Natural Religion* (1779) (see especially Part V).

Ah! Sunflower

123 l. 5. *pined away with desire*. Blake seems to be remembering the actual phrasing of the account of Clytia, who was deserted by Apollo and turned into a sunflower, as given in Lemprière's Classical Dictionary.

The Little Vagabond

124 l. 12. *bandy*. The connection between the disease of rickets (of which bandy-leggedness is a characteristic symptom) and lack of sunlight was not understood in Blake's day, but rickets was known to be linked to poor and overcrowded living conditions.

London

l. 1. *chartered*: pejoratively, since charters deliver boroughs into the hands of corporations. For a significant parallel expression of hostility to charters see Paine's *Rights of Man* Part 1 (1791) (e.g. 'Every chartered town is an aristocratical monopoly in itself'). Blake is either not using the term literally, or is thinking of the streets of the City of London, the only part of London to have a corporation in his day (and even that, as a matter of strict history, was not established by a proper royal charter).

124 l. 10. *appalls.* There is a play on the old sense of 'make pale'.

Infant Sorrow

125 l. 6. *swaddling bands.* The age-old practice of swaddling children was becoming unpopular in advanced circles in Blake's day.

A Poison Tree

126 l. 14. *night . . . veiled the pole.* See Cowper's 'On the Death of Mrs Throckmorton's Bullfinch' (1789) 31.

l. 16. *outstretched beneath the tree.* Compare Milton's Adam after he has eaten the fruit (*Paradise Lost* x. 850–1).

128 *To Tirzah.* 'Tirzah' is a rare and obscure biblical name used once here by Blake, and then only, but often, in *The Four Zoas, Milton,* and *Jerusalem.* Blake was no doubt mainly struck by its use as the name of one of the biblical daughters of Zelophehad (who are also important in *Milton*), but he would also have noticed its linking with that of Jerusalem at S. of S. 6: 4, and perhaps its appearance as the name of one of the conquered territories of the Israelites at Josh. 12: 24.

l. 3. *generation.* Blake's first use of a word that later became his standard term for the mortal world. Though he was echoing Neoplatonic practice this early use makes it clear that the ordinary sense of the word was in his mind too. He may also have remembered *Paradise Lost* i. 653. See also note to *Milton* II, 256.

l. 15. A formulation with a Pauline ring to it.

129 *A Divine Image.* Although never included in *Experience* this would-be counterpart to 'The Divine Image', unlike other poems rejected from the collection, was illustrated and etched.

130 *Europe, a Prophecy. Europe* is in many respects the climax of the blank-verse narratives of this period in Blake's career: the most complex, ambitious, and strange of them all. Though in its title and subtitles *Europe* seems to be a close parallel to *America* it has a very different procedure, which is due to a quite different approach to time and human history, and one that lays the foundation for all Blake's subsequent prophetic writing. Such contemporary events as can be discerned in *Europe,* and other elements from our orthodox idea of human history, are, with startling effect, placed within unfamiliar schemes that deny conventional time: the 'shadowy female's' perpetual procreation, the 1,800 years' sleep of Enitharmon, and the identity of pre-Roman and modern Britain. Blake has abandoned historical

time in the spirit of his investigation of permanent states of human nature.

l. 1. *caverned man*: the man equipped only with physical senses, as depicted in Plato's allegory of the cave.

l. 6. For the phrasing see Prov. 9: 17. Blake thinks of the sense of touch, the last of his five senses, above all the modality of sex.

132 ll. 58–9. *the secret child Descended*: in human history, the birth of Christ.

133 l. 86. *horrent*: bristling; but probably also with the sense of 'frightening'.

l. 92. *lovely Woman*. Blake echoes Goldsmith's famous line 'When lovely woman stoops to folly'.

l. 102. *skipping upon the mountains*: cf. S. of S. 2: 8.

l. 112. *Eighteen hundred years*: the time between Christ's birth and Blake's own day.

134 l. 122. *Angels of Albion*: historically, the government of Pitt, at war with revolutionary France.

ll. 129–30. *ancient temple . . . island white*. Blake generalizes the theory, due to William Stukeley, that the megalithic ruins at Avebury described a serpent-shape.

l. 132. *Verulam*: a major town in Roman times, modern St Albans.

l. 136. *colours twelve*: Rev. 21: 19–20.

l. 138. *fluxile*: presumably, here and elsewhere, 'malleable': a usage peculiar to Blake.

l. 140. *spiral ascents*: the ears, in their original form.

136 l. 178. Generally accepted to be a reference to the dismissal of Lord Chancellor Thurlow in June 1792 at Pitt's instigation.

l. 204. Cf. *Paradise Lost* i. 301–2.

137 l. 237. *seven churches*: Rev. 1: 20.

138 *From the annotations to Boyd's Dante*. Blake annotated Boyd's preface to his translation, consistently objecting to the view that Dante, or any great poetry, has a moral aim and effect.

Capaneus: one of the 'Seven against Thebes' of Greek legend and literature, struck down by a thunderbolt after defying Jove.

wine-bibber: Matt. 11: 19, Luke 7: 34.

139 *'To my friend Butts'*. This poem is contained in a letter Blake wrote to his friend and loyal patron Thomas Butts just two weeks after moving to the Sussex seaside village of Felpham.

l. 15. *particles bright*. In Blake's day the corpuscular theory of light (as sanctioned by Newton) had yet to be displaced by the 19th-c. wave theory.

140 l. 41. *friend*: William Hayley (1745–1820), the man of letters and connoisseur who had invited Blake to Felpham so that he could employ him and generally assist his career. Over the next two years Blake became increasingly distressed in his situation, and antagonistic towards Hayley.

141 *'With happiness stretched across the hills'*: also contained in a letter from Felpham to Butts, written in Nov. 1802.

l. 7. *Hayley*. See note to l. 41 of preceding poem.

l. 39. *Fuseli*. The Swiss-born Henry Fuseli (1741–1825) was a dynamic personality and a highly original painter and illustrator, in particular of frightening, erotic, and dream-like subjects. He and Blake were intimate for about ten years from 1787, and he probably introduced the latter to some of the radicals of the day. Thereafter their friendship, though it continued, became more fraught.

l. 47. *Flaxman*. John Flaxman (1755–1826), the neo-classical sculptor and illustrator, was a friend of Blake's from their earliest manhood, and throughout his life he exerted himself on behalf of Blake's career, though Blake later entertained suspicions of his loyalty.

l. 54. *weltering*. Blake's 'double vision' expresses itself in a play on words. 'Weltering' means withering, as applied to the thistle, and staggering, as applied to the old man.

l. 59. *Los*. If 'sun' and 'Los' are also outward and inward respectively in spelling, the outward form of 'Los' would be 'Sol'.

143 l. 86. *Beulah*. Isa. (62: 4) calls Jerusalem 'Beulah', i.e. married. It is Bunyan in *Pilgrim's Progress* who uses the term as a place-name. In Blake's day there was a rural hill in Norwood, on the southern edge of London, variously called Bewlay/Beaulieu/Beulah Hill, and some of his uses of the word seem to include an allusion to this site.

144 *Manuscript Lyrics of the Felpham Years*. While the poems in this section may not have been composed entirely at Felpham itself (the first three items, in particular, are of uncertain date) they are predominantly the product of Blake's residence there.

'A fairy stepped upon my knee'. The functions attributed to fairies in this poem seem to derive in some measure from Pope's sylphs in *The Rape of the Lock*.

On the Virginity . . . Joanna Southcott. Joanna Southcott was a Devonshire girl who achieved great celebrity as a mystic. She claimed in 1802 to be the bride of God and mother-to-be of the Christ of the second coming.

146 *The Grey Monk*. Blake eventually used this title for a slightly shorter version of this poem than is given here. The original conception was even longer, but several verses were adopted (together with a couple also appearing here) to make a poem at the head of *Jerusalem* III.

'Mock on'

148 l. 5. *every sand*. The sense of a single grain of sand must have been nearly obsolete in Blake's day.

l. 9. *Democritus*. The ancient Greek pioneer of atomic theory, for whom reality was composed of an infinity of uniform indivisible units, differentiated only by the equivalents of Locke's primary qualities.

l. 10. See note to 'To my friend Butts' 15.

'My Spectre around me'

150 l. 42. *infernal grove*. From the 'grove' described at *Paradise Lost* x. 547–52, which bears ashy fruit resembling 'the bait of Eve | Used by the tempter' (a phrase Blake would have noticed). Also remembered is the myrtle grove in Virgil's underworld (*Aeneid* vi. 440–76) which harbours the lovelorn, and where Aeneas last sees Dido.

'O'er my sins'. These verses obviously have a close connection with the preceding poem, though the relationship intended by Blake is not clear. They should perhaps be allotted to two speakers, as has been done conjecturally for the companion poem.

151 *The Mental Traveller*. While the title of this tantalizing and much-discussed poem refers primarily to the first-person speaker it perhaps has a secondary application to the protagonist of the poem: the male figure who passes through infancy, manhood, old age, and parenthood, till the 'maiden' of l. 56 brings about a reversal of the process (and if the latter is also the 'woman old' of l. 8 she follows, at the same pace, the opposite sequence: age—youth—age). It requires an attentive reading to see this pattern, however, since it is embellished with a number of other images of human development and transition in the sexual and social domains. Two senses of 'generation'—procreation, and the interval between old and young—are strongly operative, in a manner that recalls *Tiriel*. Indeed the special quality of 'The Mental Traveller' arises from its deployment in a ballad-like form of large, enduring human themes reminiscent of the earlier poem.

ll. 7–8. Ps. 126: 5.

Mary

157 l. 43. *face . . . human divine*: cf. *Paradise Lost* iii. 44.

161 *Milton*

From the Preface

l. 3. *Lamb of God*. The phrase is particularly associated with John the Baptist who, uniquely in the Bible, uses it to refer to Jesus in John 1.

l. 12. *chariot of fire*. Elijah is taken up to Heaven in a 'chariot of fire' at 2 Kgs. 2: 11.

161 *Book Two: 217–end.* The concluding action of Blake's extraordinarily difficult poem starts with his encounter with a girl in the garden of his Felpham cottage. This figure he perceives to be Ololon, who in the first book of the poem appears as a group of 'immortals' named after the river they dwell beside in the supernatural realm. At the beginning of this extract they fuse into a Thel-like individual for their incarnation in our world. Ololon is following the descent to Felpham of the immortal form of the poet Milton, who has already become incarnated in Blake's foot, after some opposition from Blake's own poetic genius, Los. Milton is driven by a Christ-like mission of self-sacrifice, in atonement for his contribution as a religious poet to the cause of false religion (this aspect of Milton is his 'Spectre', Satan). The arrival of Ololon provokes a stupendous manifestation of both Milton and the latter's Spectre. Satan represents the whole accumulated history of Man's spiritual life, in which contending religions have multiplied, and Milton declines to continue the process with an attack on him, but instead will himself die. Satan proclaims victory, but to his surprise and terror seems to be abetting the spiritual awakening of Man. The girl, Ololon, is still dismayed by the fact of the rationalistic religion that has held sway since Milton's time, but Milton affirms his power, having died into life as Blake, to transform mankind's spiritual being without imposing a new religion.

ll. 224–5. *fountain . . . streams*: combines Ezek. 47: 1–2 and Zech. 14:8 with Exod. 17: 6.

162 l. 240. *Slumber nor sleep.* Ps. 121: 4.

l. 256. *vegetable worlds.* This image, and the frequent use of the motif of vegetation in Blake's later writing (as in 'vegetation and generation') in connection with the physical universe, may be indebted to Hume's *Dialogues Concerning Natural Religion* (1779) (see especially Part VII).

163 l. 282. *the covering cherub*: Ezek. 28: 14–16.

l. 283. *Rahab*: a biblical term for Egypt, also a Gentile prostitute who aids the Israelites in Josh. 2. In *Jerusalem* Blake will give her name also to the Whore of Babylon of Rev. 17, probably because of Ps. 87: 4 (with the encouragement of the apocalyptic overtones of Isa. 51: 9).

l. 285. *wicker man of Scandinavia.* Multiple human sacrifices by burning in wicker effigies are only recorded of the Druids; but (contrary to *Jerusalem*) Blake seems at this stage not to wish to accuse the latter of cruelty, and transfers the anecdote to the Odin-worshipping Scandinavians.

ll. 289–90. *in him . . . churches.* In the following lines Blake seems to express this idea very directly, since the list of pagan deities is heavily indebted to Milton.

l. 291. *synagogues of Satan*: Rev. 3: 9.

l. 294. *Baal*. His worship is strongly associated with Tyre in the Old Testament.   *Ashtaroth*. Blake uses Milton's occasional form of the name of the Sidonian goddess Astoreth (e.g. *Paradise Lost* i. 422). *Chemosh*: the Moabite national deity. Blake prefers the Bible spelling to Milton's 'Chemos'.

l. 295. *Molech*: Ammonite deity associated with human sacrifice (also called Moloch).

l. 299. *Dagon*. The idea that Dagon was a fish-god is a non-biblical conjecture familiar to Milton (see *Paradise Lost* i. 462–3).

l. 300. *Rimmon*: a deity strongly associated with Damascus in all traditions.

ll. 300–1. *Thammuz, Orus*: Milton's spellings of the Bible's Tammuz and the Egyptian god Horus.

l. 304. Blake is clearly following Milton's non-biblical interpretation of 'Belial' as a deity, and association of him with Sodom (*Paradise Lost* i. 502–3).

l. 307. *Rhea*: the Greek earth-goddess (see *Paradise Lost* i. 510–21).

ll. 310–16. The first twenty names are taken from biblical genealogies at Gen. 11 and Luke 3: many of them also appear elsewhere.

l. 311. *hermaphroditic*. Blake transfers from Milton's account of the pagan deities (especially Baal and Ashtaroth) the idea of sexual indeterminacy and generalizes it to cover all three groups of 'heavens'.

l. 317. *dragon red*: Rev. 12: 3.

165 l. 320. *substances*. 'Substance' is the philosophical term used by Locke for the relatively undifferentiated matter, but possessing such Newtonian qualities as mass, volume, and velocity, which composes the universe.

l. 324. *Og*: a giant-king and opponent of the Israelites.
Sihon: king of the Amorites, enemies of Israel and conquered during their advance; his territories were given to Reuben and Gad.

l. 335. cf. Num. 35: 7.

l. 340. *paved . . . stones*: cf. Exod. 24: 10.

166 l. 350. *not . . . hands*: Heb. 9: 11.

l. 365. *one greater*: *Paradise Lost* i. 4.

167 l. 389. *Seven angels*: a recurrent motif throughout Revelation, but in association with the true deity. In this speech Blake has in effect transferred to the latter the fraudulent, Antichrist-like associations of Satan in Revelation.

ll. 402–3. *lake . . . fire*. cf. Rev. 20: 10.

167 l. 404. *four Zoas*. Blake derives his idea of these four agencies from the four beasts of Rev. 4: 6–9 (collectively *zoa* in Greek). But 'zoa' is also an acceptable transliteration of the Greek word for life and existence.

168 ll. 420–1. *Chaos, Sin, Death, Ancient Night*: ontologically the most intriguing of all the agents in *Paradise Lost*, being neither deity, angel, human, nor animal.

l. 426. *Legions*: an ancient British city of great renown, according to Geoffrey of Monmouth, where King Arthur was crowned.

l. 430. *basements*: foundations, sub-structure.

169 l. 444. *Arnon*: a resting-place for the Israelites on their way to the Promised Land. Crossing 'the brooks of Arnon' and 'the stream of the brooks that goeth down to the dwelling of Ar' is said at Num. 21: 14–15 to be comparable to the crossing of the Red Sea.

l. 464. *Bolingbroke*. The politician Henry St John, first Viscount Bolingbroke (1678–1751) is here because in his occasional philosophical writings he had enunciated a deistical Christianity.

l. 474. *Patmos*: where John is supposed to have received the vision recorded in Revelation.

170 ll. 476–7. *five . . . Philistia*: presumably the five lords of the Philistines (see Josh. 13: 3).

171 l. 514. *abomination of desolation*: Matt. 24: 15, Mark 13: 14.

ll. 515–16. *curtains . . . rent*. Blake accepts the traditional association of the veil of the temple (rent in Matt. 27: 51) with the curtains on the Old Testament ark of the covenant.

l. 519. *sixfold Miltonic female*. Milton had three wives and three daughters.

172 l. 538. *garment dipped in blood*: cf. Rev. 19: 13.

l. 539. *Written within and without*: Ezek. 2. 10.

l. 540. *literal*: perhaps 'in letters'. The next paragraph is a kind of rephrasing, in English terms, of elements in Rev. 4, 7, 10, and elsewhere.

l. 545. *Jesus wept*: John 11: 35.

Auguries of Innocence

173 l. 17. *gamecock . . . fight*. Fighting cocks have their feathers and combs heavily cut, and their natural spurs sheathed in artificial ones.

174 l. 33. *boy . . . fly*: *King Lear* IV. i. 38–9.

l. 42. *polar bar*: see note to *Thel* 108.

l. 65. *hands*: farmworkers.

175 ll. 97–8. *poison . . . crown*. The fact of the poison in laurel being prussic acid (recently isolated chemically; see note to *Jerusalem III*, 551) enables Blake to attack the militarism of the Roman Empire with peculiar intensity and wit.

l. 105. *emmet*: an ant.

176 l. 127. *born . . . night*: Jonah 4: 10.

Jerusalem. Blake composed, illustrated, and engraved *Jerusalem* in his middle-age, years in which he endured great personal hardship, and achieved no artistic recognition at all. It is nevertheless by far his most ambitious literary project, and is executed in a way that bespeaks a formidable determination and discipline. The 4,000-odd lines of verse, divided into four 'chapters', are engraved on exactly 100 plates, 25 per chapter. It is of course much harder for the reader to find a comparable lucidity in the structure of the poem's content, but *Jerusalem* is arguably an easier text than *Milton*. Blake himself is not implicated as an actor as he is so strangely in the earlier poem: he figures instead as the perceiver of a sequence of visions (five in all) involving Los, Albion, and their respective consorts, who are Enitharmon and Jerusalem. Los is in an ambiguous but basically loyal frame of mind towards the stricken ruler Albion, who is sundered from Jerusalem through the activities of his sons and daughters (Los is equally sundered from Enitharmon). The poem's single main action is the restoration of Albion to life and authority, and the reuniting of the two couples. Blake is of course implicated in the sense that Los is at one level his depiction of himself in his artistic, political, and domestic situation in early 19th-c. Britain. Los also stands for human creativity in general, and for all its strangeness *Jerusalem* is quite recognizably a poem of the Romantic era in its central concerns. Even the insistent theme of married love, triumphing over alienation and separation, while it must relate to William and Catherine Blake in a way we can never reconstruct, is of its time: *Jerusalem* can be compared interestingly to Beethoven's *Fidelio*.

From the preface to Chapter I

176 l. 9. *types*: printed lettering.

From the preface to Chapter II

177 l. 2. *Primrose Hill*. In Blake's day Primrose Hill was used for ceremonies by a neo-Druidical organization calling itself The Order of the Welsh Bards, and Druids are prominently mentioned in the prose-parts of this preface.

l. 13. *Jew's Harp House*: a tea-garden in Marylebone Park (later part of Regent's Park).   *Green Man*: a public house on the Marylebone Road (formerly New Road), just south of Marylebone Park and Willan's Farm (near the modern Great Portland Street tube station).

177 l. 15. *Willan's Farm*: also incorporated into Regent's Park.

178 l. 33. *London Stone*: the monolith in Cannon Street, which features importantly in *Milton* and *Jerusalem* as a sacrificial altar. Various ancient purposes have been conjectured for it.

l. 34. *Tyburn's brook*. Tyburn Hill (where Marble Arch now stands) was the site of public executions in London.

From the preface to Chapter III

179 l. 1. *Charlemagne*: a Christian king, but in the mould of the Roman emperors.

l. 7. *schools*: medieval theology.

180 l. 21. *Titus! Constantine!*: Roman emperors who were pro-Christian, but emperors none the less.

From the preface to Chapter IV

l. 12. *a watcher and a holy one*: Dan. 4: 13.

The confession of Albion

182 l. 932. *redound*: to surge up abundantly (almost an obsolete usage in Blake's day, though found on several occasions in the later writings).

l. 937. *relapsing*: Blake's sense of 'falling' seems to be unique to him.

183 l. 968. *Jerusalem, Jerusalem*: Matt. 23: 37–9 (one of Blake's favourite chapters), Luke 13: 34–5.

184 l. 998. *Hesperia*: Italy.

185 l. 1009. *wast dead . . . alive.* See the parable of the prodigal son in Luke 15.

l. 1010. See Christopher Marlowe, *Dr Faustus* v. ii. 187.

Los explores Albion

ll. 808–10. The sequence of images accurately follows the process of brick-making.

186 l. 816. *kennels*: gutters in the street.

ll. 823–4. *Bethlehem . . . bread*. Bethlehem here is the London lunatic asylum at this date situated at Moorfields, rather than the biblical town. The Hebrew means 'house of bread'.

187 l. 839. *temple*: probably an ancient British temple hypothesized by Blake, rather than the Inn of Court of that name.

Erin mourns at the tomb of Albion

188 l. 933. *the vale of Rephaim*. The Atlantic is associated with the valley on the borders of Old Testament Judah, where Judah's enemies encamped. For this allusion see also Isa. 17: 5.

189 l. 964. *Bashan and Gilead*. Bashan is the mountainous kingdom of Og in the Old Testament, and Gilead another mountainous area, occupied by the Jewish tribes of Gad, Manasseh, and Reuben.

190 l. 973. *Shiloh*: a precursor of Jerusalem as a political and religious centre of Israel.

l. 979. *Havilah*: the land drained by Pison, one of the rivers of Paradise.

l. 995. *chargeth . . . folly*: cf. Job 4: 18.

191 l. 1007. *Egypt . . . Philistia . . . Moab . . . Edom . . . Aram*: all in some way antagonists of Israel.

ll. 1015-16. Cf. Exod. 13: 21.

l. 1020. *Og and Anak*: enemies of Israel of gigantic stature. For Anak see, in particular, Num. 13: 33.

l. 1022. *Balaam*: the gentile (Moabite) prophet who believed in the Jewish God and blessed Israel, contrary to the commands of King Balak.

In the world of the dead Albion

193 l. 157. *Gwendolen*. As with many of the prominent female names in this section, derived from Geoffrey of Monmouth's British history.

194 l. 163. *while*: meanwhile (a sense obsolete by Blake's day).

l. 180. *Rosamond's bower*: the maze-like retreat allegedly built by Henry II at Woodstock to shelter his mistress Rosamond Clifford (where she was none the less successfully poisoned by Queen Elinor). Blake's knowledge of the legend probably comes from the 'Fair Rosamond' ballad in Percy's *Reliques*.

195 l. 189. *Rock of Ages*. The phrase, used in the Authorized Version to gloss Isa. 26: 4, became very familiar as the opening of a late 18th-c. hymn.

l. 199. *bonifying*: Blake's neologism.

196 ll. 220-1. *Hand . . . Coban . . . Hyle . . . Skofield*: Blake's disguises, of varying penetrability, for the Hunt brothers, editors of the *Examiner* (which had called Blake's art that of a 'lunatic'), Private Scolfield (the soldier with whom Blake had an altercation at Felpham, leading to a trial for high treason), and Hayley (Blake's Felpham patron—but Blake almost certainly has in mind also Greek *hyle*, 'matter', which, on a Gnostic view, the evil of creation produced). Coban could be a 'Cockburn' in reality, but he has not been identified. Although for the purposes of this edition Blake's various spellings of proper names deriving from his trial have been standardized the reader should be aware that, for whatever purpose, these names vary much more in spelling than any other group in Blake's mythology.

198 l. 297. Cf. *Exod.* 26: 7, 36: 35.

199 l. 315. *Mizraim*: Gen. 10: 6.

l. 317. *Tesshina.* Although the context and Blake's practice at this period would suggest a known name the word has not been traced.

200 l. 357. Cf. Job 38: 31.

201 l. 364. *Lo . . . always*: cf. Matt. 28: 20.

l. 365–6. *Only . . . sleepeth*: combines John 11: 23–6 and Mark 5: 36–9.

l. 367. *Elohim*: the ordinary Hebrew word for God, and used for God the creator of the world in Genesis rather than Jehovah. Blake is reported as 'triumphantly' pointing out this fact in conversation with Henry Crabb Robinson, and expounding the Gnostic doctrine that the world is not the creation of the supreme deity. *behold Joseph and Mary.* The vision that follows in the next 27 lines is Blake's rewriting of Matt. 1: 18–24 in a vein that is not only anti-moralistic but rationalist.

ll. 372–3. *more pure . . . maker*: Job 4: 17.

202 l. 388. *without . . . price*: Isa. 55: 1.

l. 390. *none . . . sinneth not.* Of several biblical texts to this effect 1 Kgs. 8: 46 is the earliest.

ll. 397–9. *Euphrates . . . Gihon . . . Hiddekel . . . Pison*: the four Edenic rivers.

203 l. 406. *to the loathing . . . person*: cf. Ezek. 16: 5.

l. 407. *Amalekite.* In the course of *Milton* and *Jerusalem* Amalek and the Amalekites appear frequently as baneful agencies in a way that goes well beyond the historical actions ascribed to them in the Bible (rather in the manner that the Bible itself deploys the concept of Egypt). Blake is, however, building on the fact that Joshua's first victory was over the Amalekites, who are declared enemies of God 'from generation to generation' (Exod. 17: 8–16).

l. 426. 'Seed of the woman' (because of Gen. 3: 15) implies descendants of Eve, and all the names that follow are those of biblical women (if 'Cainah' is taken to mean 'wife of Cain') forming a 'maternal line' to Mary, mother of Jesus, in the manner of the male-oriented genealogies at the beginnings of the gospels of Matthew and Luke. Blake also suggests, with considerable ingenuity, how this line of descent violates the idea of a licit, pure ancestry for Jesus, often with the direct authority of the Bible. Cainah, Ada and Zillah, and Naamah are respectively wife, daughters-in-law, and granddaughter of Cain (the last of these, in one alternative Jewish tradition, is an evil woman who miscegenates with angels or, in yet another tradition, is the wife of Noah, unnamed in the Bible). Shuah's daughter, and her daughter Tamar, are both Canaanites and concubines of Judah: since Tamar is an ancestor of Jesus (Matt 1: 3) his lineage is incestuous. And if the Rahab and Ruth of this genealogy are those written of at Josh. 2 and in Ruth, Jesus is also descended from a harlot of Jericho and a Moabite. Similarly Bathsheba the Hittite was the married mistress, and later wife, of King David, and mother of Solomon (Matt. 1: 6 in fact defines her as the ex-wife of Uriah). Jesus is descended from Solomon via Rehoboam, and according to 1 Kgs. 14: 21 his mother was Naamah, an Ammonite. The Bible only records of Zibeah that she was the mother of King Jehoash.

l. 433. *I know ... last day*: John 11: 24.

l. 434. *in my flesh ... God*: Job 19: 26.

204 l. 436. *I am ... life*: John 11: 25.

l. 444. *a season*: Philem. 15 and John 16: 16.

205 l. 469. *Thor and Friga*: the Norse god of war and the principal wife of Odin. Here and in the following section Blake does more justice than hitherto to the allegations in the ancient sources that the Druids performed human sacrifices, though he still in some sense wishes to implicate Scandinavian forms of religion.

l. 471. *wheels filled with eyes*: cf. Ezek. 10: 12 and Rev. 4: 8.

206 l. 499. *Druid knife*. Blake's sacrificial flint knife is perhaps an extrapolation from the celebrated golden knife with which the Druids were reputed to cut mistletoe: but see note to l. 641 below.

l. 500. *poetic vision*. Blake may have it in mind that knives and poison-cups feature in Elizabethan and Jacobean tragedies and in their descendants in the melodrama.

208 l. 540. *Ragan*: according to Geoffrey of Monmouth, an ancient British princess (better known in Shakespeare's spelling as Regan).

l. 542. *caves of Machpelah*. The cave of Machpelah was the family mausoleum of the great patriarchs Abraham, Isaac, and Jacob, and their wives.

209 l. 551. *poisonous blue*. Blake in effect suggests that woad was Prussian Blue (a characteristic ingredient of which, prussic acid, had been identified as a deadly poison in 1803).

213 l. 641. *knife of flint*. It is most significant that the Authorized Version glosses the 'sharp knives' used for circumcision at Josh. 5: 2–3 as 'knives of flint'.

ll. 644–9. Evidently closely imitative of Christ's crucifixion as described in the gospels of Matthew and Mark, with an additional allusion to Judg. 4: 2–3.

215 l. 691. *dove and raven*: Gen. 8: 7–8.

215 l. 700. *high Mona*: *Lycidas* 54.

l. 706. *blood of their covenant*. The primary use of the phrase is at Exod. 24: 8.

ll. 717–18. *Epicurean philosophy*. Underlying the Epicurean system was an atomistic physics inherited from Democritus.

216 l. 720. The rocks may be thought of as parents of men in a metaphysical system, such as the Epicurean, which holds that the inanimate and the animate (however intelligent) are constituted by the same materials. Also, Lucretius' account of Epicurus gives considerable emphasis to the phase of random and violent chaos which is supposed to precede the formation of the universe.

l. 727. *Kotope*: probably based on the name of an unidentified participant in the events of Blake's arrest and trial.

l. 728. Cf. Gen. 37: 31.

l. 732. *Horeb*: the mountain of God. Sinai (l. 771) is part of it.

l. 734. *Beth Peor*: the burial place of Moses.

217 l. 762. *Manasseh*: one of the tribes of Israel, who play an important (and increasingly free) role in Blake's mythology from *Milton* onwards. Blake makes use especially of Manasseh, Reuben (a conspicuous figure in this section of *Jerusalem*), and Gad. These were the only tribes to acquire lands east of the Jordan before Israel crossed that river, and in this sense they separated from Israel, and perhaps from her religion.   *River Kanah*: formed the boundary between Ephraim and Manasseh.

l. 770. *Ebal, mount of cursing*: cf. Deut. 27: 13–26.

ll. 771–3. *Mahlah . . . Hoglah . . . Milcah*: three of the five daughters of Zelophehad (along with Tirzah: see note to 'To Tirzah').

218 l. 775. *Shechem*: modern Nablus.

ll. 784–5. Since the non-biblical deities in this list come in male–female pairs it may be deduced that Blake thinks of Molech and Chemosh likewise. See also IV. 401.

l. 790. *valley . . . Jebusite*: where Jerusalem (the Jebusite city) is located.

219 l. 805. *from Havilah to Shur*: Gen. 25: 18.

l. 806. *Shaddai*: a common Hebrew term for God in the Old Testament, translated as 'The Almighty'.

l. 818. *Uzzah*: see 2 Sam. 6: 3–7 (also 1 Chron. 13: 7–10).

l. 822. *Rehob in Hamath*: cf. Num. 13: 21.

220 l. 828. *Meribah Kadesh*: Num. 13: 26, 20: 13–14. At Exod. 17: 7 the Authorized Version glosses Meribah as 'Chiding or Strife'.

l. 848. *Leah and Rachel*: the two contending wives of Jacob, notable for various subterfuges.

221 l. 877–9. *In the circumference*: since the tabernacle was set down at the centre of the Israelite camp, as described at Num. 1: 50–3 and 2.

222 l. 895. *key-bones*: collar-bone.

Jerusalem, Vala, and the daughters of Albion

223 l. 32. *arrows of the Almighty*: Job 6: 4.

l. 36. *Heshbon*: a city of Reuben and Gad.

l. 40. *mountain of blessing*. Cf. Deut. 11: 29.

l. 44. *Goshen*: a conquest of Joshua's.

224 l. 68. *Kishon*: a river in northern Palestine.

l. 69. *earth . . . down*. Cf. Job 1: 7.

226 l. 116. *I am . . . soul*. Cf. Ps. 22: 6.

229 l. 210. *zone*: girdle, belt.

230 l. 242. *Helle*: Hellas (Greece).

231 l. 257. *Bath Rabbim*: S. of S. 7: 4.

Reconciliation and joy

233 l. 448. *Holiness . . . Lord*: as with the frontlet worn by Aaron (Exod. 28: 36).

234 l. 463. Cf. Rev. 21: 2.

l. 471. This imagery constitutes a major motif, and derives from Exod. 13: 21–2.

l. 472. *Ammon*. The kingdom of Ammon is linked with Moab at 2 Chron. 20: 22–3 and with Amalek at Ps. 83: 7 as enemies of Judah.

l. 476. *Javan*: a figure mentioned in Genesis, usually taken to be the ancestor of the Greeks. 'Isles of Javan' thus may be the Greek islands: but see l. 624.

235 l. 521. *not as . . . I will*: Matt. 26: 39, Mark 14: 36.

238 ll. 596–7. *Pharisaion . . . Grammateis . . . Presbyterion . . . Archiereus . . . Iereus . . . Saddusaion*: intended as transliterations of terms in the Greek New Testament denoting the following elements in the Jewish religious establishment, all implicated in the persecution of Jesus: Pharisees, scribes, elders, High Priest, priest, Sadducees.

l. 609. *dragon of the river*: cf. Ezek. 29: 3.

239 l. 616. *Rabbath*: the chief Ammonite city.

l. 619. *scapulae . . . os humeri*: anatomical terms for shoulder-blades and upper-arm bone.

l. 637. *Anakim . . . Emim . . . Nephilim . . . Gibborim*: all giants, though the first two groups are giant enemies of Israel, and the latter two (in the Hebrew) the giants and their offspring of Gen. 6: 4.

240 l. 666. *Bowen*: probably another unidentified figure connected with the Scolfield affair.   *Conwenna*: one of the female names Blake dervies from Geoffrey of Monmouth.

242 l. 717. *Deists*. Deism is the common term for a religious attitude which spread in Christian culture in the enlightenment: it accepted the existence of a God (above all, as the creator and designer of the universe) but was sceptical of the more specifically Christian doctrines and institutions.

243 ll. 752–3. *heavens . . . curtain*: cf. Ps. 104: 2.

244 l. 754. *Hermes*: Hermes Trismegistus, the Egyptian God Thoth, who is supposed to have written the *Hermetica*, the foundation of alchemical tradition.

245 l. 801. *Asshur*: scarcely known in the Bible, but evidently taken by Blake to be among the enemies of Israel.

246 l. 813. See Gen. 30: 14.

l. 827. *communion of saints and angels*. 'The communion of saints' is an expression from the Apostles' creed. By supplementing it with angels Blake emphasizes that central to Christianity is the idea of a level of existence completely transcending the physical, which Man can also aspire to dwell in, such as is certainly played down, if not denied, by deism (though Bacon, Newton, and Locke have no relevant comment on the question).

l. 829. *god of this world*: 2 Cor. 4: 4.

247 l. 839. *damps*: poisonous gases.

252 l. 953. *fourfold*. The various quadruples in the passage that follows have their roots in those of Rev. 4–7.

253 l. 974. *non-ens*: non-being.

l. 987. *Priam*. For reasons that are not clear, Priam, King of Troy, is taken by Blake in his later writings as the representative of a religious system antithetical to Christianity.

254 l. 990. *accuser of sin*: see the account of Satan at Rev. 12: 9–10.

l. 992. *kingdoms . . . glory*: cf. Matt. 4: 8.

l. 993. *Gog-Magog giant*: the most relevant biblical allusion is from the apocalypse (Rev. 20: 8), but Blake would also have known of the giant statues in the Guildhall, London, known as Gog and Magog.

The Everlasting Gospel. Blake's drafts for a couplet poem, at least part of which he entitled 'The Everlasting Gospel', are dispersed through his manuscript remains. Further sections may have been lost. It is not certain which pieces of text, in which order, might have appeared in a completed form of the work. Here a version is offered in which

Blake's repetitions and false starts have been suppressed; the order chosen seems cogent and consistent with Blake's own indications. For the title of the work see Rev. 16: 6.

l. 3. *Caiaphas and Pilate*: the Jewish High Priest and the Roman governor of Judea, between them responsible for the arrest, condemnation, and execution of Christ.

255 l. 11. *Antichrist*: 1 John 2: 22.

l. 14. *Rhadamanthus*: in classical lore, one of the judges in Hades and ruler of Elysium. Hence, in Blake's version, he is the agent of moral condemnation in the afterlife as understood by false Christianity.

l. 18. *Plato and Cicero*: apparently chosen simply as two exponents of a pre-Christian world-view.

256 l. 62. *seven devils*: Mark 16: 9.   *pen*: perhaps from the dialect sense of a sow's vagina.

ll. 63–4. The mother of Jesus could have been a harlot and still a virgin if she had consorted with 'sucking devils'.

l. 73. *mocked the Sabbath*: e.g. Mark 2: 27–8.

ll. 74–6. *unlocked . . . divines*: refers to the casting out of devils from the insane, and the enlisting of Peter, Andrew, and John as disciples.

l. 83. Mark 5: 1–19, Luke 8: 27–37.

l. 87. *Obey your parents*: as instructed by the fifth commandment.

257 l. 88. John 2: 4.

l. 91. *seventy disciples*: Luke 10: 1.

ll. 101–2. *adulteress . . . law*: John 8: 3–11.

l. 108. *Sinai's trumpet*. In Exod. 19 this announced the delivery of the ten commandments.

l. 110. Luke 2: 42–9.

l. 119. Matt. 14: 3–10.

ll. 120–6. The various temptations put to Jesus by the devil are recounted in the fourth chapters of Matthew and Luke.

258 l. 128. *thunder's sound*: also part of the sound effects in Exod. 19.

l. 134. *bound old Satan*: Rev. 20: 2.

l. 139. See Matt. 33.

ll. 142–3. *gate's . . . bar*: Ps. 107: 15–18.

ll. 151–2. *scourged . . . temple*: adapts John 2: 13–17.

l. 159. *Church of Rome*. Catholic religious imagery frequently depicts the dead Christ.

259 l. 167. Matt. 7: 9, Luke 11: 11.

ll. 168–71. John 3: 1–8.

l. 173. Matt. 7: 29, Mark 1: 22.

l. 175. Matt. 11: 28–9.

l. 198. *Priestley . . . Bacon . . . Newton.* The common thread between these three is natural science (Priestley did important work on gases; Bacon was an early theorist of science). Priestley, being a Unitarian, was also an enemy of Christianity as Blake saw it. They do not literally resemble Caesar; the connection is that of militaristic values and false religion, so stressed in *The Everlasting Gospel.*

l. 231. Isa. 57: 15.

l. 240. Luke 23: 34.

l. 243. John 17: 9.

l. 244. *in a garden*: in the garden of Gethsemane, just before his arrest.

l. 246. *of woman born*: Job 25: 4. The Book of Job is generally important for this difficult section of the poem.

261 l. 252. *fiction*: apparently in the sense (generally obsolete in Blake's day) of making, creation.

l. 267. *Mary.* Blake, as is traditional, identifies the woman taken in adultery (see John 8) with the Mary Magdalen of Mark 16: 1–9. The rest of this section is Blake's version of the episode.

l. 268. Recalls *Paradise Lost* ix. 1000–3, the moment at which Adam tastes the forbidden fruit.

ll. 275–7. *heavens . . . roll*: Rev. 6: 14.

ll. 284–310. The speaker is Jesus.

l. 286. According to Exod. 31: 18 the ten commandments were 'written with the finger of God'.

l. 287. Job 15: 15.

262 l. 291. *devil.* Blake at first wrote 'God', thus clearly echoing Luke 18: 18–19.

l. 292. The angel of the presence, frequently mentioned in Blake's later writing, is his development of a solitary reference in the Bible (Isa. 63: 9). He evidently interpreted several other biblical passages as references to this figure, citing as one of them Exod. 14: 19, which mentions the 'angel of God' leading the Israelites over the Red Sea. God's guiding agency is called his 'presence' later in Exodus (33: 14–15).

ll. 301–3. Derives from Milton's picture of the punishment of the defeated angels.

l. 304. *breath divine*. Blake's anglicization of Gen. 1: 2 is a more literal translation of the Hebrew than the Authorized Version's.

l. 317. Gen. 3: 14.

l. 319. Luke 16: 20.

263 l. 370. *Melitus*: one of the accusers of Socrates (whose teachings were alleged to corrupt the young).

264 *From the annotations to Berkeley's Siris*. The thought of Bishop Berkeley (1685–1753) has affinities with that of Blake, in so far as he asserted the essential spirituality of the material world in a post-Lockian philosophical environment (indeed it was essential for Berkeley's metaphysics that Locke should be correct); these annotations are the only allusions to Berkeley in Blake's surviving works, though Blake's first biographer Alexander Gilchrist records that Berkeley 'was on the list of Blake's favourite authors'. *Siris* is Berkeley's last philosophical utterance, and an oddity in his output: an eccentrically structured work in which arguments for immaterialism are couched in a more Platonic idiom than hitherto.

I will not leave . . . to you: John 13: 33, 14: 18–21.

spiritual body . . . heavenly Father: Matt. 18: 10.

imaginative form. Berkeley had denied that harmony and proportion are 'objects of sense': in empiricist terms, they are secondary qualities. In response, Blake in this paragraph simultaneously claims more for sense-perception than empiricism (harmony and proportion are primary qualities), and less (the 'reality' of a thing is 'imaginative').

perception or sense. Blake is again, in a sense, ultra-empirical.

'If I e'er grow'

266 l. 4. *take the wall*: be accorded woman's privileges as conferred by sexual etiquette.

'You don't believe'

l. 11. *'Only believe'* Mark 5: 36.

'Why was Cupid a boy'

268 l. 18. Blake may be conjecturing that the Greek cult of male homosexual love was rooted in admiration of martial prowess.

'To Chloe's breast'

269 l. 2. *Myra*. This name, and Chloe, are probably those of imaginary women, but in the latter case Blake could have in mind the figure of Myrrha: see note to 'In a Myrtle Shade'.   *pocket-hole*; placket-hole, giving access to the genitalia.

Further Reading

Hazard Adams, *William Blake: A Reading of the Shorter Poems* (Seattle, 1963).

John Beer, *Blake's Humanism* (Manchester, 1968).

—— *Blake's Visionary Universe* (Manchester, 1969).

G. E. Bentley Jr., *Blake Records* (Oxford, 1969).

David Bindman, *Blake as an Artist* (Oxford, 1977).

Bernard Blackstone, *English Blake* (Cambridge, 1949).

Harold Bloom, Blake's Apocalypse (Ithaca, NY, 1963).

Anthony Blunt, *The Art of William Blake* (New York, 1959).

Jacob Bronowski, *A Man without a Mask* (London, 1944).

G. K. Chesterton, *William Blake* (London, 1910).

S. Foster Damon, *William Blake: His Philosophy and Symbols* (Boston, 1924).

—— *A Blake Dictionary* (Providence, 1965).

David V. Erdman, *Blake: Prophet against Empire* (Princeton, NJ, 1954).

—— and John E. Grant (eds.), *Visionary Forms Dramatic* (Princeton, NJ, 1970).

Northrop Frye, *Fearful Symmetry* (Princeton, NJ, 1947).

Stanley Gardner, *Infinity on the Anvil* (Oxford, 1954).

Alexander Gilchrist, *Life of William Blake, 'Pictor Ignotus'* (London, 1863).

D. G. Gillham, *Blake's Contrary States* (Cambridge, 1966).

Robert Gleckner, *The Piper and the Bard* (Detroit, 1959).

E. D. Hirsch, *Innocence and Experience* (New Haven, Conn., 1964).

John Holloway, *Blake: The Lyric Poetry* (London, 1968).

Jack Lindsay, *William Blake: His Life and Work* (London, 1978).

Raymond Lister, *William Blake: An Introduction to the Man and his Work* (London, 1968).

Herschel M. Margoliouth, *William Blake* (New York, 1961).

John Middleton Murry, *William Blake* (London, 1933).

Martin K. Nurmi, *William Blake* (Kent, Oh., 1976).

Morton D. Paley, *Energy and the Imagination* (Oxford, 1970).

Mark Plowman, *An Introduction to the Study of Blake* (London, 1927).

Kathleen Raine, *Blake and Tradition* (Princeton, NJ, 1968).

Alvin H. Rosenfeld (ed.), *William Blake: Essays for Foster S. Damon* (Providence, 1969).

Denis Saurat, *Blake and Milton* (New York, 1924).

Mark Schorer, *William Blake: The Politics of Vision* (New York, 1946).

Algernon Charles Swinburne, *William Blake: A Critical Essay* (London, 1868).

J. H. Wicksteed, *Blake's Innocence and Experience* (London, 1928).

Mona Wilson, *The Life of William Blake* (London, 1927).

Index of Titles and First Lines

POETRY

PROSE

GEORGE ELIOT	**Adam Bede**
	Daniel Deronda
	Middlemarch
	The Mill on the Floss
	Silas Marner
ELIZABETH GASKELL	**Cranford**
	The Life of Charlotte Brontë
	Mary Barton
	North and South
	Wives and Daughters
THOMAS HARDY	**Far from the Madding Crowd**
	Jude the Obscure
	The Mayor of Casterbridge
	A Pair of Blue Eyes
	The Return of the Native
	Tess of the d'Urbervilles
	The Woodlanders
WALTER SCOTT	**Ivanhoe**
	Rob Roy
	Waverley
MARY SHELLEY	**Frankenstein**
	The Last Man
ROBERT LOUIS STEVENSON	**Kidnapped and Catriona**
	The Strange Case of Dr Jekyll and Mr Hyde and Weir of Hermiston
	Treasure Island
BRAM STOKER	**Dracula**
WILLIAM MAKEPEACE THACKERAY	**Barry Lyndon**
	Vanity Fair
OSCAR WILDE	**Complete Shorter Fiction**
	The Picture of Dorian Gray

THOMAS AQUINAS	**Selected Philosophical Writings**
GEORGE BERKELEY	**Principles of Human Knowledge and Three Dialogues**
EDMUND BURKE	**A Philosophical Enquiry into the Origin of Our Ideas of the Sublime and Beautiful Reflections on the Revolution in France**
THOMAS CARLYLE	**The French Revolution**
CONFUCIUS	**The Analects**
FRIEDRICH ENGELS	**The Condition of the Working Class in England**
JAMES GEORGE FRAZER	**The Golden Bough**
THOMAS HOBBES	**Human Nature and De Corpore Politico Leviathan**
JOHN HUME	**Dialogues Concerning Natural Religion and The Natural History of Religion Selected Essays**
THOMAS MALTHUS	**An Essay on the Principle of Population**
KARL MARX	**Capital The Communist Manifesto**
J. S. MILL	**On Liberty and Other Essays Principles of Economy and Chapters on Socialism**
FRIEDRICH NIETZSCHE	**On the Genealogy of Morals Twilight of the Idols**
THOMAS PAINE	**Rights of Man, Common Sense, and Other Political Writings**
JEAN-JACQUES ROUSSEAU	**Discourse on Political Economy and The Social Contract Discourse on the Origin of Inequality**
SIMA QIAN	**Historical Records**
ADAM SMITH	**An Inquiry into the Nature and Causes of the Wealth of Nations**
MARY WOLLSTONECRAFT	**Political Writings**

The Oxford World's Classics Website

www.worldsclassics.co.uk

- Information about new titles
- Explore the full range of Oxford World's Classics
- Links to other literary sites and the main OUP webpage
- Imaginative competitions, with bookish prizes
- Peruse *Compass*, the Oxford World's Classics magazine
- Articles by editors
- Extracts from Introductions
- A forum for discussion and feedback on the series
- Special information for teachers and lecturers

www.worldsclassics.co.uk

American Literature

British and Irish Literature

Children's Literature

Classics and Ancient Literature

Colonial Literature

Eastern Literature

European Literature

History

Medieval Literature

Oxford English Drama

Poetry

Philosophy

Politics

Religion

The Oxford Shakespeare

A complete list of Oxford Paperbacks, including Oxford World's Classics, OPUS, Past Masters, Oxford Authors, Oxford Shakespeare, Oxford Drama, and Oxford Paperback Reference, is available in the UK from the Academic Division Publicity Department, Oxford University Press, Great Clarendon Street, Oxford OX2 6DP.

In the USA, complete lists are available from the Paperbacks Marketing Manager, Oxford University Press, 198 Madison Avenue, New York, NY 10016.

Oxford Paperbacks are available from all good bookshops. In case of difficulty, customers in the UK can order direct from Oxford University Press Bookshop, Freepost, 116 High Street, Oxford OX1 4BR, enclosing full payment. Please add 10 per cent of published price for postage and packing.